Pacific Futures

Pacific Perspectives
Studies of the European Society for Oceanists

Series Editors: Christina Toren, University of St Andrews, and Edvard Hviding, University of Bergen

Oceania is of enduring contemporary significance in global trajectories of history, politics, economy and ecology, and has remained influential for diverse approaches to studying and understanding human life worlds. The books published in this series explore Oceanic values and imaginations, documenting the unique position of the Pacific region – its cultural and linguistic diversity, its ecological and geographical distinctness, and always fascinating experiments with social formations. This series thus conveys the political, economic and moral alternatives that Oceania offers the contemporary world.

Volume 1
The Ethnographic Experiment
A.M. Hocart and W.H.R. Rivers in Island Melanesia, 1908
Edited by Edvard Hviding and Cato Berg

Volume 2
Pacific Futures
Projects, Politics and Interests
Edited by Will Rollason

Upcoming titles
Movement, Place-Making and Multiple Identifications in Oceania
Edited by Elfriede Hermann, Wolfgang Kempf and Toon van Meijl

Visible Value
Problems with Request, Reciprocity, and Community in Manus, Papua New Guinea
Anders Rasmussen

New Perspectives on Pacific Kinship
Edited by Christina Toren and Simonne Pauwels

Pacific Futures

Projects, Politics and Interests

Edited by Will Rollason

berghahn
NEW YORK • OXFORD
www.berghahnbooks.com

First edition published in 2014 by
Berghahn Books
www.berghahnbooks.com

Library of Congress Cataloging-in-Publication Data
Pacific futures: projects, politics and interests / edited by Will Rollason.
pages cm. -- (Pacific perspectives; volume 2)
Includes bibliographical references.
ISBN 978-1-78238-350-5 (hardback: alk. paper) -- ISBN 978-1-78238-351-2 (institutional ebook)
1. Oceania--Social life and customs. 2. Pacific Islanders--Social life and customs. 3. Ethnology--Oceania. I. Rollason, Will.
GN663.P317 2014
306.0995--dc23
2013044570

British Library Cataloguing in Publication Data
A catalogue record for this book is available from the British Library

ISBN 978-1-78238-350-5 (hardback)
ISBN 978-1-78238-351-2 (institutional ebook)

Contents

Figures and Tables

Introduction

Pacific Futures, Methodological Challenges

Will Rollason

The contributions to this book are devoted to demonstrating how the activities of Pacific Islanders can be better understood by analysing the future as a field of possibility, action and hopes. We envisage this future as an alternative or creative supplement to interpretations and explanations framed as cultural or social – a positioning which, as I argue in this introductory essay, serves only to locate people in the past. This is the issue which motivates all of the chapters in this volume; each serves, in different ways, to demonstrate how an understanding of contemporary life in the Pacific is advanced by a perspective rooted in the aspirations and projects of Pacific people.

Facing the Future

Achieving a future that includes some measure of prosperity, dignity, self-reliance and opportunity is an object of struggle for many Pacific people in the contemporary era. Nor is this struggle a new one. For as long as we have records of the lives of Pacific people – not considering indigenous oral records – we find a rich variety of strategies and innovations for responding to change and seeking to reproduce, reform or alter the future in line with situated projects. Indeed, taking a broad view of anthropological perspectives on the Pacific, we could say that Pacific social lives are inherently innovative in that they continuously fabricate new constellations of social relations (Crook 2007). While this is not the place for a comprehensive review, it is worth noting the rich literature on ritual innovation, deep engagements with Christianity, the state, and markets and development, to mention only the most prevalent and global themes.[1] We could trace similar evidence of innovation and critical engagement through specific projects for the future in many if not all areas of contemporary Pacific life.

The point here is not to praise the creativity of Pacific people – as though valuing creativity was in itself a worthwhile scholarly or political project. Rather, the aim of these comments is to demonstrate the need to think about Pacific life in harmony with the interests that motivate that creativity (Hau'ofa 1999).[2] Hence it is not enough to highlight the challenges, both historical – colonialism, poverty, inequality, racism, salvation – and emergent – HIV/AIDS, ecological catastrophe, neo-colonial domination, and so on. Nor is it sufficient to note with satisfaction the inventiveness of grassroots responses to these developments.[3] Rather, we need to ask why indigenous people respond to the challenges that they face in the particular ways that they do, inventively and resourcefully to be sure: where is their inventiveness and resourcefulness directed?[4] This volume proceeds from the premise that it is directed prospectively (Battaglia 1995a) into the future, articulated into projects to control, direct and alter social lives, ecological worlds and economic positions (Appadurai 2002). Thinking in this way results in a simple observation: If we want to explain what is happening in the contemporary Pacific, we need to produce an account of what Pacific people are doing to secure their futures. The questions for scholars of the Pacific are twofold: how do Pacific people imagine the future; and how are they acting today to shape their lives tomorrow?[5] The essays in this collection take up these questions in different ways. The role of this introduction is to establish the grounds on which an anthropology of the future in the Pacific might proceed.

Defining the Future

At present, the ways in which scholars phrase explanations of how indigenous people in the Pacific live consistently neglect those people's own attention to the future. On the one hand, accounts authored from the perspective of development and governance impose their own versions of the future on others' projects and aspirations. Diverse cultural practices are reduced to variants of 'underdevelopment'; all of these are to be transformed into a uniform future of 'modernity' (Stirrat 2000; Mbembé 2001; Errington and Gewertz 2004). On the other hand, anthropological accounts of indigenous Pacific people's political and ethical projects usually account for present happenings in terms of the past (my particular reference here is Sahlins 1981, 1995). Despite an extensive literature dealing with economic aspirations, millennial predictions, political fears and other concerns with the future, we usually explain the present in terms of the traditions – historical or cultural – that seem to produce it, something which Appadurai (2002) suggests is a general problem for anthropologists. To the extent that peoples of the Pacific are stubbornly identified as the 'other' to Western 'civilisation', the problem here is acute.

The Poverty of Development

Accounts authored from the perspective of development are highly problematic in these terms. Although development, an inherently future-oriented activity, appears to offer all of the people of the global South a 'better future', on closer inspection that future really consists in devaluing and invalidating specific projects entertained by particular people as manifestations of underdevelopment, and replacing them with a generalised future based on some version of 'modernity'. Whether people actually want such a future or whether it is the object of their projects never really enters the equation. Rather than engaging the future, development de-problematises and evacuates it of meaning.

As a political practice supported by authoritative discourses (Ferguson 1990; Mosse 2005), development deploys naturalistic, teleological metaphors of blossoming and fulfilment (e.g. Rostow 1971) which are closely linked, even today, to modernist assumptions about 'the good life' (Scott 1998). The good life is defined by the life of the global North; the way to get there is to stimulate economic growth and the 'creative destruction' implicit in capital accumulation (Harvey 1989). From this perspective, it appears as an article of faith that wants are (or should be) unlimited and goods are (or should be) scarce (Harvey 2005; Rist 2008).

Indigenous Pacific societies typically never did operate on this principle: goods were never engaged in the free choices of individuals or freely exchangeable against others to satisfy needs (Gregory 1982). On the contrary, they were always engaged in specific relationships that bound people to certain kinds of exchanges which demonstrated not who they were as consumers facing 'lifestyle choices' but who they were within a definite set of relationships founded on claims and obligations between people (Strathern 1988) in so-called gift economies (Gregory 1982; Mauss 2002). That these systems of production and exchange in the Pacific were most often functioning subsistence economies that offered not only food security but also dignity and identity for those involved is more than incidental.

Of course, from the perspective of economic growth, this appears as no future at all (see e.g. Hughes 2003). Subsistence economies do not grow; they sustain themselves (Taussig 1977). For this reason, indigenous societies – usually homogenised beyond recognition in policy documents (Ferguson 1990) – appear as the 'degree zero' of development (Rist 2008), the archetype of the old and outmoded. The systems that sustain and reproduce them must be broken and destroyed so that indigenous people can enter history and begin to have a future (Wolf 1982). As such, indigenous social lives enter the narrative only as the past.

As a normative discourse, development wholly neglects the specificity of the people who are supposed to benefit from it (Stiglitz 2003). Development takes the liberal, democratic, consumer societies of the global North as the norm, and defines 'the poor' as figures of lack. The poor do not have enough freedom, they do not consume enough, they do not live long enough, and so on (Escobar 1995). The food that they do eat, the goods that they do produce, the freedoms that they do enjoy are of little interest. In fact, in the moment in which the global poor of the Third World or South are defined as such, their specificities become irrelevant; only their relation of lack compared with the rich is of interest. Their future as people who have, or should have 'more' is never in doubt.

There is no room for specific futures here, independent of a future of 'modernity' in one guise or another. Hence, that the majority of the world's population, including the people of the island Pacific, despite poverty and marginalisation, live lives that make sense on their own terms – that are not lives of 'lack' – does not enter into the equation. By the same token, the futures that they pursue and the aims and projects that they entertain need not be directed towards their 'lack' of production or consumption: through dynamic, prospective practices indigenous Pacific people forge lives as projects proceeding not from lack but from the richness of the contemporary moment viewed from a specific social vantage point (Battaglia 1992, 1995a). This is a classic anthropological position, but no less valid for that. The possibility of our entering a 'post-development age' (Escobar 1995; Rist 2008) must be more or less dependent on making other people's futures visible and acceptable beyond the horizon of increasing economic growth (Scott 2009). If this is to be achieved, we need to foreground what local people actually want, what they are trying to do to get it, and why it makes sense.

Relativism is Not the Answer

As anthropologists, our responses to these and other political concerns are too often counter-productive, and take too little account of the demands and constraints of this powerful system of ideas and practices. Relativism has been the basic position from which anthropological critique is made. We have argued cogently, and largely successfully, that both from the point of view of social relations and from the point of view of cultural representations – however we choose to divide this terrain (see Wagner 1974) – the lives that indigenous people pursue are integrated, complex, beautiful and valuable: they work on their own terms regardless of how strange and undesirable they might appear from the outside (e.g. Malinowski 1922; Geertz 1973; Benedict 1989).[6] This position is no longer adequate, not because particular lives do not make sense in the ways that we propose, but because of the way we ground them in the past, a strategy that in fact undermines their validity in the struggle for recognition (Fabian 1983).[7]

How does this pastness (Appadurai 2002) come to be the defining feature of cultural others? The notion of cultural specificity demands a mechanism for its reproduction (Carrithers 1992). Socio-cultural reproduction attaches specific cultures to 'traditions' in a weak sense: because the transmission and reproduction of culture has to take place in time – specifically in inter-generational time (Toren 1999) – then to posit culture as something more or less coherent that marks a specific way of life is immediately to extend it into the past. In the sense that it takes the form of a 'social fact' transcending individuals and emergent from collective life (Durkheim 1938), culture is always about this past and not about the future. More precisely, culture as a social fact necessarily operates on a different temporal basis to any given human life (Butler 2005), which it exceeds by virtue of its social character; hence exhaustively to articulate a specific project in culture's terms is possible only insofar as that project conforms exactly to the tradition.[8] As such, particular plans and projects that respond to the temporality and horizons of human lives are impossible to articulate adequately in cultural or social terms, which overwhelm and erase the specific as a condition of culture's social meaningfulness. Hence, because cultures are imagined as more or less integrated symbolic worlds, furnishing the meanings that make the world comprehensible, the logic of culture implies that where people imagine a future it is in fact with reference to a cultural tradition of imagined futures and therefore is in fact an imagination of the past.[9]

Naturally, I am not here arguing that indigenous cultural traditions are not important or that they do not exist. I am simply raising a concern about the way in which they can be used to interpret and explain the projects and struggles that indigenous people conduct in order to secure their futures. The difficulty is that a tradition of culture deployed as a context within which current trends make sense traces those trends inexorably into the past of cultural reproduction (Wagner 1975; cf. Rollason 2010), and does not allow us to connect them into a future that might be radically different to the past that preceded it (Robbins 2007).

This is a problem that comes into sharp focus in connection with anthropology's commitment to cultural relativism as a political project. We tend to regard the indigenous as inherently valuable. This is in large part intended as an act of resistance directed against exactly the modernising narratives that supported colonialism and continue to support neo-colonialism and development (Sahlins 2000). Too often, anthropologists seek to defend the indigenous bases of culture by revealing that what appears to be new is a transformation of a cultural 'tradition'.[10]

The intent here is to resist the homogeneity implicit in development narratives (Moore 2004), narratives that see commodities and ideas such as 'democracy' and 'the market' – indeed 'development' – as goods in themselves, bound up with developmental teleology. This resistance is valuable: if we can convincingly show that 'democracy' means something specific in Fiji, or that 'the market' has a unique valence for ni-Vanuatu, then the status of these ideas and the interventions that they support can be criticised. However, the risk is always present that by 'nativising' these concepts we confine our collaborators to a tradition that we, perhaps, value in a way they would not agree with (Lindstrom 1993).

This problem is particularly acute in the Pacific. The region, and specifically Melanesia, has been the catalyst for powerful and sophisticated ethnographic theorising in the form of the 'New Melanesian Ethnography' spearheaded by Roy Wagner (e.g. Wagner 1975, 1977, 1991) and Marilyn Strathern (e.g. Strathern 1980, 1988, 1995b). The key insight of these intertwined bodies of work is that Melanesian social life cannot adequately be understood on the basis of social-scientific analyses which proceed from an ontology founded on the opposition of individuals to society and, analogously, subjects to objects. Rather, Melanesian persons are constituted out of 'things', transacted as gifts in the sense defined by Mauss (2002). These things may be pigs or pearl shells, blood, semen or nurture – but they are all conceived of as manifestations of the capacities of people to affect one another, their social being (Wagner 1967; Strathern 1992). As a result, not only are people not constituted as logically prior individuals but as relational compositions or assemblages, agency – the ability to affect others – consists exactly in entering into a relationship where such transactions take place and new people and new relations are simultaneously constituted (Strathern 1988: 272). This ontological scheme, where relations, not 'individuals', are prior, and where things are components of persons, not 'objects', emerges as a foil to a 'Euro-American' world-view in which exactly the opposite holds (this distinction itself is founded on Mauss's inversion of the commodity form in his development of the concept of the gift).[11] Importantly, this distinction operates in the theory in a very strong form, branded either 'ontological' or 'systemic' – Strathern's wording – such that there is no observable difference between the form of the commodity and the gift, which must be inferred ethnographically.

This is powerful and productive work, and has helped to make the anthropology of the Pacific region so central to theoretical development in the discipline in recent years. Yet, like the 'nativisation' of cargo cult (Lindstrom 1993), such powerful models extract a cost. Where a weak version of Strathern's reasoning, deployed as the epistemological critique it sets out to be, is productive, stronger versions exist in which the ethnographic inference of a dividual world-view is made on the basis that the people under study are Melanesians and must, *ipso facto*, subscribe to it. Hence, Mosko, in a strongly argued piece, contends that ethnographers of Melanesian Christianity who propose that missionisation represents a radical rupture with the past have got it wrong (Mosko 2010a).[12] Mosko argues that Melanesians in fact accept Christianity precisely as a gift, a component of missionaries' and God's personhood, leaving their mode of sociality substantially intact. Conceding that this process does involve change, Mosko writes:

> Although Melanesian Christianity does not exhibit quite the sort of rupture some have posited, neither does it involve the mere continuity of pre-existing religious beliefs and practices or some simple slotting in of exogenous features … Villagers have taken upon themselves some elements of Christian personhood and agency in complex transactions involving the strategic eliciative relinquishment of personal elements of indigenous heritage. (ibid.: 233)

While the actual things Melanesians do may change, their core identity as Melanesian persons remains intact insofar as the systemic qualities of their relational ontology are not accessible to changes of this sort – at least in the course of interpretation. Given the logic of the argument, it is impossible to see how they might change because Melanesian personhood is taken to be systemic and any change could be read as an extension of gift logic by a scholar committed to its continuity. Thus, an essentialised Melanesia is insulated from the possibility of ever being other than it always has been.

From the logic of Mosko's argument it is clear that Melanesians – and by extension anyone for whom we can posit a systemically integrated system of ideas, relationships and representations (that is, everyone) – must and always will act in line with their tradition because we can use it as a context for translating and neutralising what is new. From this position, it becomes impossible for 'people of culture' to do anything innovative or original.

The tension here is in the relationship between the necessity of actual ways of life and the possibility of particular readings of them. Just because you can interpret what someone does in terms of the past and a cultural tradition doesn't mean that you must do so. It is no coincidence that every one of the authors whose work is used by Mosko to support his argument launches their criticism of him by saying that his reading of their work substantially misrepresents what people in the field told them, and distorts the interests of their collaborators (Barker 2010; Errington and Gewertz 2010; Knauft 2010; Robbins 2010).[13] We must question for what purpose and with what results we might pursue the neutralisation of the new in the name of culture. Other frames of reference may be more relevant, not least to the people we work with.

Engaging the Future

Provocatively, we could say that Pacific scholarship appears to remain in thrall to an archaic distinction between tradition and modernity: on the side of modernity are accounts of development that denigrate and deny custom and culture as relevant factors in contemporary affairs, to be erased by the march of the future (e.g. World Bank 1991); from the perspective of tradition we have accounts that refer the present endlessly to the past without allowing for innovation. The combination of these attitudes means that innovation in the Pacific can never be legible as a distinctive indigenous project but must either be a reflection of development (and therefore culturally empty) or a refraction of tradition (and therefore not innovative). This introduces a fundamental conflict of interest between accounts of Pacific life and projects to secure its future: our frames of reference prevent us from saying what it is that indigenous people are doing.

It is here that the future is critical. There is no reason why what people can imagine or plan or propose needs to be identical, or even continuous, with what they have imagined in the past (Moore 1999; Josephides 2008). This is not to say that we should make assumptions about the motivations behind the specific projects that contemporary Pacific people undertake. We have already seen where that strategy leads in terms of development discourse, and it is not a model that we should emulate. However, insofar as we are interested in the specificities of other peoples' ways of life and strive to take them seriously, we must accept that when Melanesians become Pentecostal Christians, or when Fijians dream of liberal democracy, that the form of their projects makes a difference. It is important to recognise that when Papua New Guineans play football, for example, the game itself adds something to their activity beyond occupying a symbolic space in the grid of culture (Rollason 2011). To subject such activity to the logic of culture is to remove its connective possibilities in a context that goes beyond the 'local' of the field site; to render it unproblematic is to wish away the effects of specific sets of social and symbolic relations. Attention to the actual form and content of other people's projects for the future is vital because it prevents the errors of developmental modernism and compulsory relativism that we have seen above.[14]

Two observations follow. First, if we attend to the actual form and content of what people do, then we are compelled to take seriously the difference that it makes when specific people work in categories that are not necessarily the categories of 'culture' (Robbins 2004; Sahlins 2005). What difference does it make when change takes the form of development rather than a transformation of ritual practice, for example? What projects can be articulated in terms of development that cannot be spoken of easily in terms of cult?

Second, it follows reciprocally that even projects for the future that take such familiar forms as 'development' or 'environmental sustainability' have to be interrogated for what such forms mean in a specific context (e.g. West 2006). How are these ideas articulated locally, and how do they respond to a particular discursive field of political possibilities and opportunities (Smith 2002)? How are the terms of these engagements controlled, and what constraints or advantages do they present to indigenous actors?

It is usually possible to render what is happening now in terms of what has always happened. This is a necessary activity for any anthropological interpretation, and one that offers to take account of the style and shape of the projects that people pursue.[15] However, in order to speak in good conscience (Battaglia 1999), cultural traditions cannot be the only source of our interpretive imagination, any more than we can appeal to 'economic rationality' to bypass specific perspectives.

It is this task I am pointing towards when I advocate a methodological stance, open towards the future. In the context of actual lives and specific material conditions, we have to attend to what people actually want and the projects that they actually pursue. In other words, we must pay ethnographic attention to other people's futures, not to subject them to grids of culture, but to engage them as displacements from it.[16] This is a deployment of the future that essentially makes of it a methodological tool.

Recourse to practice is appropriate here, as it is clear that the future cannot be used directly as an analytic term. By this I mean that it would be difficult to identify a stable category of 'the future' to apply cross-culturally. It seems inevitably tainted, as do all anthropological generalisations, by its sources, and offers only a collapse back into cultural specificity. Hence, phenomenological approaches would regard the future as an aspect of human experience of one sort or another. An openness or expectancy towards what is to come would thereby become something shared which would dissolve cultural difference and might become the bedrock of an analysis. Yet as Crapanzano (2003) has pointed out, criticising the work of Minkowski (1970), phenomenology appears to be a hostage to the language with which it works, which in turn bears the stamp of certain operations of power and distinction. The 'bracketing' activity by which phenomenologists seek to keep their cultural background at bay and access experience is itself a feature of Western forms of knowledge production, analogous to the 'bracketing' of the social and technical context of scientific experimentation, for example (Latour 1993). Alternative languages and ways of knowing the world would deliver a very different account, therefore, of what it means to engage the future. Indigenous accounts of time and futurity can be of little help, not least because they too easily collapse into a cultural reading, and paradoxically simply index the tradition from which they are drawn.[17] Here, the future, like kinship (Schneider 1984) or gender (MacCormack and Strathern 1980; Collier and Yanagisako 1987), threatens to become culturally specific and lose its usefulness as the very possibility of entertaining a future becomes tied to a cultural tradition.

Is the future then useless to us, being either socially determined or an outgrowth of our own culture? An analogy is provided by writing on hope. Ernst Bloch (1986) has argued that hope for the future is simply a reflex of bourgeois society. To engage others in hope is to implicate them in bourgeois sentiments and the failed project of the bourgeoisie. Miyazaki, however, disagrees. He argues that to hope is to maintain a stance of openness towards the world, offering the possibility of the continuous rearrangement of social relations, resources and representations (Miyazaki 2006). These define an unfinished temporality in which transformation is expected (Miyazaki 2004). This rearrangement may become the condition for life, or of continuous struggle in difficult circumstances. Or it might simply represent an ethical attitude to subjectivity, one which is prospective rather than fixative (Battaglia 1999). Miyazaki appropriately denotes this stance the '*method* of hope' (Miyazaki 2004; see also Bloch 1986).

It is in this sense that this volume takes up the future, not as an analytic term, or as a human universal, but as a stance towards the world. There are significant theoretical debates to be had about the ontological or epistemological nature of this stance – debates which Josephides takes up in her contribution to this volume. Here, however, I wish to stress the methodological and political implications of adopting such a stance to the others of anthropology. This stance is methodological in the sense that it defines the shape of knowledge – its objects, operations and conclusions. It demands that we take people seriously when they articulate projects for the future. It asks us to entertain the possibility that these projects should not be subjected to and submerged in a cultural interpretation, or assumed to be effects of development's modernising discourse – respectively removing their distinctive prospective orientation or de-problematising them. Rather, it asks us to accept these projects on their own terms, as providing their own meaningful contexts for the representations and practices that they embed. Particularly, this stance asks us to frame what people say and do in terms of what they say they want.[18] At root, such an engagement with other people is fundamental to the anthropological enterprise; however, it forces us beyond the frames in which we are accustomed to work.

To take this stance makes the distinctions imposed by culture difficult to sustain. The future as a methodological attitude defines our field as a fundamentally relational one. When people seek different futures and craft projects to achieve them, however slight, they must move themselves, either physically or imaginatively, beyond the boundaries of their current position. This displacement is familiar to ethnographers seeking to comprehend difference (Clifford 1986), and analogous to their strategies. Trying to get at the future is like trying to engage with the 'other': it involves a consciousness of the place and time in which one 'belongs' at the same time as it pulls one into relation with other people (Rabinow 1977). That 'other' might be a counterpart in a social encounter, it might be what you would like to be in the future, or what will be revealed by a ritual action, or a combination of these and other things. But in the move to meet this other, the self must become disconnected from its 'proper place' (de Certeau 2002). As such, the boundaries established by cultures, which define the places proper to native peoples (Gupta and Ferguson 1992, 1997), must in a sense be transgressed as soon as we allow people to dream, plan and scheme in more than a culturally stereotyped way.

The alternative, to approach the future culturally, seems both implausible and objectionable. While the notion that different people and groups have different ways of remembering, living and inscribing history offers a certain kind of liberation – a point on which Lévi-Strauss (1966), Chakrabarty (1992) and Gow (2001) offer different perspectives – the suggestion that different people might have different futures has the opposite effect. A weak claim on this basis is simply to fall into the errors of cultural relativism that I have already outlined. The future becomes, paradoxically, simply a figment of the past, a component of cultural tradition in which no real difference is possible. A strong claim, in which people actually occupy different futures – or worse, that they should – raises the spectre of cultures as new Bantustans in which natives will rot, chewing over their customs forever.

To mean anything, the future must be taken as a space of openness, a relational manifold implicating people in relations that disrupt their immediate cultural location as they move beyond it. This space is, in a weak sense, cosmopolitan (Bauman 2001). Here I do not intend to re-embed bourgeois liberalism in the notion of the future, but to point to a post-cultural location (Bhabha 2004) in which relationships can be formed and imagined in a way that subverts the notion that people can and must be finally fixable (Battaglia 1990, 1995b, 1999). The future, ultimately, represents a tactic to deploy against the fixing of people and their relegation to the past.

Approaches to the Future and the Present Volume

The challenge of the future presents itself as a problem of some considerable scope. Explaining the social without recourse to the past may be politically valuable, but it makes the grounds for description and argument problematic. A number of approaches are possible. However, it is clear that to engage the future in a committed way we must ground our methodological stance in some kind of theoretical framework that will establish the necessity of working with the future in mind. Clearly, given the location of these essays in disciplinary terms, ethnographic description is equally vital: without close attention to the lives lived by the people we write about, this project is vacuous. Finally, some form of activist engagement is close to the heart of the project of this volume: to investigate the future as others aspire to and work for it inclines all of these chapters towards some form of political engagement.

The contributions to this volume take up the issues I have outlined here in a number of different ways to show how understanding the future as a field of possibility, action and hope might supplement and advance our understanding of how Pacific Islanders live. Each contributor takes up a different ethnographic or historical case and demonstrates the value of the future as a tool for understanding in their analysis. The chapters are arranged so that the more theoretically oriented open the collection, the middle chapters are the most richly ethnographic, while the final contributions are the most explicitly politically engaged – although considering the nature of the project at hand these distinctions are a matter of degree.

In keeping with the call for methodological openness that I have advanced above, the chapters are varied both in subject and approach. No attempt has been made to discipline the contributors to pursue a particular line of theory: the only condition which I have consistently imposed is that all the contributions deal as squarely as possible with the future as it is imagined and worked towards by the people whose social lives provide the chapters' subject matter.

Creating a Coherent Critique

Notwithstanding the difficulty of deploying theoretical notions of the future analytically, philosophical approaches which place the human subject as a future-oriented being (Josephides 2008; Toren 1999) are central to breaking the dominance of the past over Pacific scholarship. This methodological groundwork is vital to make the field of present activities directed towards the future comprehensible and controllable. Relating ethnographic and activist perspectives to a principled framework – one which sees people themselves as projects with specific, open-ended trajectories (resistant to homogenising narratives such as that of modernity) that exceed and build upon their origins (thus escaping the bind of cultural context) – is vital for challenging the epistemic stranglehold that the past has upon the future. There are a number of ways in which this theoretical project might be defined and employed, but some such effort is necessary to articulate dissent into a coherent critique.

Josephides's chapter concerns the Kewa of Papua New Guinea (PNG), and makes the claim that humans are existentially prospective – continuously moving into their own futures. She demonstrates this through an analysis of Kewa narratives, composed in a context of rapid social change. Through images of religious revelation and mythic references, these narratives 'show how people attempt to grasp and shape the future with the ultimate aim of gaining recognition and prestige in the new world … how they take their lives in their own hands and push themselves over the chasm to a new terrain' (Josephides, this volume). Josephides articulates her understanding through an exploration of hope, imagination and desire, which weaves Kewa accounts with philosophies of human potential. She thus establishes the necessity of the future in considering what it means to be human. Josephides's chapter is a vital starting point for this volume, in that this claim must be made at the outset in some form.

Rollason considers 'cargo cult' activities in the Louisiade Archipelago (PNG) in the early 1940s. He focuses on the suicide by hanging of the cult leader, Buliga. Rollason contends that Buliga's suicide must be understood as a powerful symbolic act in which the cult prophet executed himself, and thus appropriated the distinctive powers of the white state, the target of his movement. The events of the 1940s cannot adequately be understood through cultural interpretation, any more than through colonial narratives of savagery (which Rollason suggests have the same form), because any attempt to do so vitiates a project for the future in which Buliga and his adherents are not who they are, and thus stand outside the identities and positions defined by their 'culture' and its interpretation. For Rollason, the future is a necessarily post-cultural space.

Ethnographies of the Future

Theory aside, for anthropologists the founding approach to the future must be documentary. There is no substitute for detailed ethnographic or historical knowledge in delineating the dimensions of particular futures, entertained by people at the grassroots. This is central both to displace the certainties of 'development' futures, and to register the content and form of specific projects. This knowledge need not be gathered or disseminated by professional academics, but it is impossible to imagine these intimacies being adequately accommodated by the broad brush of policy discourse, development or economic 'science'.

A central problem lies in the relationship between faithfulness to the meaning of specific projects – issues of translation and interpretation – and to their form and content. Understanding specific projects in context inevitably risks subjecting them to the authority of that context. However, this problem simply underscores the need for ethnographic engagement, for studies which are sufficiently sensitive to trace the synergies and connections that have the capacity to displace any final cultural grid. Such an engagement lies squarely within the long-standing commitments of the discipline.

In this collection, all of the chapters have an ethnographic base. Particularly focused on the problem of producing an 'ethnography of the future' are Lind writing on kinship, contraception and the obligation to reproduce oneself amongst Paama islanders from Vanuatu; Pickles writing on gambling in Goroka, PNG; and Handman and Eriksen writing on different permutations of Christianity in PNG and Vanuatu respectively. All of these contributions begin from detailed ethnography, in the understanding that without a committed engagement with the details of people's lives, there can be no understanding of the futures to which they aspire. The emphasis in all of these chapters is on the process of displacement and the dynamics of prospective action by which the people in question pursue their projects.

Lind discusses the 'roads of kinship', which from one perspective serve people from Paama (Vanuatu), to replace people through reproduction, and thus to perpetuate relationships. Lind shows, however, that from the perspective of other aspirations – for formal education, migration to town, or the control of population – these 'roads' operate differently, prompting actions which aim to reshape the future in non-teleological ways.

Pickles considers gambling with playing cards as a model for social life in Goroka (PNG). In doing so, he seeks to demonstrate how all social interactions – potentially risky gambles in this context, where others' intentions are held to be unknowable – are necessarily prospective ventures into an unknown future.

Handman explores how for Christians in the Waria Valley (PNG), religion is not a backward-looking, past-bound aspect of social life, despite its biblical authority. Rather, in the context of the discovery by some Guhu-Samane Christians that they belong to a Lost Tribe of Israel, Christianity opens up a space for critique. This critique fosters inter-regional and inter-ethnic recognition amongst other 'lost tribes', motivated by the desire for a future of spiritual and political unity modelled on local imaginations of contemporary and biblical Israel.

Eriksen shows how people from Ambrym (Vanuatu) take a history in which they see themselves as 'cursed' for their violent rejection of Christian missions as the pretext for imagining how to access a prosperous future. Eriksen traces the divergent schemes of a senior man and a younger woman healer to demonstrate how their projects for lifting Ambrym's curse involve radically different visions of personhood and agency in the island's future.

Reflexive Activism

Activism of all kinds dwells on and in the future. Activist perspectives have a huge amount to contribute to the interpretation of contemporary Pacific lives, insofar as they represent or form part of specific approaches to the future on the part of the people who pursue them or are represented by them. Because of the nature of the struggles often waged by people in different situations throughout Oceania, cultural traditions commonly figure centrally in indigenous activism (Keesing 1992: 199; Linnekin 1992), often alongside demands and strategies that have their sources in discourses of development. However, a reflexive activism is capable of positioning itself relative to a fixed tradition – avoiding, for example, traditionalist and often less than egalitarian views on gender relations or seniority – and of displacing the 'common sense' of development by phrasing itself exactly in indigenous terms. Activist texts written from committed positions in these politics are therefore both ethnographic documents of specific futures and material interventions in particular projects (e.g. Kasaipwalova 1974; Narakobi 1983; Hau'ofa 1999). Activism and political engagement appear in this collection in a variety of forms. Pascht, Schieder and Robinson make different descriptive and interpretive passes at activism.

Pascht demonstrates how the role of chiefly title holders on contemporary Rarotonga (Cook Islands) can only be understood in terms of the political projects which both title holders and non-chiefly Rarotongans entertain. While the position of chiefs in Rarotongan society has a definite historical trajectory, Pascht shows how that history has been shaped by leaders' conflicting aspirations for their nation – particularly how custom and tradition are valued in those futures – and the shifting opportunities perceived by titleholders themselves.

Schieder's essay explores the development and perpetuation of a 'coup culture' in Fiji, which sees a defined elite continuously generating political instability for their own political ends. He argues that in order to comprehend this coup culture – and perhaps to limit its effects – it is not sufficient to understand or to recuperate the past or tradition, but to understand how a history of colonisation, class formation and appeals to Fijian cultural integrity are deployed in the prospective strategies of coup perpetrators and their allies. These strategies, he shows, are not simply reflexes of social or cultural determinants, but have very specific personal and political goals for the future of Fijian society at large, and the individuals involved specifically.

Robinson's chapter considers the different ways in which the Dread, Rastafari members of the Ngāti Porou tribe of eastern Aotearoa/New Zealand, seek to secure their future as traditional guardians of the land. This involves bringing aspects of customary life into dialogue with diverse knowledge and practice: geomorphology, forestry, road maintenance and conservation interweave with Ngāti Porou visions of the world. Robinson does not simply describe an activist moment, but through his articulation of these various elements contributes to it by making Ngāti Porou visions of the future apparent.

Hereniko's closing contribution to the collection shifts the emphasis from anthropological analyses of 'other' societies to a Pacific Islander scholar's reflection on the future of his home. While the other contributions to the collection consider their material against the foils of culture, tradition and other social-scientific devices, Hereniko situates the future of Rotuma and Tuvalu, Pacific island nations whose existence is threatened by climate change, squarely within the interests of grassroots Pacific people – a turn of phrase I take to index a material constituency that can be set against the abstractions and tropes which he identifies in much social-scientific literature on the Pacific. If the other contributions to this collection offer analysis, and with it the illusion of some kind of mastery, Hereniko's offers up the doubt and anxiety of someone for whom the issues at stake are infinitely more pressing. His chapter serves as a fitting endpoint by highlighting both the intensely personal nature of the futures described here, and the necessary uncertainty of any attempt to gain control over events as they unfold.

The ambition of the project described in this introduction is considerable, and not one that can be completed within the space of a single volume; the aim here is the elicitation of debate rather than conclusions. The chapters which are presented here are exactly essays – first steps towards a potential reimagining of anthropology in the Pacific. Like the projects for the future that they describe and interpret, these are prospective ventures.

Notes

1. On ritual innovation, see e.g. Lindenbaum (1979), Lindstrom (1990, 1993), Jebens (2004, 2010) and Harrison (2007); on Christianity, see e.g. Robbins (2004), Scott (2005) and Eriksen (2007); on the state, see e.g. Dinnen (2001),

Goddard (2005) and Lattas (2006); and on markets and development, see e.g Smith (1994), Filer (2006) and Alexeyeff (2008).

2. See also Battaglia (1990) on the notion of 'ethnographic congruence'.
3. Hence, e.g., the Comaroffs' claim that African ritual innovation promotes creative global 'multilogues' appears complacent from this perspective (Comaroff and Comaroff 1993).
4. In many respects this may offer a return to political-economy discourses that predate independence and the focus on economic growth which marks recent political and economic thinking in the post-colonial world. Such discourses focus on the resilience of indigenous ways of life as resources for redefining the ultimate aims of policy rather than simply charting routes to them. See e.g. Kasaipwalova (1974) and Narakobi (1983), to mention only sources for PNG.
5. The questions which are posed here are clearly similar to those raised by Appadurai under the banner of 'the capacity to aspire' (Appadurai 2002). At a superficial level, Appadurai is a natural ally of this collection: his interest in the capacity to aspire leads him to argue that anthropologists must begin 'to place futurity, rather than pastness at the heart of our thinking about culture' (ibid.: 84) in order to forge a relationship with the poor and with development agencies in which culture is not a necessarily critical position on development, but one which fosters the all-important (meta-)capacity to aspire from which other capacities to organise and act derive (ibid.: 59). However, read more closely, Appadurai's 'capacity to aspire' is in fact of little use in the form in which he presents it. Capacities to aspire are rendered as components of culture. This is a problem because, given a relatively strong theory of culture – itself a tradition, as Appadurai recognises (ibid.: 60) – the location of the future as a function of cultural tradition calls into question the extent to which it can refer to a future as such in distinction to a traditional representation of futurity (cf. Butler 2005). The total lack of ethnographic data supporting the concept – which is drawn from Sen (1999), amongst others – while understandable given the short essay format in which it is presented, nevertheless makes it difficult to judge exactly what is at stake.

   Perhaps as a result of this location of the future in culture, development as its opposite number is de-problematised. The futures defined by development – founded on improved material conditions of living – are left unquestioned: Appadurai's interest lies in how poor people realise them, not the sense in which they desire them. While development is no doubt founded on goods which would be recognised as such by almost anyone, their articulation with specific projects is not a matter which can be taken for granted. Furthermore – and more troublingly – development is removed from the social situation within which poor people operate (cf. Uvin 1998; Green 2003). Rather than representing a powerful mode of discourse and practice with important implications for poor people's lives, and around which they must negotiate their way to their aspirations (Rollason 2009), development is envisioned as exogenous to the cultural situation of the poor – the central claim of Ferguson (1990); see also Scott (1998). Revealingly, Appadurai opposes culture to development, describing the latter as 'the real world' (Appadurai 2002: 70). Concomitantly, the 'cultural' factors affecting the terms of recognition for the poor are none of them to do with development and all to do with localised and 'indigenous' forms of life – caste in India, for example; hugely important no doubt, but surely not the whole picture.

There is much to value in Appadurai's article, and I cite it as a source of considerable inspiration at certain points in this Introduction. However, 'the capacity to aspire', to my mind, remains an inspiration requiring considerable development in specific ethnographic contexts to operationalise effectively. As such, while I freely draw attention to its valuable contribution and political commitment, the concept is not of itself capable of articulating the project I am pursuing here.

6. Indeed, 'indigenous people' is superfluous here: all people must be recognised as 'people of culture' – Schneider's demonstration is notable here (see Schneider 1980, 1984). The relativisation of 'Western' ways of life is an integral component of anthropological critique (Marcus and Fischer 1986; Sahlins 1996).
7. Although it is import to acknowledge Fabian's seminal contribution to these issues (Fabian 1983), the critique on offer here is different from the one that he advances. Mainly this is because, while Fabian's argument moves in the domain of ethnography as text, the argument here aspires to engage with material political conditions.
8. Note that this argument is somewhat different to, but consonant with, Robbins's critique of 'continuity thinking' in anthropology (Robbins 2007). Robbins points out the same dynamic I elaborate here. However, because his particular target is the anthropology of Christianity, he dwells on the way in which anthropologists construct time. I focus rather on the interpretive devices by which the authenticity of culture is established, and the political implications of that interpretive activity. However, as I make clear in the argument which follows, I am wholly in agreement with Robbins's conclusions.
9. This is, as Wagner (1975) shows, the fiction of ethnographic abstraction at work, but it is nevertheless the theoretical logic of the term. In Strathern's terms, through the device of analysis, culture becomes a position from which to view and comment on social happenings (Strathern 1995a).
10. See e.g. Englund and Leach (2000). This point is made more fully in Rollason (2011).
11. Note that Strathern explicitly states that 'the intention is not an ontological statement to the effect that there exists a type of social life [that of Melane-

sians] based on premises in an inverse relation to our own' (Strathern 1988: 16) – a disclaimer which I think has largely been ignored by subsequent scholars. Strathern is very explicit in *The Gender of the Gift* that her intention is to make apparent the process and effects of anthropological knowledge production. My use of 'ontology' here is intended to emphasise that the 'fiction' of Melanesia Strathern proposes is intended to be equivalent to the basic underlying truths of conventional sociological analysis – and to suggest the way in which the notion has been taken up by later scholars.

12. Mosko's target here is really the school of New Melanesian History, which evolved as a complement to and sometimes critic of the New Melanesian Ethnography (Carrier and Carrier 1989; Carrier 1992; LiPuma 1995; Foster 2002), insisting on the importance of colonial and postcolonial relations to an adequate anthropology of Melanesia.
13. There is no value in mounting a more extensive critique of Mosko here. The responses to his 2010 essay (Barker 2010; Errington and Gewertz 2010; Knauft 2010; Robbins 2010) elegantly expose the numerous flaws in his reasoning. Here, I take Mosko's essay as a particularly striking example of 'continuity thinking' (Robbins 2007) in anthropology, aggravated by a rigid use of a theory of culture. This is, as Barker has it, 'a throwback – albeit a sophisticated one – to an older style of analysis more concerned with preserving village-centred ethnography than grappling with the lived complexities of Christian Melanesians' (Barker 2010: 249). In the reduction of all Melanesian life to a 'procrustean scheme' (Robbins 2010: 242), Mosko's argument throws into sharp relief the challenges of cultural interpretation I highlight in this essay.
14. Of course, this does not close off the empirical question of whether change happens, or whether 'believing in change' (Eriksen, this volume, commenting on Robbins 2007: 21), is an adequate condition for social transformation. However, insofar as anthropology since the 1970s has moved away from questions of empirical adequacy and towards an analysis of the implications of representations, this really constitutes a question apart from the political task of making our research chime more effectively with the interests of our collaborators, something which may also pay explanatory dividends (see Schieder, this volume).
15. We can draw inspiration here from Robbins (2007), an article which examines the failure of a sub-field to develop around the notion of an anthropology of Christianity. Robbins suggests that anthropology is hostile to Christianity at a 'deep structural' level. He points out, exactly as I am suggesting here, that anthropologists are inclined to view cultures as long-lasting and difficult to change. Change takes place incrementally, with clear causal linkages. This makes it hard for us as scholars to credit Christian converts' claims to radical transformation, or to accept the millennial models of time on which they

are premised. As a result they tend to work to diminish their importance and seek to 'reveal' the 'true' congruence of current activity and the cultural past, much as Mosko (2010b) does. In order to avoid this error, Robbins argues, we must seek to understand the values which govern a system of life and representations. Regardless of the symbolic forms people make use of, he suggests, we are justified in calling a culture 'Christian' when the things people do and care about are substantially motivated by Christian values. While Robbins confines himself to talking about Christianity, the broader implications of his argument are consonant with the position I take up in this essay. Where change is at stake, it is our job as ethnographers to find out what our collaborators' frames of reference are, and how they motivate particular projects in a specific historical conjuncture.

16. In this regard, 'the future' could be seen as filling an analogous place to accounts of 'resistance' to 'power' (Scott 1985). While tracing the future as a resistance to culture is clearly a possibility, this is not my aim. Rather, I suggest that projects for the future must be seen as diverse tactics, unfolding within the total relational manifold of the present, where distinctions of culture represent only one, albeit major, strategic feature (de Certeau 2002).
17. This is by no means to denigrate extensive and important ethnographic work on specific notions of time, both in the Pacific and elsewhere (see Munn 1992). It is merely to point out that elevating any one of those representations of time to the status of an analytic category is unhelpful, both because it is unlikely to be applicable beyond its site of origin, and because 'indigenous futures' too easily collapse into cultural traditions – which is to say, pasts.
18. The problem of translation cannot simply be wished away of course (Geertz 1983). It is here that cultural interpretation must continue to have a key role, anchoring our work in ethnographic detail. The methodological importance of the future lies in prising open interpretation, so that it does not finish in the completion of a pattern, be it hermeneutic or structural, but pursues synergies, connections and possibilities for relationships that exceed analytic patterns and bring them into question. Naturally, this work entails a tension at the very heart of the project – between the development of the cultural models which enable us to understand others, and openness to innovation which allows us to extend the kinds of recognition which attention to others' futures entails. Just as ethnography in general presents us with the problem of representing other people in the language of our peers (Wagner 1975; Strathern 1988), attention to the future forces us to confront a conflict between the multi-cultural pluralism and humanistic universalism which coexist within the project of anthropology – an issue thoughtfully highlighted by Douglas (2002: xii–xiii).

References

Alexeyeff, K. 2008. Neoliberalism, Mobility and Cook Islands Men in Transit. *Australian Journal of Anthropology* 19(2): 136–49.

Appadurai, A. 2002. The Capacity to Aspire: Culture and the Terms of Recognition. In V. Rao and M. Walton (eds), *Culture and Public Action*, pp.59–84. Stanford: Stanford University Press.

Barker, J. 2010. The Varieties of Melanesian Christian Experience: A Comment on Mosko's 'Partible Penitents'. *Journal of the Royal Anthropological Institute* 16(2): 247–49.

Battaglia, D. 1990. *On the Bones of the Serpent: Person, Memory, and Mortality in Sabarl Island Society*. Chicago: University of Chicago Press.

——— 1992. Displacing Culture: A Joke of Significance in Urban Papua New Guinea. *New Literary History* 23(4): 1003–17.

——— 1995a. On Practical Nostalgia: Self-prospecting among Urban Trobrianders. In D. Battaglia (ed.), *Rhetorics of Self-making*, pp.77–96. Berkeley: University of California Press.

——— 1995b. Problematising the Self: a Thematic Introduction. In D. Battaglia (ed.), *Rhetorics of Self-making*, pp.1–15. Berkeley: University of California Press.

——— 1999. Towards an Ethics of the Open Subject. In H. Moore (ed.), *Anthropological Theory Today*, pp.114–50. Cambridge: Polity Press.

Bauman, Z. 2001. Identity in the Globalising World. *Social Anthropology* 9(2): 121–129.

Benedict, R. 1989 [1947]. *The Chrysanthemum and the Sword: Patterns of Japanese Culture*. Boston: Houghton Mifflin.

Bhabha, H.K. 2004. *The Location of Culture*. London: Routledge.

Bloch, E. 1986 [1959]. *The Principle of Hope*. Cambridge, MA: MIT Press.

Butler, J. 2005. *Giving an Account of Oneself*. New York: Fordham University Press.

Carrier, J.G. (ed.). 1992. *History and Tradition in Melanesian Anthropology*. Berkeley: University of California Press.

Carrier, J.G., and A.H. Carrier. 1989. *Wage, Trade, and Exchange in Melanesia: A Manus Society in the Modern State*. Berkeley: University of California Press.

Carrithers, M. 1992. *Why Humans Have Cultures: Explaining Anthropology and Social Diversity*. Oxford: Oxford University Press.

Chakrabarty, D. 1992. Postcoloniality and the Artifice of History: Who Speaks for 'Indian' Pasts? *Representations* 37: 1–26.

Clifford, J. 1986. On Ethnographic Allegory. In G.E. Marcus and J. Clifford (eds), *Writing Culture: The Poetics and Politics of Ethnography*, pp.98–121. Berkeley: University of California Press.

Collier, J.F., and S.J. Yanagisako (eds). 1987. *Gender and Kinship: Essays toward a Unified Analysis*. Stanford: Stanford University Press.

Comaroff, J., and J.L. Comaroff. 1993. Introduction. In J. Comaroff and J.L. Comaroff (eds), *Modernity and Its Malcontents: Ritual and Power in Postcolonial Africa*, pp.xi–xxxvii. Chicago: University of Chicago Press.

Crapanzano, V. 2003. Reflections on Hope as a Category of Social and Psychological Analysis. *Cultural Anthropology* 18(1): 3–32.

Crook, T. 2007. *Anthropological Knowledge, Secrecy, and Bolivip, Papua New Guinea: Exchanging Skin*. Oxford: Oxford University Press.

De Certeau, M. 2002. *The Practice of Everyday Life*, 2nd edn. Berkeley: University of California Press.

Dinnen, S. 2001. *Law and Order in a Weak State: Crime and Politics in Papua New Guinea*. Honolulu: University of Hawaii Press.

Douglas, M. 2002 [1966]. *Purity and Danger: An Analysis of Concepts of Pollution and Taboo*. London: Routledge.

Durkheim, E. 1938 [1895]. *The Rules of Sociological Method*, trans. S. Solovay and J. Mueller, ed. G. Catlin. Chicago: University of Chicago Press.

Englund, H., and J. Leach. 2000. Ethnography and the Meta-narratives of Modernity. *Current Anthropology* 41(2): 225–48.

Eriksen, A. 2007. *Gender, Christianity and Change in Vanuatu: An Analysis of Social Movements in North Ambrym*. Aldershot: Ashgate.

Errington, F., and D. Gewertz. 2004. *Yali's Question: Sugar, Culture, and History*. Chicago: University of Chicago Press.

——— 2010. Expanding Definitions, Contracting Contexts: A Comment on Mosko's 'Partible Penitents'. *Journal of the Royal Anthropological Institute* 16(2): 250–52.

Escobar, A. 1995. *Encountering Development: The Making and Unmaking of the Third World*. Princeton: Princeton University Press.

Fabian, J. 1983. *Time and the Other: How Anthropology Makes Its Object*. New York: Columbia University Press.

Ferguson, J. 1990. *The Anti-politics Machine: 'Development', Depoliticization, and Bureaucratic Power in Lesotho*. Cambridge: Cambridge University Press.

Filer, C. 2006. Custom, Law and Ideology in Papua New Guinea. *Asia Pacific Journal of Anthropology* 7(1): 65–84.

Foster, R.J. 2002. Bargains with Modernity in Papua New Guinea and Elsewhere. *Anthropological Theory* 2(2): 233–51.

Geertz, C. 1973. *The Interpretation of Cultures: Selected Essays*. New York: Basic Books.

——— 1983. *Local Knowledge: Further Essays in Interpretive Anthropology*. New York: Basic Books.

Goddard, M. 2005. *The Unseen City: Anthropological Perspectives on Port Moresby, Papua New Guinea*. Canberra: Research School of Pacific and Asian Studies, Australian National University.

Gow, P. 2001. *An Amazonian Myth and Its History*. Oxford: Oxford University Press.

Green, M. 2003. Globalizing Development in Tanzania. *Critique of Anthropology* 23(2): 123 –43.

Gregory, C.A. 1982. *Gifts and Commodities*. London: Academic Press.

Gupta, A., and J. Ferguson. 1992. Beyond 'Culture': Space, Identity and the Politics of Difference. *Cultural Anthropology* 7(1): 6–23.

——— 1997. Discipline and Practice: 'The Field' as Site, Method and Location in Anthropology. In A. Gupta and J. Ferguson (eds), *Anthropological Locations: Boundaries and Grounds of a Field Science*, pp.1–46. Berkeley: University of California Press.

Harrison, S. 2007. *Fracturing Resemblances: Identity and Mimetic Conflict in Melanesia and the West*. New York: Berghahn.

Harvey, D. 1989. *The Condition of Postmodernity: An Enquiry into the Origins of Cultural Change*. Oxford: Blackwell.

——— 2005. *A Brief History of Neoliberalism*. Oxford: Oxford University Press.

Hau'ofa, E. 1999. Our Sea of Islands. In V. Hereniko and R. Wilson (eds), *Inside Out: Literature, Cultural Politics, and Identity in the New Pacific*, pp.27–38. Lanham, MD.: Rowman and Littlefield.

Hughes, H. 2003. Aid Has Failed the Pacific. *Issue Analysis* 33: 1–32.

Jebens, H. 2004. *Cargo, Cult, and Culture Critique*. Honolulu: University of Hawaii Press.

——— 2010. *After the Cult: Perceptions of Other and Self in West New Britain*. New York: Berghahn.

Josephides, L. 2008. *Melanesian Odysseys: Negotiating the Self, Narrative and Modernity*. New York: Berghahn.

Kasaipwalova, J. 1974. 'Modernising' Melanesian Society: Why, and For Whom? In R. May (ed.), *Priorities in Melanesian Development*, Sixth Waigani Seminar, Royal Society for Pacific Studies, Australian National University and University of Papua New Guinea.

Keesing, R.M. 1992. *Custom and Confrontation: The Kwaio Struggle for Cultural Autonomy*. Chicago: University of Chicago Press.

Knauft, B.M. 2010. Beyond Polarization and Partition in Melanesian Anthropology: A Comment on Mosko's 'Partible Penitents'. *Journal of the Royal Anthropological Institute* 16(2): 244–46.

Latour, B. 1993. *We Have Never Been Modern*. Cambridge, MA: Harvard University Press.

Lattas, A. 2006. The Utopian Promise of Government. *Journal of the Royal Anthropological Institute* 12 129–50.

Lévi-Strauss, C. 1966. *The Savage Mind*. Chicago: University of Chicago Press.

Lindenbaum, S. 1979. *Kuru Sorcery: Disease and Danger in the New Guinea Highlands*. Palo Alto, CA: Mayfield.

Lindstrom, L. 1990. *Knowledge and Power in a South Pacific Society*. Washington: Smithsonian Institution Press.

_______ 1993. *Cargo Cult: Strange Stories of Desire from Melanesia and Beyond*. Honolulu: University of Hawaii Press.

Linnekin, J. 1992. On the Theory and Politics of Cultural Construction in the Pacific. *Oceania* 62(4): 249–63.

LiPuma, E. 1995. The Formation of Nation States and National Cultures in Oceania. In R.J. Foster (ed.), *Nation Making: Emergent Identities in Postcolonial Melanesia*, pp.33–69. Ann Arbor: University of Michigan Press.

MacCormack, C.P., and M. Strathern (eds). 1980. *Nature, Culture, and Gender*. Cambridge: Cambridge University Press.

Malinowski, B. 1922. *Argonauts of the Western Pacific*. London: Routledge and Sons.

Marcus, G.E., and M.M.J. Fischer. 1986. *Anthropology as Cultural Critique: An Experimental Moment in the Human Sciences*. Chicago: University of Chicago Press.

Mauss, M. 2002. *The Gift: The Form and Reason for Exchange in Archaic Societies*, trans. W.D. Halls. London: Routledge.

Mbembé, J.-A. 2001. *On the Postcolony*. Berkeley: University of California Press.

Minkowski, E. 1970. *Lived Time: Phenomenological and Psychopathological Studies*. Evanston, IL: Northwestern University Press.

Miyazaki, H. 2004. *The Method of Hope: Anthropology, Philosophy, and Fijian Knowledge*. Stanford: Stanford University Press.

_______ 2006. Economy of Dreams: Hope in Global Capitalism and Its Critiques. *Cultural Anthropology* 21(2): 147–72.

Moore, H.L. 1999. Whatever Happened to Women and Men? Gender and Other Crises in Anthropology. In H.L. Moore (ed.), *Anthropological Theory Today*, pp.151–71. Cambridge: Polity Press.

_______ 2004. Global Anxieties: Concept Metaphors and Pre-theoretical Commitments in Anthropology. *Anthropological Theory* 4(1): 71–88.

Mosko, M. 2010a. Partible Penitents: Dividual Personhood and Christian Practice in Melanesia and the West. *Journal of the Royal Anthropological Institute* 16(2): 215–40.

_______ 2010b. Partible Penitents: A Response to Comments. *Journal of the Royal Anthropological Institute* 16(2): 253–59.

Mosse, D. 2005. *Cultivating Development: An Ethnography of Aid Policy and Practice*. London: Pluto Press.

Munn, N.D. 1992. The Cultural Anthropology of Time: A Critical Essay. *Annual Review of Anthropology* 21, 93–123.

Narakobi, B. 1983. *The Melanesian Way*. Port Moresby/Suva: Institute of Papua New Guinea Studies/Institute of Pacific Studies.

Rabinow, P. 1977. *Reflections on Fieldwork in Morocco*. Berkeley: University of California Press.

Rist, G. 2008. *The History of Development: From Western Origins to Global Faith*, 3rd rev. edn. London: Zed Books.

Robbins, J. 2004. *Becoming Sinners: Christianity and Moral Torment in a Papua New Guinea Society*. Berkeley: University of California Press.

——— 2007. Continuity Thinking and the Problem of Christian Culture. *Current Anthropology* 48(1): 5–38.

——— 2010. Melanesia, Christianity, and Cultural Change: A Comment On Mosko's 'Partible Penitents'. *Journal of the Royal Anthropological Institute* 16(2): 241–43.

Rollason, W. 2009. Diving One Man: Disconnection and Recontexualization among Panapompom Bêche-de-mer Divers. *Cambridge Anthropology* 28(2): 45–62.

——— 2010. Working Out Abjection in the Panapompom Bêche-de-mer Fishery: Race, Economic Change and the Future in Papua New Guinea. *Australian Journal of Anthropology* 21(2): 149–70.

——— 2011. We Are Playing Football: Seeing the Game on Panapompom, Papua New Guinea. *Journal of the Royal Anthropological Institute* 17(3): 481–503.

Rostow, W.W. 1971. *The Stages of Economic Growth: A Non-communist Manifesto*, 2nd edn. Cambridge: Cambridge University Press.

Sahlins, M.D. 1981. *Historical Metaphors and Mythical Realities: Structure in the Early History of the Sandwich Islands Kingdom*. Ann Arbor: University of Michigan Press.

——— 1995. *How 'Natives' Think: About Captain Cook, For Example*. Chicago: University of Chicago Press.

——— 1996. The Sadness of Sweetness: The Native Anthropology of Western Cosmology. *Current Anthropology* 37(3): 395–428.

——— 2000. What Is Anthropological Enlightenment? Some Lessons of the Twentieth Century. In *Culture in Practice: Selected Essays*, pp.501–29. New York: Zone Books.

——— 2005. The Economics of Develop-man in the Pacific. In J. Robbins and H. Wardlow (eds), *The Making of Global and Local Modernities in Melanesia: Humiliation, Transformation and the Nature of Cultural Change*, pp.23–42. Aldershot: Ashgate.

Schneider, D.M. 1980. *American Kinship: A Cultural Account*, 2nd edn. Chicago: University of Chicago Press.

——— 1984. *A Critique of the Study of Kinship*. Ann Arbor: University of Michigan Press.

Scott, J.C. 1985. *Weapons of the Weak: Everyday Forms of Peasant Resistance*. New Haven: Yale University Press.

_______ 1998. *Seeing Like A State: How Certain Schemes to Improve the Human Condition Have Failed*. New Haven: Yale University Press.

_______ 2009. *The Art of Not Being Governed: An Anarchist History of Upland Southeast Asia*. New Haven: Yale University Press.

Scott, M.W. 2005. 'I Was Like Abraham': Notes On the Anthropology of Christianity from the Solomon Islands. *Ethnos* 70(1): 101–25.

Sen, A.K. 1999. *Development as Freedom*. New York: Oxford University Press.

Smith, M.F. 1994. *Hard Times on Kairiru Island: Poverty, Development, and Morality in a Papua New Guinea Village*. Honolulu: University of Hawaii Press.

_______ 2002. *Village on the Edge: Changing Times in Papua New Guinea*. Honolulu: University of Hawai'i Press.

Stiglitz, J.E. 2003. *Globalization and Its Discontents*. New York: Norton.

Stirrat, R.L. 2000. Cultures of Consultancy. *Critique of Anthropology* 20(1): 31–46.

Strathern, M. 1980. No Nature, No Culture: The Hagen Case. In C.P. Maccormack and M. Strathern (eds), *Nature, Culture and Gender*, pp.174–222. Cambridge: Cambridge University Press.

_______ 1988. *The Gender of the Gift: Problems with Women and Problems with Society in Melanesia*. Berkeley: University of California Press.

_______ 1992. Qualified Value: The Perspective of Gift Exchange. In C. Humphrey and S. Hugh-Jones (eds), *Barter, Exchange and Value*, pp.169–92. Cambridge: Cambridge University Press.

_______ 1995a. The Nice Thing about Culture Is that Everyone Has It. In M. Strathern (ed.), *Shifting Contexts: Transformations in Anthropological Knowledge*, pp.153–76. London: Routledge.

_______ 1995b. *The Relation: Issues in Complexity and Scale*. Cambridge: Prickly Pear Press.

Taussig, M.T. 1977. The Genesis of Capitalism amongst a South American Peasantry: Devil's Labour and the Baptism of Money. *Comparative Studies in Society and History* 19(2): 130–55.

Toren, C. 1999. *Mind, Materiality, and History: Explorations in Fijian Ethnography*. London: Routledge.

Uvin, P. 1998. *Aiding Violence: The Development Enterprise in Rwanda*. West Hartford, CT: Kumarian Press.

Wagner, R. 1967. *The Curse of Souw: Principles of Daribi Clan Definition and Alliance in New Guinea*. Chicago: University of Chicago Press.

_______ 1974. Are there Social Groups in the New Guinea Highlands? In M. Leaf (ed.), *Frontiers of Anthropology*, pp.99–122. New York: Van Nostrand.

_______ 1975. *The Invention of Culture*. Englewood Cliffs, NJ: Prentice-Hall.

_______ 1977. Analogic Kinship: A Daribi Example. *American Ethnologist* 4(4): 623–42.

——— 1991. The Fractal Person. In M. Godelier and M. Strathern (eds), *Big Men and Great Men: Personifications of Power in Melanesia*, pp.197–214. Cambridge: Cambridge University Press.

West, P. 2006. *Conservation Is Our Government Now: The Politics of Ecology in Papua New Guinea*. Durham, NC: Duke University Press.

Wolf, E.R. 1982. *Europe and the People Without History*. Berkeley: University of California Press.

World Bank. 1991. World Development Report 1991: The Challenge of Development. Washington: World Bank.

1

Imagining the Future

An Existential and Practical Activity

Lisette Josephides

Hope has been described as being about the sense of possibility that life can offer; its enemy is a sense of entrapment (Hage 2001; see also Hage 2003). This sense of possibility, I argue, is existential. It was certainly experienced and expressed many times by different Kewa people of the Southern Highlands of Papua New Guinea during my long period of fieldwork. In an attempt to elucidate people's own imaginings and hopes for the future, I consider the relationship between the following concepts and activities: imagining; the future; hope and desire; the existential human condition; and practical activity. I ask: What does it mean to want a future that is different from the past? How do people experience desire for a different future? How do they act on such desires? Why is the need to retain a prospective outlook an 'existential' one?

Ethnographic and theoretical enquiries allow me to assert that people everywhere want to move forward, and in this they can only start from their selves, as individuals who know and experience the world from their own perspective. Naturally what I present here is a perspective that I find interesting, but this interest developed during fieldwork and did not precede it. What I as an ethnographer saw on the ground was desire, expressed as inquisitiveness: about all sorts of things not known locally but fast becoming part of the local world, a fervent wonderment about everything. This is what leads me to suggest that imagining as an activity is first of all existential. People 'take themselves out' out of sheer interest (see the example of Walali below). Even welcoming the anthropologist is an act that imagines the future.

To see imagination as forward propelling is to follow a different route from one that forces a choice (from either the ethnographer or the villager) between past/tradition on the one hand and modernity/development on the other. As I argued elsewhere, 'what defines each modernizing strategy is not whether it is an attempt to localize modernity or embrace it in an alienating foreign form, but whether it is undertaken in the spirit of an active, bold self-externalization, or a desperately anxious submission' (Josephides 2005a: 123–24). I offered this argument as a response to Sahlins's 'humiliation hypothesis', where he suggested that in order to modernise, 'people must first learn to hate what they already have', they must experience a certain humiliation' and a 'global inferiority complex' (Sahlins 1992, quoted in Josephides 2005a: 116). Sahlins used my ethnography (Josephides 1985) to develop his distinction between local and colonial understandings of development: '"You know what we mean by development?" says a leader of the Kewa people to the ethnographer. "We mean building up the lineage, the men's house, killing pigs. That's what we have done"' (Sahlins 1994: 388). Below, I refer to this attitude as an attempt to understand change by 'bringing the outside in' (soon to be replaced by the strategy of 'taking oneself out'). At times people did laugh at their old practices or describe them as bad, but this is an established aspect of wry Kewa self-deprecation.

During our fieldwork in 1993, Marc Schiltz (my husband and fellow-anthropologist) and I received requests for help in 'development projects', such as the starting up of a saw mill with Marc as manager. But Rimbu's decision to sell his shares in Lake Kutubu Oil showed prescience as well as a concern with the outcome of the sort of 'anxious submission' mentioned above. 'Since oil was found in Kutubu, all people think about is money', he told me.[1] For Rimbu as for others, these acts did not signal a rejection of the past or a desire for development. They were a striving. As Ernst Bloch put it, we live in the future because we strive (cited in Crapanzano 2004: 111). Imagination is always moving into the future, and this is what distinguishes it from recollection and nostalgia.

A crucial trait of imagination as outlined by Edward Casey (1976) is indeterminacy and pure possibility. As a musing on what is purely possible, imagination can never be in the past, but demands independence and freedom of the mind. Ernst Bloch (1989) talks of hope as being similarly radically indeterminate, and open in a future-oriented direction, not addressing itself to what already exists but committed to change and thus incorporating the element of chance. Bloch's 'not-yet' is not something forgotten but 'something still outstanding', as Heidegger has said of both desire and hope (Heidegger 1962: 278). In Minkowski's words (cited in Crapanzano 2004), hope opens the future before us, putting us into contact with a becoming that is unfolding at a distance. Hope has been described as 'optimism of the intellect' opening up ways of thinking, and a method of radical temporal reorientation of knowledge (Harvey 2000, cited in Miyazaki 2004: 1). I expand the enquiry into an existentialist one, bringing knowledge together with being, thus linking epistemology and ontology. Hope persists in the face of constant disappointment because it is more than a strategy; it is part of imagining, and imagining as an activity is first of all existential. This establishes the link between 'hope' and 'future', with imagination as mediator – despite Casey's disinclination to see imagination in this 'reduced' capacity.[2]

I begin with a discussion of the key terms under three headings: imagining; hope and desire; and the future as a horizon of knowledge and being. The existential aspects will be exemplified throughout my discussion. The perspective I outline here, though philosophical, was suggested by the words, activities and expressed opinions of the Kewa people with whom I lived over many years (see Josephides 2008). For this reason it cannot be dismissed as 'Western philosophy'.

Imagining

How then is imagining the future an existential and practical activity? It is existential because it arises spontaneously in human beings who could not flourish without it, and practical because it incorporates action. 'Imagining' is the capacity; 'hope' is what is imagined. Though some philosophers conflate the two, hope is not the actualisation of desire. The horizon, where hope meets the future, is the creation of the human observer who is not satisfied with available dogmatic answers (Maleuvre 2011).

As Casey sets out in his major work on imagining, the first thing to be said about imagining is that it is easy to do – we can imagine whatever we want at any time and with the greatest ease (Casey 1976). This may be the reason why philosophers have dismissed imagining as an inferior form of mental activity. We may imagine the same thing many times over, Casey continues, but every time it will be somewhat different. Imagination is constantly innovative, which means that it is always moving into the future, towards horizons. The objects of our imagination can be fictitious or real. If somebody says to me, 'Imagine a winged horse', I can see such an image, even if I have never heard of Pegasus (ibid.: 7).

In fact, when we imagine, the actuality of 'facts' or things must be held in abeyance: 'eidetic insight is strictly non-empirical in character' (ibid.: 23). Suspending factuality – or as I shall call it, 'suspended actuality' – allows us to arrive at essential structures through the well-known phenomenological reduction, an exercise that makes an independent phenomenon 'a phenomenon-for-me' (ibid.: 23).[3] The phenomenological method makes more explicit what was implicit. Things imagined are concretely given in actual experience, but they may be either empirical intuitions or intuitions with no relation to sensory experience (ibid.: 24).

These philosophical points can be made more concrete by being applied to pertinent anthropological questions. Have anthropologists come across such cases of suspended actuality in exchanges with the people they study? Many times, I would contend. The point to be developed here concerns the role of imagining in the creation of a horizon by human actors who are not satisfied with conventional narratives, as mentioned above; it links to subsequent discussion of immanence and transcendence.

Actual episodes of imagining are always first person in character, as Casey comments: we do not imagine using someone else's imagination. Objects, events or acts, real or imagined, are taken to exemplify an essence or essential structure. Casey outlines how imagination holds in tension three pairs of traits: spontaneity and controlledness, self-containedness and self-evidence, indeterminacy and pure possibility. I will take up only the last, 'pure possibility', which is 'a kind of possibility that is posited and contemplated *for its own sake*' (ibid.: 116, original emphasis). Because imagining is pure possibility, it can never be in the past.[4]

'Pure possibility' involves entering 'into a *musing* state of mind', a state of mind that entertains an idea. 'Imagining is entertaining oneself with what is purely possible', and the purely possible 'fosters free mental movements'. 'Imagining is entertaining a given imaginative presentation as purely possible while at the same time experiencing it as inherently indeterminate' (ibid.: 123). It cannot be tied down to any one thing, or be called upon to account for itself. Thus our imagination slips out of the noose of what is actually possible, and can never be falsified. What puts itself back in the noose is no longer imagination but desire for a particular reality (see Marcel on hope, below).

While this openness has led to imagination being considered as transitional, serving to link two other acts which actualise it (ibid.: 129), Casey wants to show that imagination is autonomous. Imagination is intentional in character, not like perception, and not inferior or reducible to perception, but 'self-delimiting and able to control its own activity' (ibid.: 179). Casey thus critiques the romantic view that imagination is spontaneous creativity. Rather, its autonomy is linked to the 'independence and freedom of the mind'; pure possibility 'is the thetic expression of imaginative freedom of mind' (ibid.: 199). This imaginative autonomy has an important role in art – that of 'possibilizing' (ibid.: 205) – but beyond art, I would argue, the concept of possibilising is relevant in everyday life. Imaginative activity, as

Casey puts it, 'directs itself to what *might* be than to what must be, or to what is, has been, or will be', representing 'an exercise of imaginative freedom'. This freedom concerns itself exclusively with the purely possible. In William James's words, 'The mind is at every stage a theater of simultaneous possibilities' (ibid.: 231). Casey concludes that the 'projection and contemplation of pure possibilities is not only a matter of instrumental significance'; pure possibilities '*are themselves ends* and experienced as such'. (This is the case with Lari's bid to escape normal life, as will be seen below.)

Borges: The Traitor and the Hero

Before giving instances from my own ethnography, I offer an exercise in pure possibility from the imagination of the Argentine writer Jorge Luis Borges. In one of his short fictions, 'The Theme of the Traitor and the Hero', Borges (1999) imagines the following scenario: While carrying out research into the assassination of a hero of a liberation struggle, a descendant of the hero reads various signs (he suggests they were left there deliberately) that lead him to conclude that his illustrious ancestor was in reality a traitor who instigated his own unmasking, then asked, in the interests of the revolutionary struggle, that his execution be staged as an assassination carried out by another, undiscovered, traitor. Having deciphered these signs, the descendant decides to leave the hero unexposed, and write a conventional account of the betrayal instead. (What Borges does not say, but leaves us free to imagine, is an equally credible *über*-Borgesian scenario in which the signs were planted in order to pervert the true history, in which the hero was not a traitor.) What Borges does in this story is to open up pockets (or crevices) in time, then close them up again. If they had been left open, they would have entered history, and we would have known about them. Borges rescues these possible realities, shoring up for them the possibility of existing. From this story we get a glimpse of what is possible, and the realities that may be running concurrently/parallel with the one that is recognised at a particular point and from a particular perspective. Though Borges closes the fissures up again and smoothes over the ground, he has left us with this indelible realisation: that it is imagination that opened them, that some fissures or signs remain, and that all imagination is also the reading of signs.[5]

Borges's fiction is an excursus into the possibilities of imagination. The Kewa self-narratives that I collected were based mainly on 'pure possibility', but when told as true stories they opened up innumerable crevices in time. Their purely possible scenarios indicate a consciousness informed by the experience of both tradition and development, of past and future, but slave to neither. In telling their stories, the narrators experienced them as ends. The selves they posited would always remain pure possibility; the negotiations they underwent were practical delimiting factors in the tension between immanence and transcendence (see below). As Maleuvre puts it, 'knowledge ends not where objective reality waves a stop sign, but where it runs out of ideas' (Maleuvre 2011: 2). This running out of ideas, or the vanishing, is also the horizon where imagining has the opportunity to push against the 'open unknown' (ibid.: 2). The act of perceiving oneself perceiving is, 'inevitably, to look inward; it is to become conscious of the reach of human experience' (ibid.: 2).

One conclusion to be drawn from this discussion is that imagination is never in the past; it is forward moving and different from recollection or reminiscence. It is not nostalgia but hope for a future. Its forward-looking character does not mean that it abandons all the ways it has known, because these ways are not in the past, as tradition is not in the past and does not have to take one 'back'. Though I use the palimpsest analogy in my discussion of Kewa self-narratives from three generations of informants, I am careful to clarify that what is at issue 'is not erasure of the past but a condensation and an embedding' (Josephides 2008: 222). Each story 'painted over' other claims, but the whole story of people's understandings moves forward as a result. What is important is not so much to distinguish between past/tradition and modernity/development, but to see the imagination as always forward propelling.

To develop these points further, I turn to a discussion of hope and desire. But first I must provide some ethnography and conceptual terms to ground the theoretical discussion. Two key conceptual terms in particular are elaborated: elicitation, and rehearsed and rehearsing talk and action. I begin by considering the different strategies at the heart of the debate on hope: 'bringing the outside in' and 'taking oneself out'. They can be understood in relation to different historical moments.

Into the Future: Kewa Elicitations and Strivings

The Kewa people of the Southern Highlands experienced first contact with colonial government representatives during the Hides patrol of 1935.[6] Many villagers were shot and killed during the patrol. Fifty years on, Marc Schiltz and I talked to villagers who lived through the event as children or youths. The story of Walali emerged from many accounts. He was said to have been a Kewa man who had left the village very young, and returned with the Hides patrol as a trained policeman. In their attempts to understand the killings of local people by that patrol, villagers summoned the figure of Walali as the trickster behind the shootings. He was depicted as a man seeking revenge for the death of his clansmen in battles more than a decade earlier, who was given carte blanche by the white patrol officers to settle old scores. Our analysis of the situation (in Josephides and Schiltz 1991) introduced the distinction between two different social and cultural responses by relating them to different historical moments: 'bringing the outside in' and 'taking oneself out'. Kewa villagers were faced with the task of explaining to themselves an utterly inexplicable event: the provenance and business of these strange-looking outsiders who came into their midst, and the reason for the killings that ensued. Their explanation in terms of local events brought the outside in; but their desire to understand was the strongest motive for their accounts.[7]

But during my fieldwork, half a century after the Hides patrol, the strategy of Kewa villagers was to 'take themselves out'. I write about this activity as a testing of the limits of oneself, 'by means of a stretching, to see how much of the outside one can encompass'; thus it is 'a form of self-exploration, self-control, and personal commitment' (Josephides 2005a: 122). As a technique for negotiating social knowledge, it replaces more conventionalised morality understood as simply following norms. I refer to it as 'eliciting' talk and action, understood as 'a measure of the absence of clear, culturally conventionalized frames of metacommunication' (Josephides 1999: 152). All Kewa make strong claims in their statements, which indicate their understanding of their world and their own place in it, and elicit recognition and agreement from their interlocutors; but they are prepared to beat a retreat if there is strong objection to the position expressed. Thus, though eliciting talk is a measure of the absence of culturally conventionalised frames of metacommunication, it still serves as a sort of frame by delimiting expectation and requiring negotiation.

I indicate this eliciting activity by the use of another pair of concepts, rehearsed and rehearsing talk and action. Habit is 'rehearsed talk' which covers over its origins as 'rehearsing talk', a claim that may at any moment be overthrown. Neither rehearsed nor rehearsing talk can escape the challenge posed by the ambiguity of all Kewa talk, which is able to spread, withdraw or be modified when challenged – and all this without loss of the speaker's credibility (Josephides 2008: 109).

From what kind of ethnographic data can I draw examples of suspended actuality and pure possibility, where possibility is posited for its own sake? I consider two expressive forms: self-narratives (including religious epiphanies) and myths. Though there is no space here to discuss everyday interactions – what I call 'minimal narratives', following Carrithers (1995) – it should be noted that they also use the eliciting strategies found in self-narratives.

Self-narrative is a cultural form that joins the past, the present and the future. It is important to stress that I am not making a claim that this is a 'traditional' Kewa form. Traditional storytelling, as far as my fieldwork uncovered, consisted of two forms: myths (*lidi*) and stories of origin (*re agele*, 'base-stories'). The first recounted fantastical events not taken to be literally true but nonetheless containing cosmological, ecological, cultural and political truths about the beginnings of the world and human beings, flora and fauna, social and political organisation (see Josephides 1982). The second were supposedly true stories of clan origins, usually told by clan members in the context of claiming rights to particular land. As I have argued elsewhere (Josephides 2005b: 179), stories of origin are routinely constructed out of the rich corpus of myths, with the intention of creating specific cultural meanings such as claims to land and special relationships to other clans. While the myths may be interpreted in many different ways, not only reinforcing order but also showing order to be a sham that upholds oppressive hierarchies, stories of origin by contrast make narrow claims for particular clans and thus become contestable.

When my interest in collecting life stories became known, people in the area began to arrive at my house prepared to tell their stories. Their motives were multiple and the narrators were conscious of them to varying degrees, but the narrative sessions soon became arenas for negotiating social, political and cultural meanings, and constructing selves in relation to a changing world (Josephides 2008). Though the stories were told in my house, many people crammed in to listen and to comment, and this gave the occasions a semi-public aspect that stressed their role as modes of communication. In this regard the stories operated as standard Kewa modes of everyday interactions. They used the eliciting strategies of strong claims that seek acknowledgement and agreement, followed by a readiness to withdraw or modify the claim in the face of strong objections. But given the changed world with which (at least) the two younger generations grappled, their claims were not more tentative so much as a little more wild, uncertain of their ground. Their nets were cast wider, because they were cast into unknown waters, part blindly. Narrators were aware that the negotiated agreement with other villagers about the status of the world in which they lived was no longer the 'last word', in the sense that this new reality could not be called into existence only by the decision of Kewa villagers. While this openness left space for the 'imaginative freedom of the mind' (Casey 1976: 199), it also made the stories and their claims 'pure possibility' in a particularly poignant way. The purely possible posited for its own sake took wing and lost its grounding, but this is the promise and the risk entailed in such freedom.

Below I give a brief account of the narratives by Rimbu, his wife Lari, his brother Hapkas, and his cousin/brother, elder and political rival, Mapi. Rimbu interprets his own heroic experiences in a picaresque account of adventures in plantations and other travel. Throughout these travels, which may be seen as replacing rites of passage, Rimbu maintains a humorous and somewhat sardonic mien. He describes the easy time he had with Bill, a white man he sees as clueless, who takes him on what Rimbu deems to be a fruitless, cushy and well-paid reconnaissance trip (Josephides 2008: 127). Though narrating confusing events, Rimbu takes charge and puts himself at the moral centre of his story, acknowledged as a person by the faraway people he meets.

In contrast to these picaresque travels, Lari is forced to run away from her own home under the canopy of torrential rain in the pitch-black night, in a desperate attempt to escape her father's marriage plans for her. She breaks her crucifix in anger when the priest turns down her plea to baptise her immediately, a ploy she hoped would stave off marriage and allow her to continue at school. In her narrative, Lari positions herself differently from other women, who describe their courting activities with relish, marriage as the aim of their lives and love magic as a way to achieve it. Instead, her young eyes turn towards the horizon that Maleuvre describes as 'infinite longing', the desire for what is beyond the line of vision, but gathers to it all her life's hopes (Maleuvre 2011: 128–29).

The aspects of Hapkas's and Mapi's stories relevant to this discussion are the accounts of their religious epiphanies. From a humdrum existence as a very ordinary man Hapkas, who claims to have 'received life' before Mapi, became a 'dreamer' whose visions foretell the future and comment on what is 'the good life'. This prophetic capacity is a way of seizing the present by predicting the future, through the reading of signs that include actual events. Hapkas realised that God had 'got him' following his arrest after a fight with men from another clan. His name was written down on the list of those arrested, but it had disappeared from the list by the time Rimbu came to pay the fine and secure his release. 'Who else but God would have removed my name?' Hapkas reasoned. His accounts of visions idealised white people, who symbolised purity and the good life (Josephides 2008: 137). In his dreams, the skin of those chosen by God turns white, in what is clearly a symbolic colour change. Previously a shy man, after his election Hapkas began to draw pictures of his visions and hold forth about them in church.

Like Hapkas, Mapi identified signs of election retrospectively, and arranged them in a coherent narrative (ibid.: 99–101). His account strings together dreams and visions – 'signs scattered in the world' (Ricoeur 1970: 46, see above) – and connects them to actual events and actual experience. The elm tree central to his epiphany really had been struck by lightning – I saw the scorched tree myself. In accordance with Casey's discussion (see above), the events Mapi describes were given in his experience, but the 'eidetic insight' was non-empirical in character. That is,

Mapi's interpretation of the events following the lightning, when high up in the sky he saw beautiful houses in many colours and lovely open spaces, was not an empirical observation but an 'eidetic insight', going beyond actual experience and seeing the form – as indeed can be said in the case of Hapkas's name missing from a list of arrested persons. Moreover, the visions of both men recalled scenes from older Kewa myths.

All the stories I collected, but especially those of the two younger generations, revolved around claims of being different and singled out (Josephides 2008: 102). They show how people attempt to grasp and shape the future with the ultimate aim of gaining recognition and prestige in the new world (ibid.: 105); how they take their lives in their own hands and push themselves over the chasm to a new terrain – 'which is the lot of all human beings who want to live' (ibid.: 109). The narratives can be seen through a double perspective – as personal texts of a perceived world, and face-value claims about the narrators' own positions (ibid.: 141). For instance, Mapi, a former village magistrate who lost political office, now found a new source of prestige. As personal texts, the narratives 'make claims, seek approval, and try out particular understandings for general agreement' (ibid.: 146). While Casey talks of 'possibilizing' and imagination as the exercise of the 'purely possible', Ricoeur injects a moral perspective: he observes that telling a story 'is deploying thought experiments in which moral judgement operates in a hypothetical mode' (Ricoeur 1992: 170). This mode of operating, in allowing 'suspended judgement', is reminiscent of Casey's 'suspended factuality'. In the Kewa case it allows, simultaneously, new understandings and the withdrawal of unsuccessful claims. In this state of suspended actuality, 'signs scattered in the world', referring to what is given in actual experience or empirical intuition, lead to changed consciousness, as in the case of religious epiphanies.

It should be clear that 'suspended actuality' is a precondition for the imaginative freedom of the mind – which, as Casey tells us, is a 'musing' state of mind concerned with the purely possible posited for its own sake. Such a musing state suggests simultaneous possibilities, as in Borges's story of crevices in time and my own analysis of Kewa myths. In their narratives, Rimbu, Lari, Hapkas and Mapi all suspend actuality in the creation of a horizon full of pure possibilities that are themselves ends and experienced as such: Lari in her attempts to escape normal life, Hapkas and Mapi in their religious epiphanies, Rimbu at the centre of any milieu in which he finds himself. Imagination is presented here through narratives, dreams and visions which combine and are informed by themes both old and new, linked by a straining into the future and resulting in a changed consciousness.

Hope and Desire

In a book on hope, Mary Zournazi puts the question in a way that resonates with my perspective: 'what hopeful visions of the future may arise, based on reconsidering what it means to be human, and how we relate to the world around us' (Zournazi 2002: 17–18). For her, this is 'an existential question about our sense of being in the world and our perceptions of it' (ibid.: 18). From a contrasting perspective, Crapanzano follows Minkowski in seeing hope as 'desire's passive counterpart' (Crapanzano 2004: 100). While 'desire is effective', presupposing human agency and leading to action, hope 'depends upon some other agency – a god, fate, chance, an other – for its fulfilment' (ibid.: 100).

But I begin with Gabriel Marcel's 1952 treatise on hope. Hope is so different from our experience, or established experience, he writes, because it is a going forward and not a looking back (Marcel 2010: 46 et passim). Does hope depend upon me or is it an innate disposition? Or, as I put it, is imagining an existential activity? Hope is faithfulness: for Marcel, with Christian overtones, to the origin (ibid.: 57); for me, to our humanity. Marcel argues that connecting hope to our reason for hoping is to stifle hope because it is to treat it as an external phenomenon (ibid.: 57), and from the perspective, position or viewpoint of the observer who thus questions the grounds for hope (ibid.: 58). But the one who hopes may have a different perspective, invisible to the observer. While this recalls Casey's argument from William James, that the contemplated (imagined) pure possibilities are themselves ends, Marcel offers additional philosophical reasoning. Can the one who hopes, he asks, ever admit that there are insufficient grounds for hoping? (ibid.: 58). Such an admission would be nonsensical, as it would nullify the claim that they hope. If a subject hopes, this is in itself sufficient grounds; 'hope and the calculating faculty of reason are essentially distinct' (ibid.: 59). In that case, the words 'reasons for hoping' have no meaning (ibid.: 59).

Nonetheless, Marcel must contend with the critique that experience shows that it is absurd to 'subscribe to an irrationalism or a radical fideism' (ibid.: 59). Citing the example of the mother who hopes to see her son again even though his death has been witnessed and certified, Marcel argues that at the root of the mother's statement is 'a loving thought which repudiates or transcends the facts' (ibid. 59). Seen in this way, it would be 'absurd or even scandalous' to dispute 'her right to hope, that is to say to love, against all hope' (ibid.: 59). While he conflates hope with love, Marcel reminds us of another distinction, that between hope and desire, where the latter designates, or indicates, a centring upon or an obsession with the subject and denotes a more egotistical love, rather than enjoying the unconditional quality of communion, an 'us' for whom 'I hope in Thee' (ibid.: 60).

In reasoning thus, Marcel is veering towards the transcendental aspects of hope that find their origin in an other, as Crapanzano has said. Hope, Crapanzano writes, 'always invokes an ever-further horizon – a beyond of a mysterious, transcending, if not transcendental, nature' (Crapanzano 2004: 104). While desire presupposes human agency, hope is predicated on an other, transcendent agency for its fulfilment.[8] But what Crapanzano does not acknowledge here is the perception (or experience) of hope as beyond fulfilment (see the discussion of Marcel, above; and Miyazaki on placing one's agency in abeyance, below), in the same way that imagining as pure possibility is its own end and does not depend on actualisation (Casey, above). In the Kewa example cited above, Lari broke her cross in anger, but still hoped to avert her fate. (See also the examples below discussing illocutionary acts and perlocutionary effects.)

For Minkowski, desire surpasses hope 'as it contains activity' (Crapanzano, 2004: 103). In desire there is a withdrawal 'towards the insides of the active ego' (ibid.: 104). 'Hope shares the same direction as expectations … towards the future-present' (ibid.: 104). 'Hope allows me to take refuge in myself in order to see life unfold around me' (ibid.: 104). Minkowski continues: 'Desire contains activity within itself, while hope liberates us from anxious expectation. And yet, it holds us breathless' (ibid.: 104). And he concludes: 'We are charmed by hope … because it opens the future broadly before us' (ibid.: 103). It puts us into contact with a becoming that is unfolding at a distance.

Hope, then, invites imagination and an expectancy, a going forth. In Bloch's words, it is an 'expectant emotion'. 'Imagining the future' is thus an existential and practical activity. In understanding desire and hope in terms of 'something still outstanding', Heidegger gave to both 'the essential characteristic of care (*Sorge*) of human life' (ibid.: 103). Kierkegaard, by contrast, and in opposition to Marcel, considered hope to be an untrustworthy guide, a poor alternative to the real knowledge of the immortals (ibid.: 116). The links between hope and knowledge (Miyazaki), and immanence and transcendence as part of the horizon of knowledge, beyond the plane of human knowledge (Maleuvre), will be discussed next.

Agency in Abeyance: Hope as Method of Knowledge

In his discussion of the place of hope in knowledge formation, Miyazaki follows Bloch and Benjamin in defining hope as a method of radical temporal reorientation of knowledge (Miyazaki 2004). Hope is not 'an emotional state of positive feeling about the future or a religious sense of expectation'; it is an 'optimism of the intellect' (ibid.: 1, citing Harvey 2000) which opens up ways of thinking and whose absence seriously obstructs progressive thinking. Miyazaki argues that, 'Unlike the subject of desire, which inherently invites one to analyze it with its infinitely deferrable quality … the conceptualization of hope as a method invites one to hope' (ibid.: 5). It is its own end, as Casey claims for imagination. But Miyazaki has other goals: to show that by 'thinking through hope as a method' we may begin to confront the fundamental problem of 'what knowledge is for' (ibid.: 9).

I reconsider two ethnographic moments that exemplify Miyazaki's meaning.

First moment: The Suvavou people have over a long period petitioned the Fijian government for compensation for seized ancestral land. These actions, Miyazaki argues, 'represent an enduring hope to confirm their self-knowledge, the truth about who they really are' (ibid.: 3). Being alienated from their land, Fijians are alienated from their own self-knowledge.

I take the liberty of adding another perspective. Suvavou people's petitions could be seen as a strategy to construct a worthwhile self. Miyazaki writes that for the Suvavou what is true is effective, but the logic could also be reversed – what is effective is true. What this understanding would stress is that it is not some 'truth' which is being pursued, but the desire to construct worthwhile selves, and to have those selves acknowledged. This is what Kewa do in their self-narratives – or what I interpret them to be doing (Josephides 2008: 109).

Second moment: There is a moment in the course of Fijian gift-giving at which the gift-givers subject themselves to the gift-receivers' evaluation. They wait and quietly hope 'that the other side will respond positively'. In this wait, Miyazaki argues, they are '[placing] in abeyance their own agency, or capacity to create effects in the world … at least temporarily' (Miyazaki 2004: 7).

Continuing with an alternative interpretation, it can be seen that Suvavou people have actually already 'offered' their agency as an act of elicitation and are merely awaiting its outcome, in the way we all pause to see the effects of our actions following an illocutionary act (see below). Elicitation, as discussed earlier, 'denotes the contestability and negotiability of meanings and intentions' (Josephides 2008: 107). In equivalent (though not strictly similar) circumstances, when Kewa people ceremonially give pigs at a pig kill, receiving no immediate return, their agency has not been put in abeyance; on the contrary, having made their prestation they are in the ascendant position. It is now up to the recipients to experience the anxiety of 'matching' them.

A brief excursus into a discussion of illocutionary acts will clarify the points above. Searle criticises Grice for confusing illocutionary and perlocutionary acts when he '[defines] meaning in terms of intended effects' (Searle 1969: 44). He elaborates: 'To say that speaker *S* meant something by *X* is to say that *S* intended that utterance of *X* to produce some effect in a hearer *H* by means of the recognition of this intention' (ibid.: 43). Saying something and meaning it is a matter of performing an illocutionary act; the hearer may understand and even recognise what I want to achieve, but will not necessarily experience the 'effect' of my intentions. This is because there are no perlocutionary acts, only perlocutionary effects. An act can be registered as perlocutionary only after it has had the desired effect on the hearer.

Searle further states that analyses of illocutionary acts must 'capture both the intentional and the conventional aspects [of meaning]' (ibid.: 45). What one means, and what the words one uses mean, are not the same thing. To give a Kewa example: When Lari caught her husband Rimbu in an embrace with another woman, she told him angrily that he should marry the woman. It was not seemly, she said, for a grown man to snatch embraces like an unmarried boy. But her intention was actually to shame her husband into stopping his love-making. Rimbu understood her meaning, but still married the woman. This was an illocutionary act that did not have the desired perlocutionary effect. Lari's meaning, as desire, was understood, but it did not have the effect of averting the marriage. A listener may recognise what the speaker intends when uttering a proposition; this is illocutionary effect. Whether the utterance has the desired effect in the listener is another matter. 'Intentions are from the speaker's side, but effects concern the hearer'. This is why I would argue that there are no perlocutionary acts, only perlocutionary effects.

To return to the second moment in the Suvavou example. Hope, Miyazaki continues, is deferred at this crucial juncture, when the recipients accept the gifts 'but then collectively present the gifts to God' (Miyazaki 2004: 7). This has the effect of denying the importance of the act of gift giving among humans, and as the gift is passed on it is treated as a prestation for heavenly blessing that is to descend on both giver and recipient. 'At the moment at which the gift-givers' hope is fulfilled, it is replaced by another hope, hope of God's blessing on all those involved … The first moment of fulfilment in ritual is an intimation of God's ultimate response. The production of hope of God's blessing, then, is a product of a carefully orchestrated discursive play of human agency' (ibid.: 8). In this instance, hope is not passive, as Minkowski and Crapanzano think, but is an activity that constructs itself. I would add that hope is not deferred but fulfilled, leading and expanding to further hopes – or a sort of paradigmatic shift. The bid is on the table; one round has been won and a new player is introduced.

Miyazaki realised that his analysis of the ritual process proceeded from 'the vantage point of its effects' (ibid.: 10). Following my discussion above, the effects would be the perlocutionary aspect of the interaction, which the speaker (or donor) cannot control. More broadly, to foresee the end point of any transaction is in effect to foreclose it and deny the agency of the respondent. However, in this case, 'ritual participants maintained a forward-looking orientation at every step of the ritual', and 'the maintenance of a prospective perspective was at the heart of ritual performance' (ibid.: 11). This was so despite the fact that the same people engaged in the same ritual at different times and were aware of its outcomes or effects. Though their hope may not be as desperate as the mother's refusal in the face of all evidence to accept her son's death, it has aspects of what Casey has called 'suspended factuality'.

Miyazaki's stated ultimate goal 'is not to theorize hope but to construct an analytical framework for approaching concrete moments of hope' (ibid.: 12). Hope, he concludes, 'cannot be argued for or explained; it can only be replicated. Hence the potential danger of hope transforming itself into self-aggrandizement and self-righteous anger' (ibid.: 110–11). What Miyazaki stresses is the way in which Suvavou people, like many philosophers and other theorists, generate hope, so that the 'idea of hope as a method … *unites* different forms of knowing' (ibid.: 3, 4). But while hope may be a method, even a sort of strategy, I would argue that it is also an existential condition.

In his major work on the *Principle of Hope,* Bloch identifies a tension: while the world is full of propensity-towards, philosophy is retrospective and presupposes 'a closed world that has already become' (ibid.: 13). Three themes are central to Bloch's notion of hope: its radical indeterminacy, its repetitive quality, and the backgrounding of agency. Bloch introduces the notion of the 'not-yet' consciousness as the antithesis of the Freudian notion of the subconscious – not something forgotten but 'something new that is dawning up', the radically indeterminate nature of hope (ibid.: 14). For Bloch:

> hope must be unconditionally disappointable, *first,* because it is open in a forward direction, in a future-oriented direction; it does not address itself to that which already exists. For this reason, hope – while actually in a state of suspension – is committed to change rather than repetition, and what is more, incorporates the element of chance, without which there can be nothing new. (ibid.: 69)

But as for everything, once hope has been realised, it does not resemble what was previously hoped for (ibid.: 70). This is so even in the case of a repetitive ritual.

Do we need to change the temporal direction of knowledge (as retrospective philosophy) in order to change the world, or ever see hope as directed to the future? The point about viewing history 'as a teleological disclosure' of the essence, or truth about humanity, reminds me of cultural functionalism, a perspective I critique in Josephides (1991).[9] However, I share the pragmatists' belief that 'the introduction of hope to philosophy reorients philosophy to the future' (Miyazaki 2004: 16), a future without a predetermined end that will 'astonish and exhilarate' (ibid.: 15, 14). I have two caveats. First, a belief that 'humanity is an open-ended notion' (Rorty, cited in ibid.: 16) does not entail a rejection of the essence of humanity in the sense that I discuss it, and to have regard for human beings as human beings does not require a completed project. Second, in response to the objection to a theorisation of hope as predicated on a concept of transcendent agency, viewed as a concept of God and thus limiting human agency (ibid.: 17), I would argue that transcendence and immanence are both aspects of being human and not limited to a relation with God and a Christian teleology.[10] These points will be developed in the next section, which takes a marvellously titled book by Didier Maleuvre as its starting point.

The Future as a Horizon of Knowledge and Being: Human Knowledge and Transcendent Knowledge

In *The Horizon: A History of Our Infinite Longing*, Didier Maleuvre (2011) writes that to the extent that the horizon is 'the child of curiosity' – 'inquiring, expectant, far-looking' – it is 'wedded to the concept of transcendence'; but for him this concept is not inherently mystical 'but underpins everyday human knowledge' (ibid.: 3). He distinguishes between transcendence and religion, arguing that transcendence 'designates the second-guessing nature of human consciousness, the fact that, self-limiting as it is, knowledge is moved to wonder about the space beyond its perimeter' (ibid.: 3). Transcendence, he continues, 'is the mental experience that consists in regarding the plane of known reality as open-ended'; the horizon beckons towards transcendence but does not fulfil it (ibid.: 3). Furthermore, this 'going-to-the-limit is innate to human intelligence'; to it we owe the idea of truth, 'which endeavors to line up our conceptions toe-to-toe with what they stand for' (ibid.: 3).

To paraphrase Maleuvre, we may say that the horizon is the creation of the human observer who is longing for the unseen, but who is not satisfied with available dogmatic answers – that is, answers previously developed by others – canonised, limiting answers, grand narratives, or as I have called them, 'rehearsed talk'. Lari's bid to escape the normal lot of a Kewa woman is a good example of this longing. We cannot stop ourselves wondering about what we cannot know, despite both commonsensical and philosophical admonitions of the type, 'Whereof one cannot speak, thereof one must be silent' (Wittgenstein 1975: 7). However undiscoverable those 'realms beyond human intelligence', still we persist in our belief that it is our business to discover them, rather than pass them over in silence – thus walking 'the tightrope between immanence and transcendence' (Maleuvre 2011: 6).

When we 'commune with celestial entities' in the hope of transcending human knowledge, the horizon disappoints this expectation (for Melanesians, leading to belief of the torn first page of the bible and cargo cults). We are left planted in immanence, as our experience cannot transcend our consciousness. Transcendence and immanence create a Deleuzean 'disjunctive synthesis', rather than a unity (cf. Badiou 2007), just as for Maleuvre our infinite longing is a 'tension rather than a synthesis' (Maleuvre 2011: 5). There is good reason for this: 'Let either transcendence or immanence tip the balance to its own camp and the horizon vanishes. The horizon is just the forever-suspended eventuality that one may dominate the other' (ibid.: 4), a condition of the 'unfinished and interminable balance between the known and the unknown' (ibid.: 5).

Maleuvre argues that while we as 'horizon gazers' can record our 'transcendence sighting', we cannot provide a teleological theory of the end-aim of humanity. The horizon itself causes us to be 'analytic and not synthetic' (ibid.: 5); our existential condition as human beings is to be moved by transcendence, to strive beyond the limits of what can be known and expressed. But always we remain on the 'human immanent plane' – the Deleuzean plane (I would add) of unqualified immersion or embeddedness of being, which rejects a separate transcendent realm.

What I have presented here are various traits concerning what it is to be human from debates within Western philosophy, accompanied by ethnography from Melanesia. But I consider these traits to be foundational. They describe responses from human beings everywhere, not only in the Papua New Guinea highlands, and for that reason I have called them existential. Specifically, I have addressed the forward-looking aspects of human lives. In the words of Ernst Bloch, 'we all live in the future because we strive. Past things come only later' (cited in Crapanzano 2004: 111). To end with a quote from Maleuvre, 'Human intelligence is a going forth; where to, it does not know' (Maleuvre 2011: 7).

Notes

1. This remark is taken from my fieldnotes (8 August 1993). The *Sydney Morning Herald* (20 September 2009) reported an incident that occurred in June 2007.

The Australian-owned oil and gas company, Oil Search Pty Ltd, was drilling for oil near Lake Kutubu, when locals began to report the water changing colour. 'When they washed their skin blistered, and when they drank water they got sick. One girl died in pain days after drinking chemical-laced water'. Though at the time no link was proved between run-off from chemicals used at the drill site and the deadly pollution, Rimbu's early concern and scepticism were noteworthy.

2. While this chapter engages themes of hope and a going forward into the future, it does not assume that the future is always bright. I do not engage political and social questions here. There is unfortunately no shortage of ethnographic monographs that record scenes and expressions of loss accompanying social change. Kirsch (2006), for instance, describes such a sense of loss in the face of environmental degradation among the Yonggom people. But at the same time he gives an account of the expansion of people's 'geographic imaginary' and their ability to map new global connections to help them in their suit against the mining company. Yonggom people continue to imagine the future, albeit in competing forms (ibid.: 206–8).
3. Following Husserl, Sloterdijk (2012) explains the phenomenological reduction (*epoche*) as defining a stepping back from all forms of existential involvement and abstaining from judgement.
4. In a similar vein, Will Rollason (this volume) talks about Ponapompom actions as projecting out into a future in which they will be masters. But right now their endeavours are pure possibility.
5. Compare Ricoeur's (1970: 46) remark that reflection itself is nothing without the mediation of 'signs scattered in the world'.
6. These events were published in a sensationalised account by Hides (1936).
7. A different highland group's curiosity about these outsiders – this time gold prospectors – was powerfully depicted in the film *First Contact* (dir. R. Anderson and B. Connolly, 1982).
8. Crapanzano's chapter on hope, though it considers the work of mostly existentialist and phenomenologist philosophers plus a Marxist one (Minkowski, Kierkegaard, Heidegger and Bloch), offers a critique of phenomenology: 'We have to remember that phenomenology is the product of a particular cultural era: one that gives, for example, evidential priority to the individual, inner experience, consciousness, and a particular take on language that at once recognizes and denies its formative specificity' (Crapanzano 2004: 106).
9. Cultural functionalism, I have argued, shows how an 'already completed' culture 'works in smooth reproduction, recreating the values that structure it' (Josephides 1991: 159), and the task of the analysis is merely to clear the ground and uncover what was already there. Melanesian persons themselves, as 'agents' for their culture, are seen to be enacting rituals whose dual purpose is to cover up and reproduce the core relations that make sociality possible.

10. Immanence denotes the bounds of possible experience. Transcendence is a going beyond any possible knowledge of a human being. In phenomenology, it is what transcends our own consciousness, thus it is objective rather than a phenomenon of consciousness. Deleuze rejects the distinction, while Kant's transcendental *a priori* is concerned with our cognitive faculties: how we can know objects without experiencing them.

References

Badiou, A. 2007. *The Century.* Cambridge: Polity.

Bloch, E. 1989 [1959]. *The Principle of Hope*, 3 vols. Cambridge, MA: MIT Press.

Borges, J.L. 1999. The Theme of the Traitor and the Hero [1944]. In *Collected Fictions*, trans. A. Hurley, pp.143–46. London: Penguin.

Carrithers, M. 1995. Stories in the Social and Mental Life of People. In E. Goody (ed.), *Social Intelligence and Interaction*, pp.261–76. Cambridge: Cambridge University Press.

Casey, E.S. 1976. *Imagining: A Phenomenological Study.* Bloomington: Indiana University Press.

Crapanzano, V. 2004. *Imaginative Horizons: An Essay in Literary-Philosophical Anthropology.* Chicago: University of Chicago Press.

Harvey, D. 2000. *Spaces of Hope.* Berkeley: University of California Press.

Hage, G. 2001. The Shrinking Society: Ethics and Hope in the Era of Global Capitalism. Retrieved from: http://subsol.c3.hu/subsol_2/constributors2/hagetext.html, accessed 1 July 2010.

_______ 2003. *Against Paranoid Nationalism: Searching for Hope in a Shrinking Society.* Annandale, NSW: Pluto Press Australia.

Heidegger, M. 1962 [1926]. *Being and Time*, trans. J. Macquarrie and E. Robinson. London: SMC Press Ltd.

Hides, J. 1936. *Papuan Wonderland.* London: Blackie and Son.

Josephides, L. 1982. Kewa Stories and Songs. *Oral History* (special issue) 10(2).

_______ 1985. *The Production of Inequality.* London: Tavistock.

_______ 1991. Metaphors, Metathemes and the Construction of Sociality: A Critique of the New Melanesian Ethnography. *Man* 26(1): 145–61.

_______ 1995. Replacing Cultural Markers. In D. de Coppet and A. Iteanu (eds), *Cosmos and Society in Oceania*, pp.189–211. Oxford: Berg.

_______ 1998. Biographies of Social Action: Excessive Portraits. In V. Keck (ed.), *Common Worlds and Single Lives: Constituting Knowledge in Pacific*, pp.137–67. Oxford: Berg.

_______ 1999. Disengagement and Desire: The Tactics of Everyday Life. *American Ethnologist* 26(1): 139–59.

——— 2001. Straight Talk, Hidden Talk, and Modernity: Shifts in Discourse Strategies in Highland New Guinea. In J. Hendry and C.W. Watson (eds), *An Anthropology of Indirect Communication*, pp.218–31. London: Routledge.

——— 2005a. Moral and Practical Frameworks for the Self. In J. Robbins and H. Wardlow (eds), *Humiliation and Transformation: The Making of Global and Local Modernities in Melanesia*, pp.115–24. Aldershot: Ashgate Press.

——— 2005b. The Aesthetics of Politics: Transforming Genres and Meanings in Melanesia. In P. Stewart and A. Strathern (eds), *Expressive Genres and Historical Change*, pp.173–200. Aldershot: Ashgate Press.

——— 2008. *Melanesian Odysseys: Negotiating the Self, Narrative and Modernity.* Oxford: Berghahn.

Josephides, L., and M. Schiltz. 1991. Through Kewa Country. In E. Shieffelin and R. Crittenden (eds), *Like People You See in a Dream: First Contact in Six Papuan Societies*, pp.198–224. Stanford: Stanford University Press.

Kirsch, S. 2006. *Reverse Anthropology: Indigenous Analysis of Social and Environmental Relations in New Guinea.* Stanford: Stanford University Press.

Maleuvre, D. 2011. *The Horizon: A History of Our Infinite Longing.* Berkeley: University of California Press.

Marcel, G. 2010 [1952]. Sketch of a Phenomenology and a Metaphysic of Hope. In *Homo Viator: Introduction to the Metaphysic of Hope.* Southbend, IN: St Augustine's Press.

Miyazaki, H. 2004. *The Method of Hope: Anthropology, Philosophy, and Fijian Knowledge.* Stanford: Stanford University Press.

Ricoeur, P. 1970 [1965]. *Freud and Philosophy: An Essay on Interpretation*, trans. D. Savage. New Haven: Yale University Press.

——— 1992. *Oneself as Another.* Chicago: University of Chicago Press.

Sahlins, M. 1992. The Economics of Develop-Man in the Pacific. *Res* 21: 12–25.

——— 1994. Goodbye to Tristes Tropes: Ethnography in the Context of Modern World History. In R. Borofsky (ed.), *Assessing Cultural Anthropology*, pp.377–94. New York: McGraw-Hill.

Searle, J. 1969. *Speech Acts: An Essay in the Philosophy of Language.* Cambridge: Cambridge University Press.

Sloterdijk, P. 2012 [2010]. *The Art of Philosophy: Wisdom as a Practice.* New York: Columbia University Press.

Wittgenstein, L. 1975 [1922]. *Tractatus Logico-Philosophicus.* London: Routledge.

Zournazi, M. 2002. *Hope: New Philosophies for Change.* Annandale, NSW: Pluto Press Australia.

2

The Hanging of Buliga

A History of the Future in the Louisiade Archipelago, Papua New Guinea

Will Rollason

This chapter deals with a hanging that took place at Bwagaoia, the colonial administrative centre of the Louisiade Archipelago, in 1944.[1] The man hanged was called Buliga.[2] He had been the leader of a millenarian movement, and was sentenced to death for his part in a series of murders associated with it. The sentence was passed by the Australian administration, but carried out by Buliga, who hanged himself in his cell before his 'official' execution.[3] In this chapter I argue that Buliga's death was not a 'suicide'. To treat his actions in good faith we have to understand his hanging as the culmination of a political project that aimed to capture the power of the state. We must understand Buliga's hanging as a product of his aspirations for a different future for the people of the Louisiade Archipelago.

The argument of this chapter is in three parts. In the first, I present the basic facts of the uprising and colonial interpretations of it. I draw both on colonial reports from the 1940s,[4] and Hank Nelson's account of the events in the Louisiades (Nelson 1976). These accounts tend to depoliticise events and, in the case of the colonial records, to ascribe them to the native savagery of indigenous people.[5] In the second part of the chapter, I focus on Buliga's hanging, contesting Nelson's account of it as an unproblematic 'suicide',[6] and by extension the colonial account of natural savagery; I am concerned to draw out the problematic, political aspect of Buliga's death. Finally, I explore the limitations of this interpretation by suggesting the problems of cultural tradition as an explanatory framework for Buliga's prospective, political project.

Events in the Louisiade Archipelago

In January 1942, after governing and exploiting the island fringe of Papua for thirty-five years, the white expatriate population of the South East District (SED) fled, fearing attack by the Japanese army which had captured Rabaul two days before (Nelson 1976: 46). Government abruptly ceased. In the Louisiade Archipelago, a man called Buliga came to prominence as a leader and began organising locals for new political ends.

Buliga was from Siagara, on the north coast of the island of Misima. He enters the colonial records in 1942, identified as a 'seer'. It is clear from the outset that the people that he mobilised[7] formed what would be identified by contemporary anthropologists as a cargo cult. Thus, A.C. Hall, the district officer in 1946, three years after the Buliga affair came to an end, investigated puzzling social transformations on Iwa. He found an elaborate, but fully indigenous, organisation there headed by a king, with a second king, governor, boss, doctor, sergeant, eighteen policemen, a regional magistrate, three assistant regional magistrates, two storemen and two motor drivers in open imitation of the prewar structure of the administration. All this was the result of a 'false prophecy' promulgated by Buliga.

Hall wrote in his report: 'He said that after all the Europeans were killed the world would turn over and then any white people remaining would change into natives and natives would change into whitemen. It is said that many natives of MISIMA, PANAEATI, CALVADOS CHAIN and other islands believed this'.[8] Hall's account of indigenous organisation on Iwa, taken in light of more recent ethnographic literature on cargo cults, strongly suggests that the movement that Buliga had inspired imitated the colonial state as a means to effect this apocalyptic transformation of the world. This is consistent with other millenarian movements described throughout Melanesia, most notably by Lawrence (1967), Worsley (1968), Lindstrom (1990), Burridge (1995), Lattas (1998, 2006a, 2006b) and Jebens (2004, 2010), to cite only the best-known examples.

With the defeat of the Japanese at Milne Bay, Australian forces reoccupied the SED, establishing a military organisation under the auspices of the Australian New Guinea Administrative Unit (ANGAU). Patrolling recommenced in November 1942. ANGAU was tasked with maintaining order in the SED, detecting enemy infiltration and recruiting – often conscripting

– labour for the Allied base at Giligili. They regarded Buliga's activities as an 'uprising'.[9] The first ANGAU patrol working out of Bwagaoia Station on Misima and led by Lt. R.G. Mader aimed to secure the island and capture Buliga. However, Buliga had fled into the mountainous hinterland of Misima and could not be apprehended. Soon after, he reappeared, based on the island of Motorina, where he was joined by people from nearby islands of the Calvados Chain. When the administration moved to capture Buliga at Motorina the patrol was ambushed; Mader, a half-caste plantation owner and four policemen were killed. The killings represented the most severe incident of civil violence in the SED since the area was colonised, and they left a profound impression on locals and colonists alike.

More murders followed. A Filipino trader, Gorio Lerau, was ambushed by Sabarl islanders off the coast of Panawina. He and three people from Sudest were murdered. In a separate incident, a village constable and another indigenous man were murdered on Joannet Island. The motive for Gorio Lerau's murder may have been emulation – Bagaman people had just arrived on Sabarl after taking part in the killings on Motorina. The killings on Joannet appear to have been related to a dispute over a pig and threats of sorcery.

In response to the murders in the Calvados Chain, the Australians dispatched a punitive expedition led by Lt. Sydney Smith in February 1943. The patrol, including twenty-eight armed men and operating with three vessels, made a considerable show of force. They found most villages deserted, and destroyed houses and canoes. However, on Sabarl they surprised a large body of local people, including a number of Buliga's adherents from Bagaman. In the ensuing fracas, five people were killed, including one woman, shot through the back as she tried to escape. Overall, 151 men were arrested and eighteen jailed as a result of Smith's patrol. Nine people, including Buliga, were sentenced to hang for their part in the murders. The hangings took place at Bwagaoia in front of a crowd of people. However, of the nine sentenced, only eight hanged. Buliga was already dead. He had plaited a rope from strips of his clothing and, as Nelson puts it, 'hanged himself in the privacy of his cell' (Nelson 1976: 46).

The Colonial Account

The ANGAU administration of Papua produced large numbers of reports and vast quantities of correspondence (cf. Errington and Gewertz 2004). The account that I have presented of the events in the Louisiades in 1942 to 1944 is ultimately drawn entirely from colonial accounts of the Buliga 'uprising'. The data nonetheless remains thin, much of it negative. This is unavoidable considering the sources available, and is a constant problem for those attempting to recover subaltern voices of all kinds. The argument here therefore remains suggestive and not conclusive. What interests me here is the way in which the colonial account of native motives strips indigenous people of any capacity to appear as political – even rational – actors in events as they unfold. I will focus on Lt. Smith's account of the murders and his response to them as leader of the punitive raid. My aim is to show how Smith systematically detaches the murders from any political engagement in the colonial regime. Such a detachment completely vitiates the purpose of Buliga's movement as suggested in 1946 by A.C. Hall – the total reorganisation of the colonial political settlement.

Australian administrators initially understood these events as a reflection of the 'native' qualities of Louisiade people which they had to modify and modernise. They were more or less in agreement that the violence of the natives was a reflection of their primitive character. Lt. Smith, who led the punitive expedition, wrote: 'After these latest murders it seems quite definite that every native in the Calvados Chain from MOTORINA Is in the west to NIMOA in the east, had decided that Government control had more or less ceased to exist and they could return to their old fashions and kill with impunity'.[10] Major K.C. McMullen, district officer, considered the murders and subsequent violence as evidence of 'The speed with which the native is capable of reverting to type – showing how slight is the influence of an Administration on a native people and how slender the control'.[11]

If Buliga's movement was simply the reflex of savagery to the removal of control – a return to a past of Hobbesian warre – then it need not be interpreted or engaged with as a political project reflecting genuine or reasonable grievances. Instead, ANGAU officers regarded the management of natives as the containment of natural savagery by the techniques of civilisation, and not as any kind of political process. This is again clear from Smith's patrol report, in which he categorically denies that the violence in the Calvados Chain was anything to do with colonial rule.

> I do not think it was because of [labour] recruiting. No natives were recruited from the islands where the murders were committed … It is a point to note, also, that those islands where the natives were most in contact with Europeans – MISIMA, SUDEST and Rossel Is. – remained peaceful and did not attempt to take advantage of the absence of government.[12]

Of course, Smith's denial that the violence was the result of a positive policy – labour recruitment – does not absolve the administration from responsibility for the disorder. If the problem was insufficient contact between indigenous communities and patrols, then that is a problem of local administration as well. However, casting the violence as a question of insufficient contact rather than a principled objection to labour conscription converts the Buliga uprising into a technical issue, to be resolved by a show of force for example, rather than a political challenge to Australian rule in the SED that would have to be answered with some form of sustained political engagement (Ferguson 1990; Newbury and Newbury 1999).

Smith's account of the events in the Louisiades in 1942/43 therefore denies that Buliga was pursuing any reasonable political project. Taken with the other comments on the punitive raid, it suggests that the violence is attributable to the natural, primitive savagery of the natives. They are violent because they are not yet modern. Confined to a past that the administration long ago left, they misbehave because they have not yet learnt how to be civilised and quickly 'revert' to savagery. Simultaneously, it defines the problem as a technical one – regaining control of the natives – and the intervention made as appropriate – a show of force. Neither the problem nor the solution is political. Rather, they are technical and managerial. The prior denial of natives' coevality (Fabian 1983) – their definition as savages for whom violence is a 'reversion to type' – is the condition for this depoliticisation of the Buliga affair. Natives located in the past cannot make claims as political actors in the present.

Problematising Buliga's Suicide

In order to disrupt the colonial account of the Buliga affair, we need to gain an insight into the ways in which Buliga was acting politically and the aims and means that his project entailed. This is not easy: his voice is completely absent from the colonial record, and we depend on suggestive fragments of information, lodged in the joints of the colonial account (Gramsci 1971; Newbury and Newbury 2000). In this section, I aim to establish that events in the Buliga affair are more problematic than they appear. I examine Buliga's suicide in the context both of comparative ethnographic material on suicide from elsewhere in the region, and in terms of my own ethnographic experience in the Louisiades.[13] This is useful because an unproblematic reading of the suicide mirrors the depoliticised colonial account. Here I show that Buliga's 'private' suicide must be understood as a powerful political act. I will later deal with the nature and course of the politics he pursued.

Nelson notes that Buliga was not hanged, but hanged himself 'in the privacy of his cell' (Nelson 1976: 46). The implication of Nelson's account is that this hanging is simply a suicide, a 'private' action which spared Buliga the indignity of public defeat and death. This reading of events would regard Buliga's death as outside the public domain of politics and the enactment of sovereign power: Buliga killed himself because he did not wish to be executed. While intuitively convincing, this reading of the hanging of Buliga will not do in light of other evidence about suicide from elsewhere in the region. We must also question the unproblematic invocation of a 'private sphere' in Nelson's account.

The Method of Suicide

The first problem with the Buliga suicide is the method. Accounts of suicides from the Louisiades in the mid twentieth century are lacking. However, Malinowski's material, collected on Kiriwina thirty years before, does serve to shed some light on the issue (see Malinowski 1932).[14] Malinowski records three forms of suicide: by jumping from a coconut palm, by taking fish poison and by starvation. Starvation appears only in a myth, and is almost certainly a symbolic expression of shame (cf. Battaglia 1990). Malinowski reports death by poison as a second-rate form of suicide, favoured by those who wanted to make a display rather than actually to die: people who took fish poison could easily be saved. The dominant method in Malinowski's account of suicide is jumping from a palm tree. Malinowski introduces the practice in the context of incestuous relationships and sexual shame:

> Marriage, anyone will tell you, is quite impossible between men and women of the same clan; nor does it ever happen. As to intercourse, this would be most improper and would be censured by an indignant public opinion. A couple guilty of such an act would, if discovered, incur the anger of the whole community; they would be deeply mortified and terribly ashamed. And to the question: 'What would they do on discovery?' the invariable answer is that they would commit suicide by jumping from a coco-nut palm. This well-known method of escaping from an unpleasant situation is called *lo'u*. (Malinowski 1932: 424)

Lo'u suicide, by jumping from a coconut palm, was clearly a recognised genre of death in Malinowski's time – he reports a case of *lo'u* occurring early in his stay on the islands (ibid.: 475–76), although his informants thought that this custom was in decline. Both men and women might commit suicide in this way (ibid.: 399), although most of the accounts of actual suicides that Malinowski produces are of women.

Trobriand islanders were certainly expert rope-makers; however, there is no mention of hanging in Malinowski's accounts. Indeed, while I heard stories of people who had thrown themselves from trees and cliffs while I was in the region from 2004 to 2006, I never heard tell of hanging as a suicide method. Although none of this can rule out the possibility that hanging was a recognised form of suicide in the Louisiade region in the 1940s, it seems unlikely given Malinowski's data in light of the strong cultural continuities across the entire region.[15]

Note that at issue here is less a question of technical innovation in suicide than highlighting a provocative anomaly. If Buliga was departing from the norms of what was probably a rather well-established genre of action, the question we must ask is what he thought he was doing more than how he went about doing it (Geertz 1983). Below, I take up this issue, focusing on Nelson's ascription of privacy to Buliga's death, before returning to the racial symbolism of hanging.

Privacy

The second problem is the issue of privacy. Nelson stresses Buliga's death in the 'privacy' of his prison cell. In the context of Melanesian anthropology, the concept of a private sphere as opposed to a public domain – through tropes of domestic versus political, individual versus society or female versus male – has come under sustained critique. This critique is at the centre of Marilyn Strathern's influential analysis of Melanesian anthropology (Strathern 1979, 1988, 1991). She points out that, while the opposition between public and private makes sense to Euro-Americans, it does so on the basis of an absolute distinction between individual autonomy and social constraint (Strathern 2003). For Strathern, the foundation of the private/public distinction is the idea that individuals are prior to society; as such they require regulation or integration into a logically posterior 'social domain' (Strathern 1988). Because of this, in structural-functionalist accounts of society, some areas of social life appear 'more social' than others. These 'more social' domains take on a regulatory function in analysis, controlling the 'less social' (natural and therefore prior) components of social life (Strathern 1985). The distinction between the public domain – Fortes's 'politico-jural' domain – and the privacy of the domestic serves Strathern as a type for this hierarchical model of social life.

Feminists have had serious issues with the establishment of this kind of hierarchy of functions. Sherry Ortner famously exploits an analogous relation between public culture and the natural domestic sphere to argue that the establishment of culture's domination over nature is necessarily the establishment of men's domination over women (Ortner 1974). Strathern's critique goes further than Ortner's, however; she argues that people from Mount Hagen in the Highlands of Papua New Guinea, and Melanesians in general, do not conceive of such a hierarchical relationship between nature and culture, or between society and the individual (Strathern 1980, 1981). While they do conceive of different kinds of action or forms of relation, these are not in opposition or hierarchically arranged. Rather, they are conceived as coeval and equally significant, such that individual people or particular household relations can afford a perspective on obviously political and 'public' activity (Strathern 1988, 1991).[16] There is no relation of control, symbolic or otherwise, between the intimate and personal and large-scale group processes.

The upshot of Strathern's critique is the collapse of the idea of the public as opposed to the private. Rather than opposed and incommensurate domains occupying different analytic levels, we are faced with a fully relational manifold: Melanesians in Strathern's analysis are basically social and constituted in and by relationships (cf. Battaglia 1990). As such, Strathern shows that Hageners do not conceive of the distinction between exchange and war as one between sociality and its inverse, but a transformation in the modality of social relations (Strathern 1985). Similarly, while at certain moments relations may be hidden, enclosed and secret – for example, pregnancy and growth – they are nevertheless social relations that must be made apparent and visible in order to be effective (Strathern 1988; Gillison 1993; Kahn 1994; Leach 2003). Melanesian social life in Strathern's formulation therefore operates as an alternation between different forms of social relations, but it is not divided between a public and a private sphere.

Shame

Given this reading of Melanesian social life, we should be suspicious of the idea that Buliga's suicide was in some way a 'private' act. There is no reason to suppose that the notion of privacy was in any way relevant to him – although likely his Australian captors would have interpreted his actions in these terms. To be sure, Buliga hanged himself in secret, but secrecy does not imply a lack of sociality. Rather, what is currently secret (like a child in the womb) must be converted into openly visible knowledge, revealing the social relations that were always taking place inside an enclosure. Hence, while the unproblematic reading of Buliga's suicide would attribute it to shame, and thereby make self-destruction a withdrawal from public life into the privacy and naturalness of death, that reading is not available to us in this context. Indeed, Louisiade people today do not regard the actions that people undertake through shame to be private acts; rather, they represent a most public rearrangement of social relations, even when that rearrangement is undertaken with secrecy.

During my fieldwork, Panapompom people most often talked to me about shame (*pulowawi*) in the context of sexual relations. Sex was thought both to be something that would be shameful if other people saw it, and, as affairs are often more or less illicit, because of the disputes and ill-feeling that they have the capacity to cause. As such, lovers have sex in secret – either in the bush or when a boy secretly visits his lover in her house, a custom called *lulubwala*. However, this secrecy is neither absolute nor lasting. Rather, a girl's relatives, if they like the boy and approve of the match, will attempt to reveal the affair. Especially if they can catch the boy with the girl in her house and compel him to stay on into the morning (often by physically imprisoning him in the house), then the revelation of the relationship constitutes marriage (Rollason 2008a).

In the shame that surrounds sex, there is therefore a continuous interplay between the secrecy of an affair and the publicity of a marriage and the children that it produces. As in Strathern's theory, there is no hard domain boundary between the public and the private as radically different 'levels', rather, there is a conversion of one into another. Shame here, as Battaglia (1985, 1990, 1992) has suggested, is a powerful social force, allowing people to withdraw from visibility so as to erase or forget certain relationships – of kinship, for example – in order to establish new ones – such as affinity. Shame, as a way of expressing social relations, is therefore no less a 'public' act than marriage or sex, in that it is something in which other people have interests and which has effects on social relations (cf. Strathern, 1979).

If shame is public, then Malinowski's accounts of Trobriand suicide indicate that under normal circumstances, killing oneself was, like marriage, an open performance of personal qualities and social relations (Malinowski 1932).[17] Malinowski describes the death of one Bogonela, a younger wife of the chief of Sinaketa, who was shamed by the discovery of her affair with another man. This affair prompted a general scandal, as a result of which she was shamed. In response to her shame she committed a most public suicide involving a speech to the assembled crowd from the top of the coconut palm from which she threw herself down. Malinowski reports the tale as follows:

> Bogonela did as the custom and ideal of personal honour dictated. In her best attire and adorned with all her valuable ornaments, she climbed a tall coconut palm on the central place of the village. Her little daughter, Kaniyaviyaka, stood under the tree and cried. Many people were assembled. She commended her child to the care of the eldest wife [of her husband, the chief of Sinaketa] and jumped from the tree. She was killed on the spot. (ibid.: 101)

This diagnosis is borne out by Hollan, who argues that suicides amongst Austronesian speakers, such as Louisiade people, are most often 'indignant' – that is public – rather than 'anomic' or asocial (Hollan 1990; cf. Adorno and Horkheimer 1979).

Questions can and should be raised about Buliga's capacity to elicit a 'public' or audience for his hanging (Rutherford 2012), which was capable of seeing it in a way analogous to that I suggest here. We know nothing concrete about the responses of local people to his death. However, the fact that Macintyre, working some forty years after these events unfolded, was able to collect detailed narratives about the Buliga cult and his death from Misima people indicates that Buliga attained the kind of narrative presence that 'big men' in the region aspire to (see Munn 1983). This indicates that, at least at some level, his actions had elicited an 'audience' from his peers, figured in the memories which his acts elicited (Battaglia 1992; cf. Rollason 2011).

The reading that Nelson suggests on the strength of colonial sources deproblematises Buliga's suicide as a private, asocial and therefore 'natural' response to a difficult personal situation.[18] This reading chimes with colonial interpretations of the 'uprising' as the natural effect of Louisiade people's 'savagery'. It thereby denies indigenous people the capacity to participate in a political project to modify the order of social relations in colonial Papua, or to prospect outward (Battaglia 1995) from their 'savage slot'. Specifically, it wholly vitiates any political purpose that Buliga and his followers may have been pursuing and for which they gave their lives: the native impulse of savagery does not need to be interpreted as a political challenge to the colonial establishment because its very nature denies it the status of a principled political engagement. The unproblematic reading of Buliga's suicide as the act of a desperate man facing death denies him the capacity to imagine or work for an alternative future. As such it does not treat his project in good faith.

I suggest that, in light of Strathern's analysis of Melanesian models of social life as a seamless manifold of social relations lacking public/private distinctions, as well as contemporary Louisiade attitudes to shame and Malinowski's account of Bogonela's very 'public' suicide, that we have to regard Louisiade suicide, and Buliga's specifically, as an act intended to have a social effect. Together with the unusual circumstances of his death – the anomalous method – there seems to be enough evidence to suggest a reinterpretation of the hanging of Buliga, one which would try to trace the social potential of his curious and unusual death.

The Meaning of Hanging

Given these comments on indigenous forms of suicide, personhood and shame, we can now consider the significance of Buliga's hanging in something nearer its own terms. In order to comprehend Buliga's death, we first need to consider the meaning of hanging in the Louisiades in the mid twentieth century. We can then consider the hanging imagined as a performance of a specific form of agency.

Before the events of 1942 to 1944, Louisiade people had experienced exactly two hangings. Returning to Nelson's (1976) history, we find that in 1891 two Sudest islanders were hanged for the murder of an Australian gold miner, whom they had killed at the behest of an elder man when he had paid them too meanly for a delivery of food. The second hanging took place in 1893: a Panaeati man called Babaga was hanged for the murder of an indigenous policeman, killed as Babaga was escaping from the government cutter where he was being held after escaping from Bwagaoia gaol.

Nothing in the colonial record or Nelson's history offers to shed light directly on the meaning that local people attributed to judicial hangings in 1944. However, there are certain indications that local people conceived of hanging as a distinctive form of white-on-black violence, or at least a form of violence monopolised by the administration against its indigenous subjects. The colonial legal system was dual, with patrol officers and village authorities dealing with minor disputes and infractions amongst 'natives', while formal district courts dealt with more serious matters and crimes involving white people, who could only be tried in such courts under Queensland law (Nelson 1982). Only white-run formal courts could issue death sentences, and for a limited number of offences. While hanging as a punishment was seriously circumscribed for natives, it nevertheless appears that indigenous people thought that these formal courts would condemn a black man to hang, but not a white man.

This is made clear in connection with a double murder committed in 1955 by Harry Pierce, who accompanied Lt. Smith on the 1943 raid against Buliga. Pierce was accused of shooting dead two indigenous men from Pantava on the south coast of Sudest when they argued with him over money that they allegedly owed him. He did not deny the charges and was taken into custody and moved to Port Moresby. There, claiming to be mentally unstable, he was hospitalised. In 1955, the assistant district officer in charge of Bwagaoia Station, John S. MacLeod, led a patrol to Sudest 'to check reaction after alleged murders by European Trader'.[19] MacLeod was principally worried about the possibility that the murders would lead to a serious backlash against white planters and traders. He found local people largely calm, but he does report that Sudest people did not think that Pierce would be condemned to hang by a court administered by white men. Indeed, they were to be proved right, and Pierce returned to Australia a free man. MacLeod relates local opinion to a previous murder on Misima, when two whites, le Boutillier and Downey, had not been seriously punished for the killing of an indigenous constable after they remained in Bwagaoia causing mayhem after the evacuation in 1942 (Nelson 1976; Macintyre 1990).

While this evidence is far from conclusive, given that there is no indication of an indigenous tradition of hanging, or that hangings were adopted by indigenous people during the colonial period – there are no records of lynchings, for example – I feel that we can reasonably suggest as an interpretive gambit that indigenous Louisiade people regarded hanging as a form of violence that was exclusively practised by white men on black men. Furthermore, it is not implausible to argue that hanging was always regarded as a distinctive enactment of the special power of the colonial state – *gavman*, as Louisiade people put it. This, of course, is exactly the way in which certain forms of state violence have been understood in the West, as Foucault makes clear:

> The public execution is to be understood not only as a judicial, but also as a political ritual. It belongs, even in minor cases, to the ceremonies by which power is manifested … [I]t was a manifestation of force; or rather, it was justice as the physical, material and awesome force of the sovereign deployed there. (Foucault 1995: 47–50)

Foucault's comments relate directly to public executions in the pre-modern period. However, the executions carried out by the Australian administration in the SED up to and including those of 1944 were similarly carried out in public for the instruction of an assembled audience. This is in contrast to most executions in European countries, which were carried out inside prisons out of sight of the population (ibid.: 15). We can reasonably argue that execution by hanging represented to Louisiade people not just racial violence, but the distinctive form of white power represented by the state.

Seem in this way, Buliga's suicide becomes intriguing: it begins to look like a mimetic performance of white, state power (cf. Argenti 1998).[20] It is anomalous as a suicide, because he hanged himself – not a common or recognised method of suicide in the region. Given indigenous ideas about shame and personhood, it must be regarded as a public act, not a private withdrawal from social relations. Finally, we can suggest that hanging represents a distinctive form of white, state violence. Taken together, I would argue that these features of Buliga's death point towards an act that is indeed not private, but part of a sophisticated political project that aimed at a mimetic co-option of state power through its performance.[21]

Nor was Buliga the only person in the Louisiades at that time who was pursuing a strategy of this type. Again, the evidence is brief at best, but Smith's report contains a very pregnant detail. He writes:

> Among those natives still in the bush on JOANNET … there is a man named KAIWATA of MAMANILA. He is known to have assisted in the murder of Lieut. Mader and his party on MOTORINA. I heard that, when he returned to his village, he boasted of his deeds and hoisted a flag made out of scraps of calico, saying that the government had now been killed and they would fly their own flag … I hear that they are preparing to fight the police should they meet them and have even cleared a space for the battle.[22]

Here we clearly see a distinctive form of the state as an agency of organised violence – on a battlefield, under a flag – co-opted by indigenous people. Smith's tone here is unmistakably mocking and exoticising, pointing out the childish whims of the natives. Understandably, as an agent of the colonial state he is unwilling to take this project seriously – indeed, anything other than mockery would undo the carefully constructed absence of politics that governs his account of the rising in the archipelago. If our project is to understand and engage with local aspirations, hopes and dreams for the future, however, we will find ourselves compelled to alter the register in which we read these events. That means that we must entertain the idea that the production of a flag from 'scraps of calico' is, in local terms, a legitimate and productive response to the death of government, holding out hope for its renewal in new hands.

Seen in these terms, Buliga's hanging can be reread as the very enactment of that future. Hanging is not a genre of suicide, but the distinctive violent act of the white state against the black body. Buliga's hanging might be regarded less as a suicide than the destruction of his present black self by the white future he strove towards, and which Iwa people related to A.C. Hall, his white alter ego hanging his worthless and devalued black body.

The Limits of Culture

The hanging of Buliga represents an attempt on a future in which white people are black and black people become white. If we accept this position, then we can begin to understand in good faith the political project that the hanging represents. However, understanding Buliga's actions in his own terms is insufficient for the purpose of understanding his political project as a project – as a meaningful series of acts directed towards a specific future. Up until this point, I have been concerned to demonstrate how his actions make sense in terms of what we might loosely call local culture or sociality. Put differently, that means in terms of a local tradition of living. Here I want to explore the conflict of interest that this contextualisation inevitably introduces into the account, and to suggest ways in which we might ameliorate it.

The difficulty with any explanation of action in terms of culture is that it inevitably ties what people do to what they have always done. In the account that I have advanced up to this point, I have contextualised Buliga's actions in terms of indigenous modes of agency, methods of suicide and understandings of privacy and shame. Strictly speaking, the account which I have given is interpretive in that it makes sense of what went on rather than claiming to explain why particular events took place (Geertz 1973). This is a typical strategy in anthropology – indeed, the driving force behind both social and cultural variants of the discipline. The resources which an anthropological interpretation draws on in making an account of why people act in the way they do are exactly the symbols of culture or the relations of society – structures which, by their very definition are formally prior to any of the persons (in the sense of socially or culturally appropriate members of a social group) who make use of them.

Given the priority and enduring quality of socio-cultural forms, we can reasonably claim that conventional anthropological interpretation takes the form of a contextualisation in terms of a 'tradition' – here with a small 't', not the hypostatised 'Tradition' of cultural essentialism. Anthropological interpretations are therefore exercises in 'prospecting', in Battaglia's (1995, 1999) terms: a movement along lines of continuity with culture or society, seeking the relationships that will reveal current action as a comprehensible transformation of what went before.

Thus Sahlins, writing about the adoption of new consumer goods in the Papua New Guinea highlands in the 1970s, comments that the things that were adopted by Mendi people must be understood as signs, where 'a sign is precisely something whose meaning is not contained in its physical presence' (Sahlins 2005: 25). New goods and relationships are adopted by Mendi people not in the form intended by their originators, but as cultural elements in the symbolic universe inhabited by Mendi people. As such, they find meaning and a place in interpretation not as new eruptions into Mendi consciousness, but as rephrased and reformed elements of what was available already. Sahlins coins a phrase to articulate this process: 'Develop*man*: the enrichment of their own ideas of what mankind is all about' (ibid.: 24).[23]

This kind of operation is typical of anthropological approaches to the excessive and bizarre mimetic ritual enactments which we call cargo cults – clearly the sort of activity that we are dealing with when we discuss the Buliga affair. Faced with the irrational masquerading as practical action (recall A.C. Hall's account of the 'government' on Iwa), the anthropological instinct is to perform the kind of contextualising activity that Sahlins suggests, and discover how this is not in fact irrational in local cultural terms. However, Lindstrom points out the critical weakness of this approach: 'This cultural reading … extracts a cost. Translation is always a reciprocal operation. Reading cargo and cult in terms of Melanesian culture rephrases that culture in terms of cargo and cult … The nativisation of cargo and cult unavoidably converts Melanesians into normal cargo cultists' (Lindstrom 1993: 61).

In this context, the movement of an anthropological account, prospecting back down seams of transformation in the tradition of a people, is imposed on them as a model of their modes of consciousness. Indigenous people are identified as themselves searching their pasts for resources to help them in their confrontation with the present. Writing of Bush Kaliai 'cargo cult' responses to colonial interventions, Lattas claims, 'People searched inside their culture for tools of transformation and metamorphosis that would allow them to use ritual representations to control and direct the changes around them' (Lattas 1998: 261). In other words, there is a powerful thread of continuity, linking culture and all actions that might be undertaken in its terms as transformations of one another, such that the native self cannot escape its own tradition (Robbins 2007).

This problem becomes critical in the case of the hanging of Buliga. As we have seen, to understand Buliga's action, we need to entertain the possibility that a person can act in order to be someone other than themselves – here, to split his being along racial lines, such that an imaginary white self can enact the sovereign violence of the state to which he lays claim on his black body (cf. Fanon 1967, 1982). While the terms on which this action might be identifiable and comprehensible can be drawn from a cultural tradition, it is clear that the form of the past is wholly inadequate to account for this act. While the anthropological interpretation prospects back into culture, Buliga is surely prospecting outwards from his place as a native, aiming to capture the position of someone else – to break the ties of continuity that enduring symbols or systems of relationships would establish (Taussig 1993; Rollason 2008b). Interpreting the hanging of Buliga in cultural terms is surely necessary – in order to identify a locally significant event buried in the dismissive colonial record for example – but it is not a sufficient account. This is because an interpretation of this kind introduces a conflict between the backwards prospecting of anthropological interpretation and the forward impetus of the sense of the act.

How are we to ameliorate this conflict? In this chapter, I began with a colonial account of Buliga's 'uprising'. In order to escape the ethnocentrism of that account and make the political importance of the events in the Louisiades of 1942 to 1944 apparent, I have engaged in a straightforward process of cultural interpretation which transcends the colonial record. Yet it is clear that this new interpretive account must itself be transcended if we are to treat Buliga in good faith, as a man whose interest was not in the reproduction of his own culture but the fundamental transformation of the native self. Culture may be an interpretive framework for action, but it cannot be explanatory or exhaustive (Butler 2005).

Buliga must be understood as a subject not in terms of the culture that provides his history, but in terms of the relations that constituted his future. To understand his actions, we must get to grips with the project that he pursued in relation to his others and use this as the frame of explanation. It is this scene that makes sense of his dramatic seizure of sovereign power. Of course, on the strength of the evidence, such an explanation is unavailable. What this essay can do is to gesture towards the limits of an interpretation phrased in terms of culture and to open the space beyond those limits. This space is vacant in my account, but it lays claim to ethnographies that would populate it with others' projects for the future, displacing culture as the frame of their actions.

Acknowledgements

I would like to thank Joel Robbins and Kathy Kreely of the University of California, San Diego, who supported my work in the Don Tuzin Archive gathering the material on which much of this chapter is based. Debborah Battaglia, Karen Sykes and Eric Hirsch offered valuable comments on earlier drafts.

Notes

1. Kinch (2001) compiles a useful chronology.
2. Multiple spellings of this name exist. In the colonial record, the man in question is called Buriga, Buliga, Bulega and Bursiga. Nelson uses 'Bulega'. I prefer 'Buliga' on the strength of Macintyre's recent rendition from Misiman vernacular (Macintyre 1990), and because this spelling avoids inconsistencies where I quote Macintyre.
3. Two principle published sources describe the events in question here. Importantly, they differ as to how Buliga met his end. While Nelson (1976) attributes the death to suicide, Macintyre has it that Buliga 'was found hanged in his cell – probably by his fellow prisoners, who hoped to avert their own punishment' (Macintyre 1990: 86). I have chosen to engage Nelson's account in this argument because his evidential base is colonial documentation, whereas Macintyre's is oral history; Nelson's account is therefore easier to bring into dialogue with the colonial records at my disposal. Macintyre's version of events appears to be an entirely independent interpretation: while she cites Nelson and colonial sources in passing, it is clear that her sources are wholly separate. This is predictable given that her data consists principally of oral historical accounts collected in 1986. As there is no obvious means of discriminating between these two independent accounts – with sources whose interests must have been very different – and their differences can plausibly be traced to their different evidential bases, I have chosen to engage deeply with Nelson's version, which makes more sense of the data available to me. Indeed, this factual discrepancy with Nelson does not substantially alter my argument, which hinges on a problematisation of the apparently transparent circumstances of Buliga's death. If for Nelson suicide in 'private' is unproblematic, for Macintyre it is the 'aversion' to punishment which is obvious. Nelson serves my rhetorical purposes because the figure of suicide has so long served as a social disruption of the unproblematic nature of

'private death' (Adorno and Horkheimer 1979). I note important differences between Macintyre's and Nelson's versions of events where they bear on my argument.

4. The colonial sources on which I draw are patrol reports, completed by administration officers on the basis of tours through certain areas of the district. This was the pattern of colonial governance throughout the territory. Reports are cited by patrol station, report number and government year. All of the patrols in question operated out of Misima patrol station at Bwagaoia. Use of full capitals in quotations follows the originals. The records I consulted are held in the Don Tuzin Archive at the University of California, San Diego. They are copies of the records now held in the National Archives in Papua New Guinea.
5. In this chapter, my approach is influenced by the genre of subaltern studies. In the study of marginalised (subaltern) groups, scholars using this approach actively seek to reconstruct and recover the lives of the marginal from dominant forms of discourse. As dominant sources of evidence often intentionally or coincidentally suppress and delete the voices of subalterns, the scholar's task is actively to reconstruct them. On occasion this involves interpretive moves which are, because of the suppression of subaltern perspectives in archives and other official sources, necessarily flimsy and lacking in authoritative support. In such cases the task of the analyst is to posit a position reading against the grain of the colonial account. Given the nature of the evidence at my disposal, such an interpretive strategy has been vital at several points in this essay, notably where I comment on indigenous attitudes to white men.
6. I am well aware that Nelson's account of Buliga's suicide is brief and probably not intended to undergo the kind of scrutiny that I bring to it here. Nelson summarises the contents of the report of a commission of inquiry that investigated the circumstances of the suspension of civil administration in Papua during the war (Barry 1945), newspaper articles and the court records of the trial of Mader's murderers. His account is useful in gathering together these colonial sources.
7. It is not clear that Buliga 'organised' any of the activities later attributed to him, although it does seem likely that his visions of the new world to emerge from the war were highly influential throughout the region.
8. Misima Special Report No. 1, 1946/47 (A.C. Hall D.O., Woodlark, Trobriands, Calvados. 5 October 1946 to 14 October 1946), p 4. Again, Macintyre's account differs somewhat from the colonial record here. She notes that Buliga insisted that his adherents wore traditional clothing. Clothing was an important marker of difference in colonial Papua, and was explicitly deployed to keep natives in their place. This suggests that his cult involved a 'proto-nationalist' element in which black people were first to become equals to whites

(as citizens, for example) before the apocalypse – an aspect of these events which merits further investigation. Macintyre concurs with Hall's ultimate diagnosis, however: 'there can be no doubt that Buliga wished to identify himself and his movement with both Church and State, and that in organizational terms his aim was not only to emulate, but to gain complete control of the power their agents wielded on Misima' (Macintyre 1990: 87).

9. Misima No. 2, 1942/43 (Lt. Roy G. Mader, Giligili, Gaibobo, Narian. 21 November 1942 to 2 December 1942).
10. Misima No. 3, 1942/43 (Lt. Sydney Smith, Calvados Chain, Misima. 18 Feberuary 1943 to 28 March 1943), p.2.
11. Misima No. 3, 1942/43, D.O.'s comments.
12. Misima No. 3, 1942/43, p.3.
13. I undertook eighteen months of ethnographic fieldwork on the island of Panapompom in the western Louisiades between 2004 and 2006. This research was supported by an ESRC studentship.
14. For comparative material on Kiriwina life, see Malinowski (1922, 1935) and Weiner (1976).
15. For comparative accounts from the region, see Leach and Leach (1983), Damon and Wagner (1989) and Damon (1990). There is certainly evidence of suicide by hanging from Papua New Guinea (e.g. Pataki-Schweizer 1985; Poole 1985), and it is not uncommon as a form of suicide in the Pacific region as a whole (Booth 1999). However, I can uncover no evidence of hanging as a widespread practice in south-east Papua.
16. See also Roy Wagner's account of the limitations of 'groups' as analytic frameworks in Papua New Guinea (Wagner 1974, 1977, 1991).
17. Durkheim of course reminds us that suicide, being socially organized, is always a social act (Durkheim 1952).
18. Macintyre (1990: 86) makes it an unproblematic response to personal difficulties on the part of the cell-mates whose aversion to punishment, rather than their shame, is the motive force.
19. Misima No. 2, 1954/55 (J.S. MacLeod A.D.O., Sudest Island, Misima Sub-district. 25 January 1955 to 19 February 1955), cover sheet.
20. Agency in Melanesia is often interpreted as taking a mimetic or performative form (e.g. O'Hanlon 1983; Wagner 1986; Merlan and Rumsey 1991).
21. Macintyre's (1990: 86) suggestion that Buliga was killed by his fellow prisoners offers a simpler route through these issues. In her version, Buliga's suicide appears more obviously as an execution in which it is the other prisoners (also, recall, cultists) who directly co-opt the power of the state.
22. Misima No. 3, 1942/43, p.3.
23. Later in the same article, Sahlins introduces the possibility of total cultural collapse and reinvention through a process of self-objectification and abnegation that he terms 'humiliation' (Robbins 2005; Sahlins 2005). As I have

argued elsewhere (Rollason 2010) this theory implies a subject who is able to objectify themselves and their culture from a non-cultural position at the point of cultural collapse. As such, while suggestive, it can do no more than gesture towards a fundamental problem with accounts of cultural continuity (see also Robbins 2004, 2005; Robbins and Wardlow 2005).

References

Adorno, T.W., and M. Horkheimer. 1979. *Dialectic of Enlightenment*. London: Verso.

Argenti, N. 1998. Air Youth: Performance, Violence and the State in Cameroon. *Journal of the Royal Anthropological Institute* 4(4): 753–82.

Barry, J.V. 1945. Commission of Inquiry into the Circumstances Relating to the Suspension of the Civil Administration of the Territory of Papua, February 1942.

Battaglia, D. 1985. 'We Feed Our Father': Paternal Nurture among the Sabarl of Papua New Guinea. *American Ethnologist* 12(3): 427–441.

_______ 1990. *On the Bones of the Serpent: Person, Memory, and Mortality in Sabarl Island Society*. Chicago: University of Chicago Press.

_______ 1992. The Body in the Gift: Memory and Forgetting in Sabarl Mortuary Exchange. *American Ethnologist* 19(1): 3–18.

_______ 1995. On Practical Nostalgia: Self-prospecting among Urban Trobrianders. In D. Battaglia (ed.), *Rhetorics of Self-making*, pp.77–96. Berkeley: University of California Press.

_______ 1999. Towards an Ethics of the Open Subject. In H. Moore (ed.), *Anthropological Theory Today*, pp.114–50. Cambridge: Polity Press.

Booth, H. 1999. Pacific Island Suicide in Comparative Perspective. *Journal of Biosocial Science* 31(4): 433–48.

Burridge, K. 1995. *Mambu: A Melanesian Millennium*. Princeton: Princeton University Press.

Butler, J. 2005. *Giving an Account of Oneself*. New York: Fordham University Press.

Damon, F.H. 1990. *From Muyuw to the Trobriands: Transformations along the Northern Side of the Kula Ring*. Tucson: University of Arizona Press.

Damon, F.H., and R. Wagner. 1989. *Death Rituals and Life in the Societies of the Kula Ring*. DeKalb: Northern Illinois University Press.

Durkheim, E. 1952. *Suicide: A Study in Sociology*. London: Routledge and Kegan Paul.

Errington, F.K., and D.B. Gewertz. 2004. *Yali's Question: Sugar, Culture, and History*. Chicago: University of Chicago Press.

Fabian, J. 1983. *Time and the Other*. New York: Columbia University Press.

Fanon, F. 1967. *The Wretched of the Earth*. Harmondsworth: Penguin.

_______ 1982. *Black Skin, White Masks*. New York: Grove Press.

Ferguson, J. 1990. *The Anti-politics Machine: 'Development', Depoliticization, and Bureaucratic Power in Lesotho*. Cambridge: Cambridge University Press.
Foucault, M. 1995. *Discipline and Punish: The Birth of the Prison*. New York: Vintage Books.
Geertz, C. 1973. Thick Description: Toward an Interpretive Theory of Culture. In *The Interpretation of Cultures*, pp.3–30. New York: Basic Books.
——— 1983. *Local Knowledge: Further Essays in Interpretive Anthropology*. New York: Basic Books.
Gillison, G. 1993. *Between Culture and Fantasy: A New Guinea Highlands Mythology*. Chicago: University of Chicago Press.
Gramsci, A. 1971. *Selections from the Prison Notebooks*, ed. and trans. Q. Hoare and G.N. Smith. London: Lawrence and Wishart.
Hollan, D. 1990. Indignant Suicide in the Pacific: An Example from the Toraja Highlands of Indonesia. *Culture, Medicine and Psychiatry* 14: 365–79.
Jebens, H. 2004. 'Vali Did That Too': On Western and Indigenous Cargo Discourses in West New Britain (Papua New Guinea). *Anthropological Forum* 14(2): 117–40.
——— 2010. *After the Cult: Perceptions of Other and Self in West New Britain (Papua New Guinea)*. New York: Berghahn.
Kahn, M. 1994. *Always Hungry, Never Greedy: Food and the Expression of Gender in a Melanesian Society*. Prospect Heights, IL: Waveland.
Kinch, J. 2001. 'Social Evaluation Study for the Milne Bay Community-based Coastal and Marine Conservation Program PNG/99/G41', UNOPS contract for services, ref: C00-1076. New York: UNDP.
Lattas, A. 1998. *Cultures of Secrecy: Reinventing Race in Bush Kaliai Cargo Cults*. Madison: University of Wisconsin Press.
——— 2006a. Technologies of Visibility: The Utopian Politics of Cameras, Televisions, Videos and Dreams in New Britain. *Australian Journal of Anthropology* 17(1): 15–31.
——— 2006b. The Utopian Promise of Government. *Journal of the Royal Anthropological Institute* 12: 129–50.
Lawrence: 1967. *Road Belong Cargo: A Study of the Cargo Movement in the Southern Madang District, New Guinea*. Manchester: Manchester University Press.
Leach, J. 2003. *Creative Land: Place and Procreation on the Rai Coast of Papua New Guinea*. New York: Berghahn.
Leach, J.W., and E.R. Leach (eds). 1983. *The Kula: New Perspectives on Massim Exchange*. Cambridge: Cambridge University Press.
Lindstrom, L. 1990. *Knowledge and Power in a South Pacific Society*. Washington: Smithsonian Institution Press.
——— 1993. *Cargo Cult: Strange Stories of Desire from Melanesia and Beyond*. Honolulu: University of Hawaii Press.

Macintyre, M. 1990. Christianity, Cargo Cultism and the Concept of the Spirit in Misiman Cosmology. In J. Barker (ed.), *Christianity in Oceania: Ethnographic Perspectives*, pp.81–100. Lanham, MD: University Press of America.

Malinowski, B. 1922. *Argonauts of the Western Pacific*. London: Routledge.

_______ 1932. *The Sexual Life of Savages in North-Western Melanesia*. London: Routledge and Kegan Paul.

_______ 1935. *Coral Gardens and Their Magic*. London: Allen and Unwin.

Merlan, F., and A. Rumsey. 1991. *Ku Waru: Language and Segmentary Politics in the Western Nebilyer Valley, Papua New Guinea*. Cambridge: Cambridge University Press.

Munn, N.D. 1983. Gawan Kula: Spatiotemporal Control and the Symbolism of Influence. In J.W. Leach and E.R. Leach (eds), *The Kula: New Perspectives on Massim Exchange* pp.277–308. Cambridge: Cambridge University Press.

Nelson, H. 1976. *Black, White and Gold: Gold Mining in Papua New Guinea, 1878–1930*. Canberra: Australian National University Press.

_______ 1982. *Taim Bilong Masta: The Australian Involvement with Papua New Guinea*. Sydney: Australian Broadcasting Commission.

Newbury, C., and D. Newbury. 1999. A Catholic Mass in Kigali: Contested Views of the Genocide and Ethnicity in Rwanda. *Canadian Journal of African Studies* 33(2/3): 292–328.

Newbury, D., and C. Newbury. 2000. Bringing the Peasants Back In: Agrarian Themes in the Construction and Corrosion of Statist Historiography in Rwanda. *American Historical Review* 105(3): 832–77.

O'Hanlon, M. 1983. Handsome Is as Handsome Does: Display and Betrayal in the Wahgi. *Oceania* 53(4): 317–33.

Ortner, S. B. 1974. Is Female to Male as Nature Is to Culture?' In M.Z. Rosaldo and L. Lamphere (eds), *Woman, Culture and Society*, pp.68–87. Stanford: Stanford University Press.

Pataki-Schweizer, K.J. 1985. Suicide in Contemporary Papua New Guinea: An Attempt at an Overview. In F.X. Hezel, D.H. Rubinstein, and G.M. White (eds.), *Culture, Youth and Suicide in the Pacific*, pp.139–51. Honolulu: University of Hawaii at Manoa in collaboration with the Institute of Culture and Communication, East–West Centre.

Poole, F.J.P. 1985. Among the Boughs of the Hanging Tree: Male Suicide among the Bimin-Kuskusmin of Papua New Guinea. In F.X. Hezel, D.H. Rubinstein, and G.M. White (eds.), *Culture, Youth and Suicide in the Pacific*, pp.152–81. Honolulu: University of Hawaii at Manoa in collaboration with the Institute of Culture and Communication, East-West Centre.

Robbins, J. 2004. *Becoming Sinners: Christianity and Moral Torment in a Papua New Guinea Society*. Berkeley: University of California Press.

_______ 2005. Humiliation and Transformation: Marshall Sahlins and the Study of Cultural Change in Melanesia. In J. Robbins and H. Wardlow (eds), *The Making of Global and Local Modernities in Melanesia: Humiliation, Transformation and the Nature of Cultural Change*, pp.3–22. Aldershot: Ashgate.

——— 2007. Continuity Thinking and the Problem of Christian Culture. *Current Anthropology* 48(1): 5–38.

Robbins, J., and H. Wardlow (eds). 2005. *The Making of Global and Local Modernities in Melanesia: Humiliation, Transformation and the Nature of Cultural Change*. Aldershot: Ashgate.

Rollason, W. 2008a. *Football and Postcolonial Subjectivity, Panapompom, Papua New Guinea*. PhD Thesis, University of Manchester, Manchester.

——— 2008b. Counterparts: Clothing, Value and the Sites of Otherness in Panapompom Ethnographic Encounters. *Anthropological Forum* 18(1): 17–35.

——— 2010. Working Out Abjection in the Panapompom Bêche-De-Mer Fishery: Race, Economic Change and the Future in Papua New Guinea. *Australian Journal of Anthropology* 21(2): 149–70.

——— 2011. *We Are Playing Football: Sport and Postcolonial Subjectivity, Panapompom, Papua New Guinea*, new edn. Cambridge: Cambridge Scholars Publishing.

Rutherford, D. 2012. *Laughing at Leviathan: Sovereignty and Audience in West Papua*. Chicago: University of Chicago Press.

Sahlins, M.D. 2005. The Economics of Develop-man in the Pacific. In J. Robbins and H. Wardlow (eds), *The Making of Global and Local Modernities in Melanesia: Humiliation, Transformation and the Nature of Cultural Change*, pp.23–42. Aldershot: Ashgate.

Strathern, M. 1979. The Self in Self-decoration. *Oceania* 49(4): 241–57.

——— 1980. No Nature, No Culture: The Hagen Case. In C.P. MacCormack and M. Strathern (eds), *Nature, Culture and Gender*, pp.174–222. Cambridge: Cambridge University Press.

——— 1981. Culture and a Netbag: The Manufacture of a Subdiscipline in Anthropology. *Man* 16: 665–88.

——— 1985. Discovering 'Social Control'. *Journal of Law and Society* 12(2): 111–34.

——— 1988. *The Gender of the Gift: Problems with Women and Problems with Society in Melanesia*. Berkeley: University of California Press.

——— 1991. One Man and Many Men. In M. Godelier and M. Strathern (eds), *Big Men and Great Men: Personifications of Power in Melanesia*, pp.197–214. Cambridge: Cambridge University Press.

——— 2003. Redescribing Society. *Minerva* 41: 263–76.

Taussig, M.T. 1993. *Mimesis and Alterity: A Particular History of the Senses*. New York: Routledge.

Wagner, R. 1974. Are There Social Groups in the New Guinea Highlands? In M. Leaf (ed.), *Frontiers of Anthropology*, pp.99–122. New York: Van Nostrand.

_______ 1977. Analogic Kinship: A Daribi Example. *American Ethnologist* 4(4): 623–42.

_______ 1986. *Asiwinarong: Ethos, Image, and Social Power among the Usen Barok of New Ireland*. Princeton: Princeton University Press.

_______ 1991. The Fractal Person. In M. Godelier and M. Strathern (eds), *Big Men and Great Men: Personifications of Power in Melanesia*, pp.197–214. Cambridge: Cambridge University Press.

Weiner, A.B. 1976. *Women of Value, Men of Renown: New Perspectives in Trobriand Exchange*. Austin: University of Texas Press.

Worsley, P. 1968. *The Trumpet Shall Sound: A Study of 'Cargo' Cults in Melanesia*, 2nd edn. London: MacGibbon and Kee.

3

Why the Future is Selfish and Could Kill

Contraception and the Future of Paama

Craig Lind

Limiting female reproductive capacities using contraception is a contentious subject for ni-Vanuatu (people of Vanuatu), not least so among and in response to Paama islanders – the country's largest out-migrating community, with a long-established proclivity for permanent urban settlement (Haberkorn 1989). For some, contraception presents a useful means of reducing birth rates so that limited resources can be concentrated on one child, in the hope of ensuring that child a good education, a professional career and an income to afford the comfort of a place in town in the future. Others, however, complain that limiting birth rates amounts to the selfish denial of a person's obligation to replace their precursors within the clan to which they belong (*raleha*).[1] These days this is often achieved in a way that deliberately extends relations towards a future in urban Vanuatu. I discuss these evaluations of a person's responsibility in light of conflicts that arose on Paama Island, and in Vanuatu's capital, Port Vila, on Efate Island, during 2003. Rather than focus on their oppositional aspects, however, I consider these as creative alternatives, which inventively draw on local perceptions concerning movement and stasis in the hope of establishing conditions for a favourable future.

Rationale

It strikes me that an analysis focused on the opposition of ideals, glossed in these opening disagreements, will lead to the conclusion that 'simplistic "progressive-conservative" dichotomies' (Wagner 1981, p.: xiii) are organising people's motivations. The choice to use contraception, for example, suggests a progressive break from past obligations grounded in kinship, while the choice to replace one's predecessors (*raleha*) appears comparatively conservative. However, such a project draws on a 'genealogy' of knowledge-making where 'subject/object' thinking (Bamford and Leach 2009) invites exogenous and hierarchically organised (Bell 2010) forms of analysis that reflect Euro-American values more clearly than ni-Vanuatu concerns (Strathern 1988; Jolly 1992). An alternative analytical strategy emerges when ethnographic description (e.g. Strathern 1999) takes its terms of argument from how islanders' talk about and plan for their future.

For Paama islanders at least, prospects for the future invariably invoke talk about a person's place (*ples*), mobility (*rod*), residence and claims of legitimacy – subjectivities that have significantly informed anthropology's understanding of Vanuatu's ethnography, particularly 'gender' and 'kinship' (Bolton 1999; Jolly 1994; Eriksen 2008). From the point of view of Paama then, the future is posited in the movement and stability of people and things between and within places, such that it is not simply a matter of temporality, nor is it entirely beyond one's grasp. Indeed, Paama islanders prospect and seek to shape the future through the people that, including themselves, they direct towards it through marriage, work, education and so on, which in turn limits or extends a person's capacity to establish legitimate residence and produce desirable circumstances in which to thrive (cf. Bolton 1999). In such terms, the future does not appear to be a conservative reproduction of the past or a simple break from it; rather, it emerges as a range of potentials that must be responded to creatively, with an aim in mind.

As a creative project, the future is approached with an attitude that reflects a particular understanding of 'kinship' that my Paama friends described as a 'game' (*gem*). That is, Paama islanders approached what anthropology recognises as kinship, prospectively and strategically, drawing on its flexibility (e.g. Wagner 1977) as a way of creatively thinking about how to align one's interests with emerging possibilities in contemporary Vanuatu (cf. Hirsch 2004). This 'game' is most evident in the way that people talk about opportunities that appear open when considered through various life-cycle possibilities, concerning marriage and childbirth, for example. Indeed, a person can significantly increase their chances of reaching preferred opportunities through inventive adoptions that reconfigure relations by limiting the scope of exogamous marriage, while enabling favourable, though previously unmarriageable, unions to take place (cf. Battaglia 1990). Persuasion, naming, support for specific childhood friendships (Lind 2010) and conversion to Christianity or denominational change (Lind 2012) share a part in this 'game', and all have consequences for the future, insofar as they each represent a means (*rod*, discussed below) by which a person might orient their activity towards the future.

In such terms, the future-directed aspirations of Paama islanders always involve creatively thinking about and attempting to influence, and reorder, relationships among people, things and locations, with the intention of producing favourable conditions by doing so. Of course, the future cannot be known from experience (Hirsch 2004), though its various possibilities can be imagined, and the clearest form in which Paama islanders reveal this knowledge is through talk about the relational attachments and detachments, of people, places and occupations, within which possible future events and configurations appear possible (cf. ibid.).

My rationale for describing Paama islanders' concerns with the future in this way may not be immediately obvious. However, as urban populations in the Pacific increase at twice the rate of their rural counterparts, anthropology faces a question: What terms of description are best suited to understanding islanders' perceptions and engagements with opportunities for travel to and settlement in new forms of residence, within contested urban locations? The limitations imposed by framing islanders' prospects and practices as either conservative (traditional) or progressive (modern) should be clear given the significant implications that such a dichotomy will have for legitimating and excluding people's interests in urban and rural planning. Here, I suggest one way of moving beyond such conceptual restrictions for imagining and representing the future by describing instead how female contraception invokes 'ethnographic descriptions' that shed new light on old anthropological concerns. I suggest that Paama's perspective on the future offers a novel way for reimagining anthropological debates concerning migration, urbanisation, urban conflict and settlement in Vanuatu, and perhaps more broadly within the Pacific, today.

Before moving on, I want to note one final argument regarding the use of contraception, which underscores my point that a Paama future entails spatial consideration, such that it implicates movement and dwelling – contestable subjects given that they also assume legitimating conditions (Jolly 1994), in expressions of kinship, for example. This last argument stems from outside Paama communities, and suggests that contraception should be used to reduce the number of people from Paama so that they can be contained by their island. Those maintaining this argument express concern that Paama islanders are increasing in number, spreading uncontrollably in town and forming new residences in places where their 'belonging' is disputed. To be sure, this demand expresses an underlying tension and potential for violent unrest associated with land disputes within the Pacific, though it also observes the spatial concerns raised by reproduction, through which a future is imaginable where Paama has grown to a position of dominance (discussed below).

This third argument is most provocative because, from a Paama point of view, legitimate childbirth establishes the basis upon which a person is shown to be replaced (*raleha*) where they belong (Lind 2010: 174–264; see also Wiener 1977, 1980; Mimica 1988; Rio 2007) – and this is publicly acknowledged in chiefs' speeches following childbirth. These speeches define legitimacy with reference to a person's movement into their birthplace (*anu*) along a particular route (*rod*) in a way that renders them analogous with their MMM/FFF. It is an analogy in which a child and their MMM/FFF are shown to constitute a oneness (*tāi*) (Lind 2010), a similarity shared only by siblings (*tuak*) (cf. Bamford 2007). I will discuss these points in more detail below. For the moment, suffice to say that a person's 'kinship' is conceived in a process of moving between and dwelling within places, such that those who are said to share a particular route and birthplace are 'one'.

Reproduction Reconsidered

Before moving on to Paama in more detail, I want to say a few words about reproduction, because contraception touches most obviously upon this well established subject in Melanesian anthropology (e.g. Malinowski 1916; Weiner 1977, 1980; Damon and Wagner 1989; Battaglia 1990; Foster 1990). It is a subject from which the discipline has gained much, and regarding which important analytical refinements have offered increasingly nuanced descriptions concerning the power of social institutions to reproduce persons and society (Weiner 1977; Battaglia 1990). However valuable these insights have been, these studies reflect anthropology's preference for village-based fieldwork (Clifford 1997), such that their relevance for understanding migration and urban dwelling is narrowed, not least so because reproduction emerges as a force for conservation (Weiner 1977) in the face of social change (Foster 1995).

Given that my own analytical lead stresses the productiveness of movement and the fact that Paama islanders have been establishing permanent dwellings in Port Vila for many years (Haberkorn 1989), neither conservation nor a focus limited by the extent of the 'village' provide convincing ethnographic subjects. Moreover, given my argument that a Paama future depends on creativity, society cannot be looked to as a blueprint of overarching order (Strathern 1985; Bamford 2007). Rather, a more inventive approach needs to be taken in order to keep pace with Paama islanders' future prospecting.

Anthropologists studying 'reproduction' in Melanesia have long noted that childbirth is only one aspect of people's reproductive concerns (Malinowski 1916; Damon and Wagner 1989; Battaglia 1990). Malinowski's classic account of *baloma* (posthumous humans), for example, described how island life, garden magic, childbirth and the world of the dead formed a socially contained Trobriand gestalt, revealing a 'belief in reincarnation' (Malinowski 1916: 404). 'Death' is no end to things; rather, posthumous Trobriand islanders travel as *baloma* to the island of Tuma, where they lead an existence parallel to living sociality. Eventually *baloma* age, shed their skin, transform into *waiwai* (spirit children), who reside in the sea, floating among flotsam and jetsam, awaiting a woman that they can impregnate and through whom they will return, in birth, to the world of the living. Notably, males are rendered obsolete in Trobriand knowledge of conception, which is achieved as the dead make their return to the lived social world.

Trobriand reproductive knowledge is gynocentric to the extent that Malinowski (ibid.) notes only one universally agreed notion: the perception that those involved in conception and reproduction (e.g. *baloma*, *waiwai*, living mother and new-born child) must all belong to a single *dala* (a configuration expressive of female descent), or else conception is impossible. Put otherwise, the transit from birth to death and birth again is perceived to be contained by a conceptually female cycle, responsible for regenerating persons within a single territorial, social unit, a *dala* (see Weiner 1977, 1980). Nonetheless, Malinowski attributed no 'important role in social life' (Malinowski 1916: 407) to this local knowledge, and insisted that meaningful anthropological observations had to be derived 'by referring the variety of individual opinions to the social structure' (ibid.: 426). In short, local difference had to be filtered through an exogenous idea (a theory of society) which provided an overarching order for rendering ethnographic variance intelligible.

Fifty years later, Annette Weiner argued that Malinowski's unwillingness to take emic perspectives seriously, coupled with his failure to view 'women's activities worthy of particular study' (Weiner 1977: 59), had distorted his understanding of Trobriand society. In short, Malinowski had failed to realise that the fundamental units of Trobriand social organisation, *dala*, depended on the reproductive activities of women (ibid.: 66). Weiner showed that women's exchange and reproductive activities maintained social purity by enabling 'identities and values … to be replaced … and regenerated through generations' (Weiner 1982: 56, cited in, Jolly 1992: 43). Women could achieve this because they were in a unique position to enable *baloma*, the epitome of *dala* identity (cf. Battaglia 1990), to remerge in birth as pure *dala* members among the living. Thus, what Malinowski had taken to be ethnographically insignificant appeared in Weiner's (1977) eyes as the reproduction of Trobriand society itself – scaled to the rebirth of social persons, renewed, pure and untouched by change over time.

Changes in anthropology (Clifford and Marcus 1986) eventually meant that the appearance of the field would have to follow. No longer able to contain society apart from passing time, as Malinowski had, or reset the cultural clocks as Weiner suggested, Foster (1995) presented a field in which historical engagements with capitalist interests (*bisinis*) was clear. According to Foster, economic activity was so centred on 'individual men or households' that it threatened clan identities and their territorial interests (Foster 1992: 288). Tangans' responded to this threat by objectifying and separating out their cultural concerns as *kastam* (see also Jolly and Thomas 1992). Seeking to account for the perpetuation of culture amidst significant social change, Foster (1995) sought to reconcile a historically sensitive account with a cultural account, much as Weiner (1977) had done by dichotomising male and female activities. Like Weiner, Foster (1995) placed mortuary exchange at the centre of Tangan social reproduction: without institutionalised mortuary exchange, in which collective commitment was reproduced, Tangan 'social order' could not withstand the vagaries of historical change.

A few points taken from this very partial discussion will serve to show that Paama's futures cannot be contained within their analytical scope. With the exception of Malinowski's (1916) contribution, which pays little heed to the passage of time, a common thread runs through these ethnographies: historical change is viewed as a destructive force, which is balanced by a form of 'historical denial' (Eliade 1971). Moreover, this temporal inertia, and here I include Malinowski (1916), is equated with the promise of absolute 'social structure', located in a 'pure', timeless (Weiner 1977) and transcendent form as 'culture'. Hence, culture emerges as a fixed mould for recasting social organisation in a pure form – that is, culture is made to act as an object for its social subjects, though it can only exist if imagined apart from the idiosyncratic particularities of people. This organising/purifying force emerges first as a theoretical necessity in Malinowski's (1916) description, then in the form of women's activities in Weiner's (1977) work, where it necessarily counters and resets damage wrought on Trobriand social order by men's activities. Lastly, structural stability appears as a cultural imperative against the 'terror of history' (Eliade 1971) in the form of individualising capitalist forces (the other) in Foster's (1995) work. In short, 'reproduction' is given the conservational role of countering, rather than engaging or taking advantage of, novelties that emerge as time progresses, such that any sense of the future collapses into a static cultural past, protected from social change.

Aside from restricting analytical engagement with the future, recourse to a transcendent, overarching order is ethnographically problematic in a Melanesian context. As Bamford has stated for Kamea, 'the world is not seen to rest upon a ready-made system of cultural distinctions in need of being perpetuated'; rather, 'it is the act of constituting those distinctions in the first place that is ... primary' (Bamford 2007: 168; cf. Wagner 1972, 1977).

The significance of this last point is unmistakable. Without a prior condition upon which to model replication we have to consider each event, however similar in representation or appearance, to be an achievement, an act of creation and not an occurrence of reproduction at all. This productive focus resonates with my suggestion that the growing numbers of Paama islanders, and new locations in which they dwell, throughout Vanuatu should be viewed as an achievement rather than a demographic trend signifying either conservative commitments or progressive departures. Indeed, Paama islanders are quick to note their achievements among themselves in claims that they are taking over Vanuatu. However, they remain understandably quiet about this boast in conversation with other islanders with whom they share space in town. I say 'understandably quiet' because of the conflictual responses that the idea of being taken over elicits. Indeed, Paama presence in Port Vila routinely gives rise to resentment among other ni-Vanuatu, drawing them into violent clashes, subjecting them to the sublimated threat of destruction that the demand to impose contraception expresses.

I move on now to follow a Paama Island description in which reproductive issues express concerns with the appropriateness of various routes and forms of movement (Weiner 1991; Bolton 1999), through which a person might come to a place, and how these routes offer vying grounds for assessing a person's legitimate belonging, their rights and even their moral dispositions (Jolly 1994; Lind 2010). What I have to say about Paama sheds light on how islanders have drawn on the potential for their reproductive rationales to accommodate a new scope and scale of mobility and settlement through their engagements with emerging interests and socialities in contemporary Vanuatu. Such a future, like reproductive concerns themselves, is inescapably spatial and relationally encompassing.

Paama in Vanuatu

In Vanuatu, the more children a household has the greater its financial burden in paying for school fees, clothing and food. Households in comparable economic circumstances, with only one or two children, have a greater opportunity to concentrate their resources or even save towards the future. As such, the use of contraception might appear to represent a 'progressivist' or forward-thinking approach towards the future, particularly when set alongside a refusal to use contraception on the basis that doing so will erode commitment to maintaining existing alliances based on past marriages. However, as I have said, I think that Paama islanders arguments about contraception are better approached less polemically, through their shared interests. I have already suggested that this concerns the *ples* (glossed for the moment as 'place') of Paama islanders in the future. Moreover, that *ples* is Vanuatu's capital, Port Vila – a location in which many island communities have become established, though in which Paama islanders figure very prominently.

While in the most obvious sense 'place' here refers to 'geographical location', the arguments concern a broader, neo-Melanesian perception of *ples*. From this perspective *ples* concerns, among other things, 'economic' and 'social' position, clan affiliation, inter-clan alliances and ancestral origins. Indeed, as Bonnemaison puts it, 'clan *is* the land, just as the clan *is* its ancestors' (Bonnemaison 1984a: 1, original emphasis; see also Toren 1997). Such issues are inseparable in the projected futures I discuss. My suggestion is that if we are to understand Paamese plans for the future we must first suspend the assumption that they express either 'progressivist' or 'conservative' values. We must put aside the idea that Paamese futures are best understood in terms of discontinuity or any simple continuity (Robbins 2007) and instead try to understand how reproductive (Weiner 1980) concerns are centrally concerned with emplacing persons in the future.

Ples

Place is centrally important for understanding Pacific socialities (Feld 1982, 1984; Weiner 1991; Gell 1997), and in Vanuatu, as elsewhere in the Pacific, ideas of the person, self-representations, kinship and clan organisation cannot be fully understood without reference to it (Jolly 1994; Toren 1997; Bamford 1998). Indeed, both substantial and insubstantial expressions of 'culture', including mat designs, songs, dances and stories are described as having being conveyed to humans by non-human co-habitants of a 'place'. 'Place' is, at best, a loose translation of the Bislama *ples* (see Weiner 1991; Bolton 1999). The importance of *ples* cannot be overstated: it is such that the origins of everything can be perceived by islanders to be inscribed in the landscape or having emerged from it when 'the world broke open' (Jolly 1994: 231, see also Lindstrom 1996; Bamford 1998; Bolton 1999). Persons themselves are 'virtually a material manifestation of … place' (Toren 1997: 164), and 'places are themselves like persons' (Leach 2003: 212). Paama islanders are quite clear about this. Indeed, *out* (place) is deemed to be fundamental to a person's constitution, while simultaneously existing as the material manifestation of persons. Indeed, both place and person are so mutually constituted that they are inseparable.

Taking this unifying concern with the *ples* of Paamese islanders as a serious analytical starting point allows me to think about their future-directed aspirations without characterising them as a desire to maintain, or inability to break from, 'tradition', or as expressive of a longing for a Euro-American style 'modernity' (Giddens 1998). In other words, it avoids reinforcing what Wagner describes as 'simplistic "progressive-conservative" dichotomies' (Wagner 1981: xiii), which leads to a problematic and misleading representation that reinforces a hegemony in which the 'other' appears either aspirant for, or unable to properly engage with, 'Western civilisation'.

The political problems of dichotomous thinking aside, neither 'traditionalism' nor 'modernism' allow local concerns to be heard in their own terms, making the analytical choice of either reduction difficult to support ethnographically. Considered in local terms, I am led to a more easily supportable conclusion in which arguments about contraception express specific strategies regarding how Paama islanders plan a place for themselves in the future. My aim then is that of finding a 'future' where exogenous terminology does not have the final word, and where Paama islanders aspirations can be heard in their terms. Doing so has the added advantage of raising questions regarding the connection between ideas about 'kinship', 'reproduction' and 'place-making' (Leach 2003; Lind 2010) that are centrally important for the future of anthropology in the Pacific region.

The Place of Paama in Vanuatu

Paama is the smallest island in the Malampa province of Vanuatu, a Y-shaped archipelago of around eighty-three islands, 1,530 miles north-east of Sydney, Australia. Although Paama is quite small (seven miles long and three wide), its population is so large that it has long exceeded the island's capacity to sustain it (Haberkorn 1989). Out-migration, for which Paama has the highest rates in Vanuatu (ibid.), and permanent residence elsewhere, particularly in urban areas, has come to accommodate the majority of Paama's people. Indeed, these days only 1,627 people reside on Paama Island, while 3,127 of these islanders live permanently in and around Port Vila.[2]

This mobility and resettlement is no new phenomenon: 'Since the 1870s, Paama has consistently supplied a large proportion of plantation labor … throughout central Vanuatu; Paamese men also have been predominant among the crews of interisland trading vessels, and from as early as the 1960s, people from the island consistently figured as the most prominent migrant group in Vanuatu's only towns' (Haberkorn 1992: 810). Paama Islanders have long embraced opportunities for travel and permanent territorial expansion into new urban areas, and in this respect they are unlike many other ni-Vanuatu, for whom 'the sole wish of those who leave their island … is often to return' (Bonnemaison 1994: 106). Indeed, the value that the people of Bunlap, the largest *kastom* community in south Pentecost, give to spending time in places like Port Vila is located in the elevated position they perceive it might offer them upon return to their island home.[3] By contrast, Paama islanders routinely perceive town as the place in which an elevated position, or an easy life, is located, and their urban migrations are often one way (Haberkorn 1989). While Paama islanders are far from unique in travelling to and staying in town, they are exemplary of the trend towards permanent urban residence that has been going on throughout Melanesia since at least the 1980s (ibid.).

In common with other ni-Vanuatu, the place of Paama people in town is marked by the island place names they bring with them and transplant there (Tonkinson 1968; Eriksen 2008), and in this respect and many others urban 'settlements reproduce the village' (Lindstrom 2010: 10). Seaside Paama, close to the centre of Port Vila and hosting people from all over Paama Island, is exemplary of this practice. Mirroring the island's constitution in its diversity, this place not only shares the island's name, for many it is the same as Paama Island itself. For example, after asking resident Paama chief, Talank Avok, when he next planned to visit Paama, he gestured to the people and dwellings around him, replying emphatically, 'This *is* Paama' (*Paama ia nao*). From a Paama point of view it is what these places on Paama Island and in Port Vila share – place names, characteristically Paama ways of doing things and crucially an abundance of Paama people – that allows them, in many important respects, to be perceived to be the same place: they are both Paama (Lind 2010).

Paama islanders have, however, contributed more than place names and people to Port Vila's urban landscape; they have influenced others living in the capital in ways that implicate their dominance there. Other ni-Vanuatu recognise this, and some even acknowledge having adopted practices known to be Paama *kastom*. Eriksen, for example, notes that Ambrym islanders have integrated 'the *kastom* of those from Paama' within their marriage ceremonies (Eriksen 2008: 66). Paama's influence is more pervasive than this, however. Richard, an employee of the Vanuatu Cultural Centre, explained that a growing concern with young women in town wearing trousers, rather than skirts or dresses, originated in strict (*strong*) Paama *kastom*.[4]

Chief Talank established this concern by bringing it to the attention of others when he banned Paama girls from wearing trousers in Port Vila. Chief Talank is aware and also proud of the fact that his chiefly influence has drawn the attention of Port Vila's multicultural landscape. Many Paama islanders view this influence as testament to how powerful an impact they have made in town, and some are even led to claim that 'Paama has taken over the place' (*Paama i raonem ples finis*), boasting that Port Vila is just like Paama now (*olsem long Paama nomo*). Paama islanders have certainly made a place for themselves in Port Vila, though a town life comes at a price: it can be dangerous and, while some may boast about Paama's influence there, many living in town find their presence opposed.

Desires and Dangers of Town Life

While living on Paama island during 2002/3, I was struck by the extent of aspiration the people expressed for a future in which they might join friends and family who have made their place in town, in the hope that they might take advantage of the opportunities they perceive their home-away-from-home offers. In Lulep village, talk of travel to town is common, and many are influenced by the stories they have heard about the possibility of making money and finding adventure, while others express a desire to move away from irreconcilable disputes (Rodman 1985; Jolly 1994). Additionally, some young Paama islanders view town as an opportunity to escape the workload expected of them by elderly kin (Lind 2010). Whatever the reason for wanting to visit Port Vila, no one expresses an intention to stay there indefinitely, though in practice many do not return for significant periods while others, who find town life appealing, or who for one reason or another find themselves unable to, never return. Instead, they add to the growing number of Paama people living permanently in Port Vila.

A life in town comes at a price though, and, while a person can eat freely from their gardens on the island, they must 'eat money' (*kakae mane*), that is, pay for food to eat, to survive in town. Town life presents challenges that are, in some respects, different or more acute to those experienced on Paama Island. Money is needed much more often and in greater amounts than on Paama, and islanders arriving in town are faced with the task of finding paid employment in order to contribute to the wider community they enter into.

Urban dwelling is not simply expensive, it is also dangerous because mixing with other ni-Vanuatu is unavoidable, and this is hazardous because it is perceived to significantly increase risk of violent assault or sorcery (*posen*). However, it is impossible to avoid mixing with others in Port Vila's central market, stores, residential areas and squatter settlements, in kava bars, on buses or in many other public areas in the urban environment. Occupying such places makes a person vulnerable to various forms of attack, and a very real sense of threat is felt by Paama islanders and other ni-Vanuatu living in town. As such, while Paama islanders might brag among themselves that they have taken over Port Vila, they would never make such boastful claims to other islanders. Indeed, Paama islanders are acutely aware that their place in Port Vila is opposed by others who would prefer they did not reside in town in such large numbers.

Dangers presented by mixing with others, coupled with the difficulty of securing paid employment, might make living in town appear unappealing, though neither represent sufficient disincentive to repel those Paama islanders who want to or already reside in Port Vila. Indeed, urban dwelling is such an inescapable aspect of Paama islanders' lives that most of the people I met on Paama Island, apart from very young children, had already experienced town life, and many expressed the desire to return. While some said that life in town was not to their tastes, others failed to obtain sufficient resources and were forced to return to Paama Island. However, for those reluctant returnees to Paama, all is not lost. Failing to establish oneself in town does not mean entirely abandoning aspirations to live there, and many returnees look towards the future, always aspiring to find a new 'road' (*faenem rod*) that will give them another chance to make a place for themselves in town.

'Roads' and Kinship

A 'road' (*sise* or *rod* in Bislama, Vanuatu's lingua franca) is essential to a person's ability to access town, and a broad understanding of the term is important to what I have to say here. In addition to referring to a path or route, 'road' might also describe a means to an end, such that a university education can be considered a 'road' to a well paid job. Significantly, 'road' also refers to post-marital virilocal residence, and affinal relations, through which places are acknowledged to be connected, the significance of 'roads' within and between the islands of the archipelago is well established (Bonnemaison 1984b). Such 'roads' have been crucial in enabling patterns of travel, trade and linguistic bridging between various islands throughout Vanuatu, and they remain so (Bonnemaison 1994; Jolly 1994; Tryon 1996; Bolton 1999).

The vast majority of travel throughout Vanuatu is similarly enabled by people with whom one expresses kinship, and such people are often referred to as 'my road' (*rod blong mi*). One's 'road' into town might include a wide range of kin and even friends who can be acknowledged as siblings, if they, as one's siblings ideally should, cooperatively work (*mūm*) with one another in life cycle exchanges conducted to 'make persons' (*anu vā sau*). In offering accommodation and support, a 'road' is a 'thing' through which another might conceivably move from place to place. It is, then, the capacity that a person exhibits to facilitate another's movement from one location to another that identifies them as a 'road'. Similarly, it is this capacity to enable the mobility of a person into a particular *ples* (place) that is consonant with Paama concerns with kinship and reproduction (cf. Facey 1989).

I limit myself here to conveying how marriage and birth are viewed as processes through which persons are replaced where they belong, so that their place might grow anew.[5] To begin: 'road', in terms of kinship theory, refers to sisters and affines. As is common in Vanuatu, post-marital residence is virilocal. As such, it is a woman's movement to her husband's place that (re)establishes 'roads' between one *āmal* (agnatic clan) and another. A woman need not move physically to enable a 'road' because it is marriage that establishes her joint affiliation and her 'road'. 'Roads', then, express a form of sociality that is imagined as distinctively female (Strathern 1988). Such female socialities 'open' (Eriksen 2008) possibilities in other places, in distinction to the 'closed', agnatically exclusive *āmal*.

Although all people come to their place within a 'road', it is birth within an *āmal* that legitimates a person's right to belong there (Lind 2010). By this token, women remain partially attached to their natal *āmal*, even following post-marital relocation. This partial attachment is founded in the 'oneness' that all siblings share by virtue of their common birthplace, irrespective of gender difference. To be clear, while birthplace associates siblings singularly, marriage establishes a dual association for women (ibid.), and it is this dual attachment bridging birthplace and post-marital residence that describes the extent of a woman's part in a particular 'road'.

Through marriage, then, a woman's singular *āmal* affiliation becomes dual, imbuing her with a social identity that extends from her place of birth into the place in which she will ideally give birth to children. As I have said, a person is acknowledged as a 'road' on the basis that they enable the movement of another. As such it is not a woman's own movement, into her husband's place, that her marriage facilitates. Rather, the 'road' that in-married women establish enables children to come to their husband's place. Unsurprisingly then, the legitimacy of a person being born in the correct place is attested to with reference to the 'road' along which they arrived, and this is traced matrilaterally (see Figure 3.1).

Having been returned to an *āmal*, a person is ethically obligated to work (*mūm*) to continue the 'road' that enabled their birth, and they do this by continuing to configure marriages that follow and perpetuate their 'road' by returning it to places where children should be born. To be clear, Paama islanders' concerns with kinship and reproduction, reflect these concerns with movement and stasis, such that an agnatically stable place, an *āmal*, provides the location through which a constant ebb and flow of persons move, leaving in marriage or death before being replaced along their matrilateral 'road' in birth, an event that acknowledges the growth of an *āmal* as it begins again.

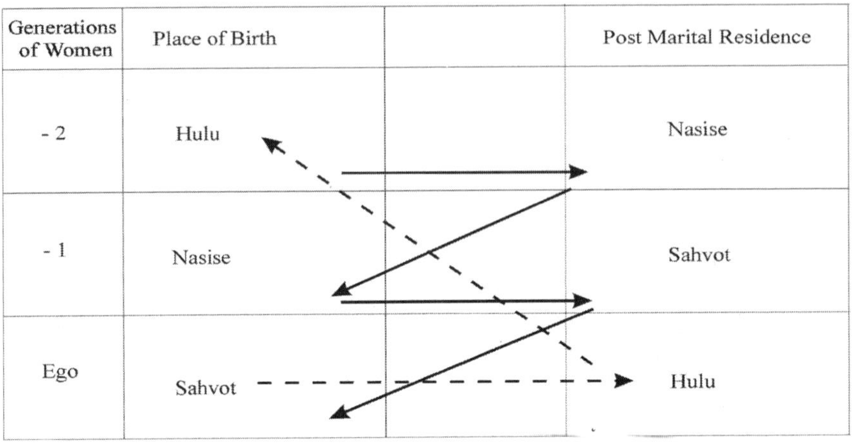

Figure 3.1: Putting people in place: Paama, marriage and reproduction.
Notes: The unbroken horizontal arrows indicate the direction of post-marital female mobility, from Hulu *āmal* into Nasise *āmal* in the first row, for example. The unbroken diagonal arrows show the routes by which people return to their places of birth by moving down one generation vertically in the diagram. Following this series of unbroken arrows as it moves to the bottom left cell, we reach the position where a female ego, born in Sahvot *āmal*, returns in marriage to her MM's place, represented by the dashed horizontal arrow. When ego gives birth to a daughter, the child is registered as the replacement (*raleha*) of her MM in Hulu. A 'road', then, reaches fruition when a child is born, replacing a person who, three generations previously, departed as a woman in marriage or as a man in death (Lind 2010).

Paama islanders present a person's birth as a welcome recurrence: it is the return of a person to the place, an *āmal*, to which they belong. As such, each person, through the very fact of their birth, is obligated to work cooperatively (*mūm*) to replace those who enabled their own birth to occur in the right place. The imperative to make efforts to this end is clear when we consider that ensuring the replacement of persons within one's own *āmal* in the future entails working to enable one's 'road' to continue to grow along its own outward path.

While much more could be said about these issues, I wish to stress one crucial point about Paama representations of kinship and reproduction as it bears on the issue of contraception: from the Paama point of view, birth is the replacement of a person within the *āmal* to which they belong, and it is the post-marital movement of women, constituting a 'road', that enables this to occur (see also Mimica 1988; Rio 2007). Through giving birth, then, a woman is described as a 'road' because she enables a person to be replaced (*raleha*) where they belong. As such, Paama concerns with kinship and reproduction are most correctly understood in terms of the 'movement' and 'emplacement' of people and things.

A 'road' is crucial to a person's ability to move between places, and this idiom of mobility is drawn figuratively from Paama concerns with kinship and reproduction. In short, a 'road' is embodied in a person's capacity to partially detach from one place in order to propagate another. In such broad terms it is easy to see why the idea of a 'road' lends itself to representing a person's move into town as it is to descriptions of how persons come to a place through processes of kinship and reproduction, because both forms of mobility describe how a person moves from one place in a way that is productive in another. While a 'road' is essential for facilitating the many Paama islanders who desire to move towards a life in town, from the point of view of kinship and reproduction, a 'road' is more than just a means for mobility. A 'road' is both the grounds upon which a person's life is enabled within an *āmal* and upon which each person is morally obligated to give life to others.

Introducing Contraception

I have taken time to discuss these issues because they are central to understanding why contraception is such a contentious issue for Paama people. It should be clear that the choice to restrict birth rates could be perceived to limit the number of people obligated to the continuance of 'roads' along which persons might be returned to their place of origin. Someone choosing to use contraception might appear selfish for refusing to return life to the source from which their own arguably stems (Figure 3.1). I move on now to look at these concerns and how they figure in the future-oriented aspirations of Paama islanders by presenting cases both for and against the use of contraception.

Why Lily Chooses to Use Contraception

Lily was born fifty miles south of Paama, on Mataso, a small island in the Shepherds group. Describing her youth on Mataso, Lily presents an idyll, clearly expressing discontentment with where she now lives, in Lulep village. Lily never imagined that her future lay in Lulep when she left Mataso in her late teens and moved in with kin in Port Vila. Lily enjoyed her urban life and her job as a waitress in Jill's Café, a popular burger joint in the centre of Port Vila.

It was here, in Port Vila, that she met Sem, a Paama islander working in construction. After some time the couple chose to marry and planned towards their future in town. However, the future did not accommodate their plans, and their hopes for a life in town were dashed when Sem lost his job. The financial burden on Lily was too severe and, unable to earn enough money from her job, the couple reluctantly chose to move to Sem's place in Lulep village, on Paama Island.

Lily and Sem are a rare couple in Lulep because they only have one child, their son Alan, and rarer still because Lily uses contraception to avoid having another child. Lily explained that she made this choice because she found life in Lulep difficult, and that she hoped for a better future for Alan. Contraception allowed Lily and Sem to concentrate their resources so that they could put Alan on the 'road' (*rod*) to a better future, which they imagined would send him to university in Suva, Fiji, where he would train to become a teacher or a lawyer. Lily told me about a future she imagined in which Alan would return from university with a good education, allowing him to move into a well-paid job in Port Vila – as such, it is education that constitutes Alan's 'road' to Port Vila. Should her plans work out, then Alan will be in a position to help his parents, either sending them money to make life on Paama more comfortable or ideally by sending for them to live with him in Port Vila, where they might all enjoy the kind of comfortable life in town that money allows for.

Chief Silas Demes

Like Lily, Chief Silas Demes resides in Lulep and has, in the past, tried to make a place for himself and his family in town. After some years of trying to establish himself, and failing to find sufficient paid employment, Silas was forced to return to Paama. While he continues to aspire to return to town, he is different from Lily and Sem in one important way: both he and his wife, Lacien, are firmly opposed to the use of contraception. From Silas's point of view, Lily and Sem's future is selfish. Who, if she avoids having more children, would make sure that Lily's mother is returned to her place? Who will replace the people who made Lily's own birth possible? If all people were so selfish, from Silas's point of view, then without anyone working to replace them Paama people would eventually die out altogether.

Perhaps Silas's response seems exaggerated. After all, Lily may reconsider her choice and have more children when Alan's future seems secured. However, Silas cannot foretell what Lily's future choices will be; he can only respond to what is evident in the present and how this appears to him to neglect the obligations that Lily and Sem have to others. Moreover, Lily's choice to have no more children presents Silas with the potential that other 'roads' will be closed off, including those leading into his own *āmal*. As I have said, the birth of a single child is described at the larger scale of renewing the growth of an entire *āmal*. Similarly, denial of birth, through the use of contraception, presents a threat to an entire *āmal* and its future existence in much the same way that the death of an unmarried woman is perceived as a general danger because such events stop a 'road' from moving on (Lind 2010).

In short, Lily's view of a better future seems selfish to Silas because it denies life to those others she is obligated to – choosing a better future for her son appears to deny a future for other people. It appears to Silas to be an acute act of selfishness and disregard towards those who worked so that both Lily and Sem might be born.

Silas and his wife, Lacien, who have five children, represent a more typical household on Paama Island. Having large numbers of children enables an *āmal* to establish broad reaching 'roads' – 'roads' that are extended out from an *āmal* by daughters who leave in marriage, and are returned to an *āmal* by sons whose wives come from other places. 'Roads' benefiting an *āmal* in one way or another are seldom neglected, and the commitment to maintaining them can be expressed in a variety of ways. For example, Silas has adopted his youngest child, Kristina, along his wife's 'road' to her brother, David, who lives on the outskirts of Port Vila. This form of adoption is common for Paama islanders, and its aim is that of 'tightening' families, though it also establishes grounds for more creative future marriages to take place.

Indeed, Kristina's adoption to his wife's place is part of a long term strategy that Silas has employed to encourage the future marriage of his eldest son, Sano, to one of David's daughters. When Sano went to live with David in 2003, this strategy became quite clear to Paama people, sparking discussion about what Silas might gain from this union and how imminent Sano's marriage now seemed. Such plans for Sano's future marriage could not have been considered had Silas and Lacien chosen to have only one child, because paving the way for Sano's move to Port Vila where it was hoped that he would marry necessitated that Silas commit to his wife's 'road', and this entailed Kristina's adoption back into Lacien's birthplace.

As I have said, 'roads' perceived to benefit an *āmal* in one way or another are never neglected, and Silas has much to gain from committing to his wife, Lacien's, 'road' because it leads to Port Vila. Maintaining this 'road' has given Sano a place in town where he can potentially earn money and make a successful future for himself. Moreover, should Sano marry according to Silas's plan, he will have secured a place in town because David is very well established there. Moreover, Silas, like Lily, can imagine himself in a position where he can expect some support from his son – as Sano is a member of his father's *āmal*, Silas will have a place in Port Vila that he and his wife Lacien might potentially move into, a move that Silas has long desired since failing to establish himself in town in the past.

Questioning Progressive versus Conservative Futures

I want to consider one final argument regarding contraception in order to stress why urban residence and reproduction, and not a conservative desire to maintain tradition or a progressivist urge to modernise, are central to what I have to say about Paama islanders' aspirations for the future. Each year in Vanuatu groups of men and women collect information from their home island and report on a specific topic in workshops held in the Vanuatu Cultural Centre (Tryon 1999). In November 2003, the male fieldworker (see Regenvanu 1999)[6] workshop met to report on the subject of childhood – *laef blong pikinini*. Silas, the male fieldworker for Paama, completed his presentation, proudly describing how Paama conducted life-cycle exchanges so that their children grew strong and healthy.

As Silas finished his presentation, the fieldworker from Tanna stood up to ask what Paama chiefs were doing to cut their population numbers. He complained that Paama islanders had spread all over Vanuatu and were so prevalent in town that every second person one met in town was a Paama islander. He addressed Silas, adding, 'don't you think it's time chiefs encouraged the use of contraception to cut down the number of Paama people?'[7] The statement was provocative and it was responded to by gasps of shock and muttered expletives in the room. He might as well have asked if Paama chiefs were planning to kill off their own people.

Earlier, I suggested that recourse to 'simplistic 'progressive-conservative' dichotomies' (Wagner 1981: xiii) were entirely unsuitable to describing Paama projections for the future. There are a number of reasons for this, not the least of which is the way that this line of thinking reinforces the hegemonic superiority of Euro-American projects for modernity and models of civilisation (Giddens 1998). Moreover, enforcing a language of 'progressive'/'conservative' dichotomies limits the level of ethnographic enquiry and imports inappropriate evaluations into the analysis. I have suggested that this leads to a view in which reproduction seems exclusively concerned with 'conservativism' in the face of social change.

Such an assessment cannot account for the inventive ways in which both Lily and Silas draw on ideas about creating roads appropriate to one's intentions in the hope of setting in motion the route towards a better future. To suggest that the 'future' represents more or less 'progressive'/'conservative' strategies is to neglect trying to understand how, in ethnographic terms, Lily's and Silas's children figure in their plans and how this in turn allows for a rethinking of anthropology's current difficulty in characterising urban migration and settlement except as an essentially separate analytical field from that vested in rural subjects. A conclusion based on a 'conservative'/'progressive' dichotomy is most problematic, then, because it rests on exogenous interests at the expense of seeking to understand the basis upon which 'alternative, possible, or imagined worlds' (Hirsch 2004: 35) are conceived by Paama people.

In each case discussed here it is quite clear that when one imagines the future, one also imagines where one will be. That is, it is quite impossible to try to imagine one's future without also imagining one's place in it. While one's past and present represent actual worlds (ibid.: 35), insofar as one has lived experience of them, the future opens itself to aspiration and imagination, and the choice of which 'road' to follow demands creative thinking. While education offers one particular kind of 'road' into a better future in Vanuatu's capital, so too does a creatively orchestrated marriage. Although education and David's daughter represent Alan's and Sano's 'roads', respectively, it is their children, in extending out from their place in the present, who represent the future of Lily's and Silas's 'roads'.

The aspirations that Lily and Silas have for their children are different, to be sure. Lily's use of contraception, which rearticulates kinship obligations, and Silas's denial of contraception, and his wish to extend his relationships widely, also represent significant differences. However, Lily and Silas share similarities as well as differences: they share a rationale in which the future appears as a spatial, and not just a temporal, concern.

A better way of understanding how Paama islanders imagine the future then must consider both the strategies they utilise and the aims they have in mind, which clearly show an interest in urban dwelling. Crucially, though, both strategy and aim must be considered in local terms. Here, the idea of *sise* (road) is central to understanding how Paama islanders imagine their plans to travel spatially, from one place to another, and temporally, from the present towards the future. This is because 'roads' are manifest in a thing's, including a person's, capacity to enable the movement of another, both geographically and temporally across generations.

Contraception is significant, here, for the way that it casts into relief conflicting ideas about how to control the future, and because it elicits arguments in which town and, more significantly, children appear central to the kinds of futures that Paama people perceive being open to them. Although different, both education and marriage enable Alan and Sano, respectively, to move into town, and thus both are 'roads'. Once in place and well established, Alan and Sano will, if their parents' hopes are fulfilled, become the means by which their parents might move – that is, as I have said, Alan and Sano will become potential 'roads' along which their parents might anticipate their own travel to town. Importantly, Sano and Alan do more than enable the movement of their parents: being of the same *āmal* (agnatic clan) as their fathers', Sano and Alan also offer a place in which their parents might reside.

The Tannese argument that Paama chiefs should impose contraception stresses my contention that the concerns I have discussed here are better understood through ni-Vanuatu ideas about kinship, reproduction and *ples*. This is because the demand to impose contraception is made in a bid to prevent Paama people from spreading into new locations throughout Vanuatu. In short, the Tannese chief's complaint expresses the concern that reproduction equates with the apparent Paama islander capacity to establish a place for their people in locations other than Paama Island. While seeming prosaic for the way in which it appears to be a simple demographic observation, it strikes me for the way that it implicates reproduction as a means of moving into a place. In this sense it bears out my contention that Paama islanders think about and plan for the future through the capacities that other persons, as 'roads' or joint *āmal* members, enable for them and upon which they might act (Strathern 1988) – that is, imagine and move towards a preferred future.

Instead of trying to figure out if hopes for the future are more or less about maintaining tradition or progressively breaking from the past, it has been more fruitful to consider Paama islander representations of the future in terms of where the people who make such representations would like to see themselves when they get there, and how they imagine doing so.

Further Questions

Reaching a particular future, like reaching another place, requires having a 'road' along which to move. Paama islanders plans are bound up with the support they can elicit or give to friends and kin, and these are presented in local idioms, concerning *āmal*, as a place to which one belongs, and *rod*, as a 'road' by which one arrives there; these terms are also important idioms describing processes of kinship and reproduction. When a person moves to town, they do so only because another, or others, enable them to do so, and in each case the people, whether a mother or a friend/kinsman, through which another person's arrival can be traced is referred to as a 'road'.

The choice to follow Paama strategies for the future, in their terms, raises a number of points that require further attention. In Vanuatu, as elsewhere in the Pacific region, urban populations are on the rise as Pacific islanders make a place for themselves in towns (VNSO 2009). The question of what kind of *ples* islanders make for themselves is important, as is the question of how *ples* is made and conceived as an activity and how, in turn, this is perceived in terms of ideas about kinship and reproduction (Leach 2003; Lind 2010). Such questions have relevance beyond the academy; they have very serious implications for urban growth in Vanuatu and for the ways in which islanders might seek access to places through differing means of legitimation and, consequently, for the potential that contesting notions of legitimate occupation have for prompting urban unrest and violence.

The concerns with contraception that are raised by the arguments I have discussed here – such as those raised by Lily's perceived capacity to detach from obligations grounded in kinship or the means by which a place might be made to accommodate Paama people – present only a glimpse of the potential that ni-Vanuatu have for imagining new ways of reaching out into their futures. Rather than entrench questionable dichotomies, which polarise and configure Pacific socialities as if they were composed of separable 'domains' (Wagner 1977), taking Paama islanders concerns in their own terms has presented a more sharply focused image of the futures they have in mind and how they work towards achieving their aspirations. This has had the reciprocal effect of raising important questions regarding how Paama people negotiate their movement within Vanuatu, and what implications this has for emerging expressions of Pacific sociality. In short, in suspending assumptions about what represents an expression of 'conservatism' or 'progressivism', and instead allowing the description to be led by shared concerns about urban residence, a number of important questions have arisen for anthropology to consider in the future.

Acknowledgements

This chapter is based on twenty-two months of fieldwork, funded by the ESRC (R42200134307), between February 2002 and March 2004, with Paama people living on Paama Island and in migrant communities in and around Vanuatu's capital, Port Vila, on Efate Island.

Notes

1. The term *raleha* is solely employed to describe the return of a person through whom another traces matrilateral or patrilateral kinship. My use of the phrase 'person where they belong' is derived from the Bislama phrase, *hemi mas kam bak long ples blong hem* ('s/he must come back to the place to which they belong'), adopted here because it was used to explain to me why a child is born in a particular *āmal*. In Paama vernacular, persons are not described as 'belonging' to a place; rather, they are described as being 'of a place' (*tenout*).
2. The figure is based on personal communications with Ben Lenge, manager of the Vanuatu National Statistics Office in mid 2008.
3. Thorolf Lipp (personal communication).
4. There are many complicated issues surrounding this contemporary urban concern with females wearing trousers; as it is not the subject of this chapter I

cannot go into them in detail here. At its most basic, the concern, as expressed by men, is that trousers accentuate and sexualise the female form, drawing inappropriate male attention and heightening the risk of sexual assault. Many females, on the other hand, argue that their choice of clothing should not be dictated by chiefs, expressing newly emerging gender issues in Vanuatu's urban locales.

5. See Lind (2010) for a detailed description.
6. Established with the aim of enlivening pre-Christian ideas, values and activities, the VCC fieldworker programme consists of volunteers tasked with recording and reporting kastom specific to their own island. Initially a male exclusive initiative, a female fieldworker programme was established in the mid 1990s through the work of ni-Vanuatu, Jean Tarisesei and Australian anthropologist Lissant Bolton.
7. *Mi luk se populaeson blong Paama i stap go antap – yu no gat tingting blong daonem populaeson o no. Yu no ting se, taem nao ia blong blokem pikinini?*

References

Bamford, S. 1998. Humanized Landscapes, Embodied Worlds: Land and the Construction of Intergenerational Continuity among the Kamea of Papua New Guinea. *Social Analysis* 42(3): 28–54.

_______ 2007. *Biology Unmoored: Melanesian Reflections on Life and Biotechnology.* Berkley: University of California Press.

Bamford, S., and J. Leach (eds). 2009. *Kinship and Beyond: The Genealogical Model Reconsidered.* Oxford: Berghahn Books.

Battaglia, D. 1990. *On the Bones of the Serpent.* Chicago: University of Chicago Press.

_______ 1992. The Body in the Gift: Memory and Forgetting in Sabarl Mortuary Exchange. *American Ethnologist* 19(1): 3–18.

Bell, C. 2010. *Ritual Theory, Ritual Practice.* Oxford: Oxford University Press.

Bolton, L. 1999. Women, Place and Practice in Vanuatu: A View from Ambae. *Oceania* 70(1): 43–55.

Bonnemaison, J. 1984a. Social and Cultural Aspects of Land Tenure. In P. Larmour (ed.), *Land Tenure in Vanuatu*, pp.1–7. Suva: University of the South Pacific.

_______ 1984b. The Tree and the Canoe: Roots and Mobility in Vanuatu Societies. *Pacific Viewpoint* 25: 117–51.

_______ 1994. *The Tree and the Canoe: History and Ethnography of Tanna.* Honolulu: University of Hawaii Press.

Clifford, J. 1997. *Routes: Travel and Translation in the Late Twentieth Century.* Harvard: Harvard University Press.

Clifford, J., and G. Marcus (eds). 1986. *Writing Culture.* Berkeley: University of California Press.

Damon, F.H. and R. Wagner. 1989. *Death Rituals and Life in the Societies of the Kula Ring*. Northern Illinois University Press.

Eliade, M. 1971 [1954]. *The Myth of Eternal Return: Or Cosmos and History*. Princeton: Princeton University Press.

Eriksen, A. 2008. *Gender, Christianity and Change in Vanuatu: An Analysis of Social Movements in North Ambrym*. Aldershot: Ashgate.

Facey, E.E. 1989. 'Blood' and 'Line': Exploring Kinship Idioms of Nguna, Vanuatu. *Culture* 9(2): 77–87.

Feld, S. 1982. *Sound and Sentiment: Birds, Weeping, Poetics and Song in Kaluli Expression*. Philadelphia: University of Pennsylvania Press.

——— 1984. Sound Structure as Social Structure. *Ethnomusicology* 28(3): 383–409.

Foster, R. 1990. Nurture and Force-Feeding: Mortuary Feasting and the Construction of Collective Individuals in a New Ireland Society. *American Ethnologist* 17(3): 431–48.

——— 1992. Commoditization and the Emergence of Kastam as a Cultural Category: A New Ireland Case in Comparative Perspective. *Oceania* 62(4): 284–94.

——— 1995. *Social Reproduction and History in Melanesia Mortuary Ritual, Gift Exchange, and Custom in the Tanga Islands*. Cambridge: Cambridge University Press.

Gell, A. 1995. The Language of the Forest: Landscape and Phonological Iconism in Umeda. In E. Hirsch and M. O'Hanlon (eds), *The Anthropology of Landscape: Perspectives on Place and Space*, pp.232–54. Oxford: Oxford University Press.

Giddens, A. 1998. *Conversations with Anthony Giddens: Making Sense of Modernity*. Stanford: Stanford University Press.

Haberkorn, G. 1989. *Port Vila: Transit Station or Final Stop? Recent Developments in Ni-Vanuatu Population Mobility*. Canberra: Australian National University Press.

Haberkorn, G. 1992. Temporary versus Permanent Population Mobility in Melanesia: A Case Study from Vanuatu. *International Migration Review* 26(3): 806–42.

Hirsch, E. 2004. Techniques of Vision: Photography, Disco and Renderings of Present Perceptions in Highland Papua. *Journal of the Royal Anthropological Institute* 1(1): 19–39.

Huffman, K. 1996. Trading, Cultural Exchange and Copyright: Important Aspects of Vanuatu Arts. In J. Bonnemaison (ed.), *Arts of Vanuatu*, pp.182–94. Bathurst: Crawford House Publishing.

Jolly, M. 1992. Banana Leaf Bundles and Grass Skirts: A Pacific Penelope's Web? In J. Carrier (ed.), *History and Tradition in Melanesian Anthropology*, pp.39–64. Berkeley: University of California Press.

——— 1994. *Women of the Place: Kastom, Colonialism and Gender in Vanuatu*. Chur: Harwood Academic Press.

Jolly, M., and N. Thomas. 1992. The Politics of Tradition in the Pacific. *Oceania* 62(4): 241–48.

Leach, J. 2003. *Creative Land: Place and Procreation on the Rai Coast of Papua New Guinea*. Oxford: Berghahn Books.

Lind, C. 2010. Placing Paamese: Locating Concerns with Place, Gender and Movement in Vanuatu. PhD diss. St Andrews: University of St Andrews.

_______ 2012. Not Giving, but Taking: Christian Conversion and the Destruction of Kinship in Vanuatu. Unpublished paper presented at the ASAO Annual Meeting, Portland 2012.

Lindstrom, L. 1996. 'Arts of Language and Space: South East Tanna', in J. Bonnemaison (ed.), *Arts of Vanuatu*, pp.123–28. Bathurst: Crawford House Publishing.

_______ 2010. Urbane Tannese: Local Perspectives on Settlement Life in Port Vila. Unpublished paper presented at Bergen University, October 2010.

Malinowski, B. 1916. Baloma. *Journal of the Royal Anthropological Institute* 45: 353–430.

Mimica, J. 1988. *Intimations of Infinity: The Cultural Meanings of the Iqwaye Counting and Number Systems*. Oxford: Berg.

Regenvanu, R. 1999. Afterword: Vanuatu Perspectives on Research. *Oceania* 70(1): 98–100.

Rodman, M. 1985. Moving Houses: Residential Mobility and the Mobility of Residences in Longana, Vanuatu. *American Anthropologist* 87(1): 56–72.

Strathern, M. 1985. Discovering 'Social Control'. *Journal of Law and Society* 12(2): 111–34.

_______ 1988. *The Gender of the Gift: Problems with Women and Problems with Society in Melanesia*. Berkeley: University of California Press.

_______ 1999. *Property, Substance and Effect: Anthropological Essays on Persons and Things*. London: Athlone Press.

Tonkinson, R. 1968. Maat Village, Efate: A Relocated Community in the New Hebrides. PhD diss. Eugene: University of Oregon.

Toren, C. 1997. Seeing the Ancestral Sites: Transformations in Fijian Notions of the Land. In E. Hirsch and M. O'Hanlon (eds), *The Anthropology of Landscape: Perspectives on Place and Space*, pp.163–83. Oxford: Oxford University Press.

Tryon, D. 1996. Dialect Chaining and the Use of Geographical Space. In J. Bonnemaison (ed.), *Arts of Vanuatu*, pp.170–81. Bathurst: Crawford House Publishing.

_______ 1999. Ni-Vanuatu Research and Researchers. *Oceania* 70: 9–15.

Rio, K. 2007. *The Power of Perspective: Social Ontology and Angency on Ambrym Island, Vanuatu*. Oxford: Berghahn Books.

Robbins, J. 2007. Continuity Thinking and the Problem of Christian Culture: Belief, Time, and the Anthropology of Christianity. *Current Anthropology* 48(1): 5–38.

VNSO. 2009. National Census of Population and Housing: Summary Release. Port Vila: Vanuatu National Statistics Office.

Wagner, R. 1972. Incest and Identity: A Critique and Theory on the Subject of Exogamy and Incest Prohibition. *Man* 7(4): 601–13.

——— 1977. Analogic Kinship: A Daribi Example. *American Ethnologist* 4(4): 623–42.

——— 1981 [1975]. *The Invention of Culture*. Chicago: University of Chicago Press.

Weiner, A.B. 1977. Trobriand Descent: Female/Male Domains. *Ethnos* 5(1): 54–70.

——— 1979. Trobriand Kinship from Another View: The Reproductive Power of Women and Men. *Man* 14(2): 328–48.

——— 1980. Reproduction: A Replacement for Reciprocity. *American Ethnologist* 7(1): 71–85.

Weiner, J. 1982. Substance, Siblingship and Exchange: Aspects of Social Structure in New Guinea. *Social Analysis* 11: 3–34.

——— 1991. *The Empty Place*. Indianapolis: Indiana University Press.

4

Gambling Futures

Playing the Imminent in Highland Papua New Guinea

Anthony Pickles

In a town called Goroka in highland Papua New Guinea, people have chosen to address daily uncertainties head-on through forms of betting. Card games and their material remains dominate the human landscape of settlements even while gambling remains side-lined in anthropological accounts of the region.[1] As both a present- and a future-oriented activity, gambling requires temporal presence of mind as well as motivations directed towards a future goal. These simultaneous engagements help procure relationships that participants hope will bloom into further transactions beneficial to themselves. At first utilising recent anthropological material on fortune and luck (da Col and Humphrey 2012), and later Robbins's notion of 'everyday millenarianism' (Robbins 2001), this chapter explores notions of time and the future; it does so through gaming rounds that reveal the direction of wealth in a context where knowledge is fleetingly manifested in transactions. Gorokan approaches to the future are premised on the impossibility of knowing others' thoughts, which must be made apparent in meaningful activities such as gambling. I explore the playing of cards in a settlement in town as an apt technology for people's attempts at repositioning their futures.

Other chapters in this collection consider the long-term future and the future of groups as a whole, or break new ground in the middle term (following e.g. Guyer 2007). My contribution compliments these approaches by gauging individuals' conceptions of the future in an everyday context where rival projects compete, specifically the visions of several people within a card game. I deliberately chose the game *bom* ('bomb') as the starting point of an attempt to make plain the intrinsic future orientation of gambling in Goroka because it is the lowest-stakes, most commonplace, lowest-impact game.[2]

Remaining firmly within the ethnographic approach suggested by this volume, this chapter attempts to describe the future orientation of gambling in Goroka (cf. da Col and Humphrey 2012). In so doing, I subscribe to Geertz's relativist point that the traits of different peoples surface during their games (Geertz 1973: 417), an idea pioneered by Caillois (1958). Yet both to remain true to the Gorokan context, and to avoid a relativisation that renders people a slave to their traditions, I cannot endorse Geertz's accompanying theory of 'deep play' (Geertz 1973: 433), a theory adapted from Bentham (1882). For Bentham there were certain circumstances in gambling where the total pain of moneys lost was greater than the happiness that came from winners' rewards, resulting in a net increase in suffering. Geertz adopts and inverts this 'deep play' by noting that when bettors during a cockfight in Bali make a large central bet, the magnitude indexes their support for one side within a cockfight and the significance of the relations (their brothers, cousins, and political allies and so on) that the cock signifies. Therefore, during large wagers, honour is the winner while the statuses of both parties are made explicit for all to see, maintaining their social position (Geertz 1973: 434). Everyday betting in Goroka is structured so as to avoid central, status-enacting heavy bets by which people can be measured, or in which they might tell themselves about themselves or activate hostile relations in a safe format (ibid.). In fact status is not an apt way of describing what is invested when people place money bets. I demonstrate that money is consumed in an effort to bring about people's opportunistic visions of the future, but not used as a tool of reaffirmation. As a consequence, Geertz's interpretation cannot be applied to Gorokan gambling as there are only successful and unsuccessful bets; this is surely related to the fact that social 'rank' – as Geertz characterised social position in Bali (ibid.: 448) – is, at least as people represent it, meritocratic in Goroka (Read 1959). People seem not to feel inclined towards 'metasocial commentary'; they seem quite at ease with their 'system' not being wholly knowable (Geertz 1973: 448).

Instead of Geertz's formulation, I draw the reader's attention toward a recent collection – clearly inspired by Wagner among others – that took notions of luck and fortune as 'concept-events' that could inform or reform our discipline's more familiar conceptual divides (da Col 2012: 3). The editors sum up their collective take on gambling as:

> a 'centrifugal' economic modality aimed at displaying vitality, revisiting notions of value and 'licit' wealth, and repositioning subjectivities … [Gambling is] predicated on a performative paradox. Fortune can be demonstrated only in events, yet one needs to act, to perform, in order to display its miraculous properties. When confronted with its effects, fortune seems *a posteriori* the result of a series of necessary events or actions. (da Col and Humphrey 2012: 7)

It is precisely the way gambling may be used to repositioning people vis-à-vis each other in the present, and the way gambling at *bom* seems to require contingent attempts at performing people's desired future positions, that I attempt to build from.

For Gorokans, even the most 'inconsequential' forms of gambling are a means by which people pull themselves into an unknowable but thrillingly undulating future (see Pickles 2012). This chapter leans upon Roy Wagner's observation that success in Melanesian societies rests largely upon an actor's ability to change others' perceptions of the world by persuading them that what they currently hold to be true is in fact untrue, or at the least disadvantageous; in effect Melanesians attempt to make meaningful and profitable reconstitutions of 'reality' in their dealings with each other (Wagner 1978, 1986, 1991; see also Pickles 2013a). In gambling, Gorokans are concerned with learning what relationships, manifested in which forms, will prove socially effective, and utilising that knowledge to their advantage. This shall be my focus too (cf. Pickles 2013b).

I first contextualise the nuances and parameters of Gorokan engagement with contingency – rather than 'chance', which is not a salient category in Goroka (see Pickles 2014a, 2014b) – through an ethnographic vignette, and then demonstrate how *bom* is well-suited as a starting point from which Gorokan actors prospect towards more consequential future relationships, weaving the explanation of *bom* into the story.

The Gorokan Context

Gambling generally is extremely prevalent in the Papua New Guinea highlands; you only have to visit a settlement in any highland town and look down to find the ground under your feet marbled with discarded cards; many communal village spaces are the same. I take the reader into one such settlement, known officially as Kaunsil Kem ('Council Camp'). A planned settlement, it was built and then reshaped by its residents on the steep dipping slopes of a stream-cut incision into the south-western edge of Goroka, whose public institutions and houses greedily splay out on the flat ground above.

Goroka is the provincial capital of Eastern Highlands Province; established in 1941, it is the oldest town in the highlands and was once the region's colonial administrative capital. The establishment of a town had to contend with and alienate land from an extremely diverse population, a dense pattern of local political units, enmeshed in complex systems of warfare and exchange (see Read 1965). Once a colonial peace was established, migrants were drawn to the flourishing town from far afield to help in its construction and the staffing of public and commercial facilities; some settled into government properties, others rented from local landowners. Goroka has remained heavily reliant on public-sector employment and the primary cash crop, coffee, as well as its airport and strategic location mid-way along the Highlands Highway. According to census data collected in 2000, Goroka had a population of 19,523 people, a high proportion of whom were from the surrounding province or other highlands provinces, primarily Simbu (NSO 2002). A great many migrants assumed local landowning and proprietorship rights as they became related to one another, while alienated state land was recolonised by illegal or planned settlements, creating complex webs of relatedness and more or less new social forms.

This chapter places us in the much more circumscribed context of a few rounds of cards, played on a morning in Kaunsil Kem, and the folks and transactions intermingled in the game. From this I hope to demonstrate how visions of the future are themselves staked by people who, despite their uncertainty of others' intentions and plans, attempt to mould that future to their will. Here I take inspiration from Munn, who both foregrounded space-time and its various manipulations by actors in the Kula ring (Munn 1986), and later reviewed the potential of a future-oriented anthropology (Munn 1992). In my own formulation, visions of the future that come to the fore during games of *bom* are the first step toward space-time manipulations, before they reveal what effect they have had.

There is one further complexity: to avoid traditionalising an activity Gorokans consider contemporary and future oriented. Much of the existing literature on gambling in Melanesia (excepting Mimica 2006; Mosko 2012) frames gambling in terms of a past without it, and charts the perversion of previous forms of redistribution into gambling (e.g. Zimmer 1987; Hayano 1989). In line with the conceptual aims of this volume, the chapter avoids validating gambling in terms of its relation to 'past' modes of existence that lead to a 'neutralisation of the new' (Introduction, this volume), exploring instead how in the case of Gorokans gambling, the 'form of their projects makes a difference' (ibid.).

Gambling is exogenous to Papua New Guinea; it arrived in Goroka in the 1950s, and *bom* has come to prominence only in the last ten years, now sharing the majority of the daily playing landscape of Goroka with only one other game, *kwin* ('queen').[3] *Bom* is slightly more popular than *kwin*, but the bets are usually lower, starting at 10 toea, peaking at 2 kina, though sometimes reaching 5.[4] Bet size can be so negligible as to make *bom* simply a social activity to pass the time, but I argue that the game is nevertheless a highly revealing and engaging one.

All the characters described below were known to me during fieldwork, but their confluence in this chapter is a matter of ethnographic licence. The context of town life means many people felt they knew little of each other, even those who were relatively close. Nevertheless, as I discuss below, the Melanesian form of this assumption actually unites them, as do the rules of the game in which they were engaged. I take my explanatory quotes from a single person for literary convenience, rather than lack of other candidates.

A Typical Morning in Kaunsil Kem

We (you and I) are under a tarpaulin next to a betel nut, cigarette and sweets table surrounded by sodden earth blackened into oily pools by betel nut spittle. The ripped, smeared and twisted blue-backed cards floating in the muck grew denser as we approached our shelter, graphic evidence of the intensity of card playing here. Perched on a coconut scraper brought out for us against all insistence, we look down on a square of tarpaulin used as a mat, four players crouched or cross legged around it, while some children play with shredded cards in the middle distance. At 8.30 AM the sun is beginning to appear through the clouds, and the tarpaulin draws spectators and players as magpies to a trinket.

We are playing 50 toea *bom*, a low denomination appropriate to morning gaming but still one of the fastest games you can find, giving it a high turnover. One player is a middle-aged man whose table is purveying tobacco and betel nut to the gathering. His name is Charlie and he lives next door. His thirteen-year-old son has just left the game and wanders towards the crossroads. As in the illustration below (Figure 4.1), marketeers and gamblers cluster together at the side of streets or on street corners. Playing avidly alongside Charlie is a man who sells water to thirsty people for a few toea at the altogether more impersonal main market; he goes by the name Las-wara, and is considered by some to be mentally affected. Another is a policeman in uniform; he lives at the police barracks a block away and is due at work soon. He has been playing cards in the settlement for the last nine months, ever since he moved up to the barracks. When he lived down in the settlement he shunned those amongst whom he now sits. There is a free space in the game; calls of 'one down' (a phrase shared with bus crews who use it when a passenger intends to get off) are met by a wife whose husband is away in Porgera (a mine in Enga Province) for work, and whose informal selling of fried lamb flap-snacks was curtailed by the cholera crisis that recently hit – she will resume frying in the afternoon. Three of the players are from different areas of Eastern Highlands and Las-wara is from neighbouring Simbu.

A 'free' betel nut is given by the marketeer to Las-wara, who is losing. This is a significant moment, displaying many of the dynamics of Gorokan social life in general. The marketeer Charlie transmits his knowledge of Las-wara's betel nut habit, condones his continuing to play, shows awareness and compassion for his disadvantageous position, and expresses faith in its turning around. The gift secures his custom in the future as it impregnates him with the memory of Charlie's generosity. This is very important, as in this settlement 36 per cent of all households sell betel nut,[5] so making money from it is a real skill. To convince customers of your generosity and register the gift as what is known as a 'round' by implanting it as such in their memory, good marketeers will often call out to people in the street and offer them a free betel nut. This is either a way of initiating a new patron–client relationship or used to further convince a known customer of their good nature, a gesture often timed for maximum effectiveness in generating rapport and memorability. Very often encounters are narrativised as first, second or next 'round', each of which are coupled with a gift of knowledge or wealth in one direction or the other. This one tiny event is oriented towards a particular future which is depicted in the instance of giving and resisted or restructured in its acceptance (cf. Swancutt 2012).

Figure 4.1 A game of *bom* being played in West Goroka. Photograph by Anthony Pickles

Charlie has given the betel nut just at the right time, so he thinks, when the tension of losing has made Las-wara crave for his habit, which he obviously has no money for as it is tied up in the game, and because Las-wara is one of the many who thinks that betel nut aids his concentration and skill (see Mosko 2012). This gift will be remembered, and its ripples affect the whole group. Everyone notices and appreciates the kindness of the gesture; someone comments that this is good behaviour. All of us present know that the lowliness of the recipient's position excludes the giver from having to give betel nut to the rest of us, and we also all know that the fried-snack marketeer who praised Charlie's good behaviour has black betel-nut-stained teeth and was angling for a betel nut of her own. Charlie will remember this gift as a 'round', an episodic act which may be brought up later when Las-wara passes his table.

This transaction is small, but in Goroka they say that millionaires are made by giving a single betel nut. It is forever in people's minds that if they give the right thing at the right moment (cf. Minnegal 2009) with the proper feelings of generosity, then they may profit enormously in any number of ways; by, for example, getting a government contract to fix a road, being bought crates of beer by appreciative debtors who are in the euphoria of good fortune, or even, when in want of a wife, by being considered favourably by the father of a prospective bride. The next 'round' could well be one's making; one should not be fooled by the appearance of continuing hardship. The life histories I collected during fieldwork revealing the turns in fortune which seemed to characterise many people's lives in Papua New Guinea often put paid to the snapshot-in-time impressions of this first-time ethnographer.

To elaborate on the notion of 'rounds' I put forward above, it is necessary to consider notions of time in a Papua New Guinean context. In respect of my experiences in the field, I find Robbins's concept of 'everyday millenarianism' (Robbins 2001) to be a useful one to adapt for an understanding of small-scale transactions in space-time (cf. Munn 1986). Robbins uses narrative practices among the Urapmin of Papua New Guinea to put forward a model of time that is always anticipatory and yet incomplete, about to be ruptured and remodelled in a way that is impossible to predict (cf. Miyazaki 2004). Urapmin narratives include sacred stories whose crucial details and the significance of what has already been told are concealed and later revealed as people go through life, like so many onion layers. Those exposing their truths are at the same time always uncertain if they have themselves received the full story, and so the import (depth or shallowness, we might say) of particular activities cannot be assumed at the time they are revealed (see also Strathern 1992). Urapmin people are therefore constantly in a state of anticipation; they are, since the present is always incomplete, 'waiting for a future that will always be more meaning-full than the present' (Robbins 2001: 538).

Yet the future is at the same time assured to be incomplete (cf. Crook 2007; Reed 2011). This is therefore not a space-time capable of supporting fully rational actors on the model of *Homo economicus*. Rather, it is inhabited by a population of prospectors who know that they may never know the choices that led to success or failure.

In Goroka, practical ways to gain control over wealth items were daily concerns, and so Robbins's description of the everyday revaluation of knowledge and predictability can be usefully extended to Gorokan meditations on sources of future wealth. Such 'onion-skin revelations' are akin to Gorokan understandings of the successive rounds (*ol raun*) of everyday life. As such I draw attention to Gorokan residents' tendency to view dealings with others in terms of rounds.

Returning to the game, Las-wara is concentrating hard, and, in the silent and almost violent way he accepts the betel nut from the marketeer, he expresses that it is nothing more than his right. As he sees it, he has not only been losing, but losing to Charlie on and off for the last two days. He accepts the betel nut begrudgingly, displaying that he thinks this is the least the marketeer could have done; Charlie has not been overgenerous in the last few days. Perhaps Las-wara's disgruntled air reflects the fact that Charlie always seems to win money at cards as he is constantly here, sells the cards in the first place, and then monopolises the selling of tobacco and betel nut to all the players. Charlie should really use his winnings to buy his own betel nut and give it to all the players, then they would have plenty, and he could think straight and have a chance at winning. That's what they do under the other tarpaulin all the time, where the marketing woman is a good Simbu, not an Eastern Highlander. Such complaints were commonly voiced in private. So Las-wara might reduce the gift to the status of non-significance, and anticipate a future in which the marketeer Charlie acts more generously towards him and reflects on his marketing strategy. Therefore, this gift of a betel nut can be perceived not so much as a generous act, but as guilty and insufficient compensation, and thus is not registered as something that it is necessary to pay back.[6] The betel nut stays a violent outcome for the time being, rather than contributing to satiation. This is a 'round' and that means a definite, marked 'phase' of a social relation (in which perhaps one is positioned as recipient in this moment, projected as a return donor in the next), much as Wagner talks of the epochal nature of social time.

Rounds mark a serial, episodic temporality. The punctuated, back-and-forth quality of this space-time, in which people make their fortunes (or not) in relation to others makes the future inherently uncertain in a distinctively social way: it always depends on another's response to previous rounds, in partial revelation of their own mind (Robbins 2001).

Coupled to a notion of episodic, serial, round-like temporality in which people may make (or squander) their fortune, there is a paucity of certitude in relation to upcoming events (see Strathern 1992). The anticipatory future Charlie suggests, where the customer will buy from him again, is obscured by the unpredictability of their intentions. In Goroka, as elsewhere in Melanesia, knowledge or understanding (*save*) cannot be known until it is revealed by a person's actions. In this case, Charlie has judged his customer's *save* wrongly. In a recent edited collection on the 'opacity of other's minds' (Robbins and Rumsey 2008), Stasch makes the point that 'Melanesian sensitivity about not presuming to know other's minds is intertwined with sensitivity about not presuming to impinge on other's self-determination' (Stasch 2008: 443). This relates strongly to the personalisation of the future through the image of the interpersonal system of rounds: a person appears in the past as a narrative, where actions can be used as interpretive cues for understanding knowledge; in the future no such narrative is available and one is left with the hazard of 'ideas', while every round becomes a test or challenge to others to reveal themselves and their *save*. The 'round' is the means by which prospective hazard is converted into contested narrative.

I learnt early on in my fieldwork that when walking around, the often asked 'where are you going?' should not usually be answered in any definite terms, lest the person who asks be able to infer one's wealth and intentions, and thus to intercept or thwart one's aims and desires. I was quickly advised to give statements like *mi raun tasol* ('I am just wandering about'), or to say that I was acting on the wishes of another. To my initial surprise, when I began making such statements they were not usually followed up with more questions about my purpose or destination. In fact, with those who hitherto had been privy to my intentions, such utterances usually elicited a knowing look to the effect that I was learning. The same reasoning applied when people were playing and I would ask them to divulge tactics; people would talk of their own, personal, 'ideas', which they utilise during play. They do not assume that other's 'ideas' work in the same way as their own, and there are differences of opinion over which kinds of 'ideas' constitute trickery and cheating and which ones are legitimate (Pickles 2013b). For instance, many people have charms which are said to aid winning, but these are not legitimate things to mention that one possesses when playing (see also Mosko 2012: 28–30). There is a distinct lack of common knowledge of others' ideas, and a perceived difficulty in knowing other peoples' thoughts or intentions, which are said to be revealed only through their concrete, visually observable actions (see Strathern 1992; Pickles 2013a). I would therefore elicit explanations privately that would never be made publicly. As an example of such talk about ideas, consider Charlie's account of his skill at knowing customers:

> I am a man who is very good at *skelim* [measuring, deciphering] all people. I look and I see people and I can see if someone needs betel nut or cigarettes; if they are desperate for it, I will shout out to them and give them it then ... My brain is open, I can *skelim* you, so I can give you something through the right channel ... If you walk past and you haven't chewed betel nut, your face will look different, it will show that you are hungry for betel nut, so you will come, I know that you smoke or chew; I will see that your face looks hungry. All the people are often surprised and ask me 'how do you know my needs?' I just say, 'I know, that's all', and I give to them. I don't tell them I worked it out, I just say I am supporting them and I give to them. I don't tell them because I don't want to, this knowledge stays with me. I don't want to let this thinking of mine get out to customers.

Charlie understands his technique of marketing as a process of friend-making, which he is particularly well suited for because of his cleverness as a reader of the outside appearance of persons. Charlie was not unusual in claiming a special ability to interpret people's outward signs and to infer their inner intentions. Nevertheless, such thinking is a taboo subject, and he does not want this ability to get out to his customers, testifying to the strategically secret nature of such interpretation. It is the assumed inability of average people to fully connect with another person's psyche which makes transactions of the types being discussed here such important activities. It is in the giving of betel nut that Charlie confirms his skills of interpretation and prediction, and the later return of the same customers to his stall. In other words, what is revealed in these exchanges is the effectiveness (or not) of the marketeer's 'idea'. Ideas are therefore tested as they convert themselves from the unknown quantity of another's thoughts into a social reality that can be narrated.

I next show how this understanding of daily life as a series of unknowable rounds is given open-ended form in the game *bom*. I argue that each round in card games and elsewhere is conceived as the only source of concrete knowledge pertaining to the tactics and relative efficacies of one's social others. In other words, without activities like gambling or marketing, how would you know people's intentions and efficacies (see also Mosko 2012)? The demand for evidence of intention is in turn reflected in the type of games played in Goroka.

Bom

Gambling games are an arena for elicitation, a space where the latent wealth of other people may be drawn out and towards you, but they are also a means of assessing each other's fortune. I contend that the form of such elicitations are discernible within the very rules of a game like *bom* – which is according to my informants a derivation of the game last card (cf. Zimmer 1987). By examining its procedures and tactical possibilities, it is possible to incorporate gameplay into the field of effective future-prospecting I am laying out.

Bom has no more than five players, rarely fewer. Bets are made before the start of play or as cards are dealt, and are standardised by consent of all players, such that if you were to ask what people were playing, the bet size and game name are conjoined, as in *fifti-toea-bom*. The dealer shuffles and then offers the cards to the person on their right, who cuts them, turns over the bottom card from the cut, places that card face up in the centre and lays the rest of the cards face down. The face-up card is the lead card, and if the cutter cuts the seven of hearts (the 'bomb card'), they automatically win. The dealer then deals seven cards to each player, and if they fail to do so properly, they pick up two cards (a two card penalisation applies to any mistake made by a player during the game). The deal is invalid if a player holds three twos, but if one player has four twos they automatically win. One has to put down a card of the same suit as the one that preceded it, or the equivalent value card belonging to a different suit, whereupon the suit required by the next player changes accordingly. If one cannot follow suit or value, or prefers to keep one's remaining cards for a better opportunity, then one has to pick up a card. The game ends when one player has exhausted the cards in their hand, or when the *bom kat* (bomb card), the seven of hearts, is played. The object of the game is to rid oneself of as many of one's cards as possible, especially those of a high value. The winner is the player with the lowest remaining hand when the game ends. Some cards have special properties during gameplay, and, correspondingly, count above their face value at the end of the game (see Table 4.1); all other cards retain their face value at the end of play. Queen is valued at two points, king at four and ace at one.

The person on the right of the dealer plays first; if the lead card has special properties they apply to this player. The seven of hearts or 'bomb card' is the most important as it has the power to end play, and gives its possessor a superior chance of winning because they can hold the bomb card back until the other cards in their hand have only a low total value.

On a basic level, 'masterminding' the game is achieved by knowing which cards have been played, and therefore the likely implications of playing a specific suit or value. For instance, laying a seven or a heart is risky should other players have only a few cards remaining and you are not holding the *bom* card yourself, as they would be enabled to play it. Skill is attributed to a player who elicits another to play their *bom* card and then beats them with a low score. Apart from certain decisions of strategy, such as opening an opportunity to lay a combination of cards or to change the suit playing to favour your hand, there is often a correct and incorrect way to play in any given situation, which can catch out the inattentive or inexperienced players, and force them to pick up two cards for making a mistake. However, for the most part the cards you can play are sufficiently constrained as to make much of the play mechanical and thus very speedy indeed.

Combined with the mechanics of gameplay, a player who participates in a game of cards often finds it necessary to focus their mind in some way, whether this be concentrating on a recent dream portending victory, how much one desires to win, which cards one aims to win by, or even employing reverse psychology by trying to forget one's desire to win or renounce emotional attachment to one's balance of wins and losses (see also Mimica 2006; Reed 2011; cf. da Col and Humphrey 2012). Tactics or 'ideas' are used to attract cards and money towards oneself, but they may as likely be interrupted by the thoughts of others within and outside the game, for the thoughts of others, while unknowable, are still able directly to affect one's own mind.

Table 4.1: Cards with special properties

Card	**Special Properties During Play**	**Point Value after Play**
Jack (called the J)	Known as a res kat (lit. 'rest card'), the jack can be joined by another card of the same suit during the same turn, allowing a player to get rid of two cards at once. If one cannot do so then the player who put down the jack must pick up a card from the deck.	45
2	Makes the player following you have to pick up two cards from the deck if they cannot respond with another 2. If the following player can respond with a 2 then they cancel out the penalty, and the next player may play as normal. If a player is forced to pick up two cards, the next player plays as normal.	20
4	Reverses the direction of play towards the previous player, after which the direction returns to normal, beginning again with the person who played the four.	20
8	Another 'rest card', it acts exactly like the jack, but without such a large point value.	8
7 hearts	The bom kat ('bomb card') ends play when laid, forcing players to compare the total point value of the cards remaining in their hands. The player with the lowest points is the winner.	n/a

Back in the Game

Let us focus now on the policeman and the player who sells fried food. The policeman does not know this woman directly, or even that she sells fried food, yet this is critical to their gameplay. The policeman, who was stationed in Goroka after his police training in the capital, lived in the settlement for four years. However, with the opening of a new barracks just up the road, he was finally given a place in police accommodation. While he lived in the settlement, he was concerned to be an upstanding example of good citizenship, and chastised card players for their apparent laziness. In uniform, he had publicly attacked card players. Now, he goes down to the settlement a few times a week during his time off, plays *bom*, buys food, betel nuts and cigarettes from those selling them. The aim is obvious: to remain part of the 'community', to keep up relations, preventing jealousy and accusations of abandonment. He is in the process of extricating himself from the settlement, but this is a potentially sensitive move, particularly because he remains nearby. He plays for fun at low stakes *bom* games, to relax, he says, basking in the approval of those who see that he is not one to forget others. There were thus previously many possible outcomes to his leaving the settlement, but by transacting with settlement dwellers, he attempts to whittle the possibilities into a single result: continued good feeling. In doing so, not only does he turn a blind eye to illegal gambling but actively participates – and as his concern is maintaining good relations, not winning *per se*, he is a popular member of the gambling circle. Without easing the abrupt end of relations with his former neighbours by playing *bom*, he would have left with a potentially dangerous uncertainty as to what others think of him, and thus what they might do to him in the future.

The lady frying lamb-flaps is implicated here: the ban on selling street food has been in force for the past two months, and her respect for the community's concern over the risk of widespread cholera has been slowly giving way to a pragmatic desire to earn money while her husband is away. A policeman is officially obliged to shut down her stall, and she will know this. This particular policeman poses little risk as his motives lie less in winning money than demonstrating his good intentions, but this would not be known to her. The policeman's presence might therefore be seen as disruptive to her efforts because she is aware that the police are against her trade, and so she may suspect that he is unhappy with her. Such instances are, like as not, perceived to prevent people from winning. Many women confessed that when their husbands are away their thoughts are freed up, and so it would be reasonable for her to assume that without the policeman she might be basking in success. The policeman might therefore be hindering her otherwise irresistible mind.

It is common knowledge that if those around you are not happy with you, if they think that you are miserly or uncaring, these unpleasant thoughts may go inside the game and affect not only your thinking but that of other players and, some say, the cards themselves, causing you to lose. As elsewhere in Papua New Guinea, these games are conceptualised as a series of individual rounds within which cards and money flow, and that flow is subject to the participant's powers of attraction (see Mimica 2006; Mosko 2012; Pickles 2012, 2013a). Yet that power is itself liable to be disrupted by others, just as all other acquisitive activities are. It does not necessarily matter which kind of transaction you are performing; if your powers of attraction are being hindered, all desirable things will be less drawn towards you. Yet it is only by attempting to attract things to you, by for instance playing cards, that one can gauge the efficacy of one's tactics and the present quality of one's relationships. People need to test themselves at things like cards in order to know not only whether they will be successful, but who they are, as this is constituted in one's relations to others (cf. Mimica 2006: 122). So the marketing lady, who joined the game as we were watching, did so precisely to test her efficacy (see Graeber 2012). The fact that the game has not been going well in the presence of the policeman will lead her to question whether to fry lamb-flaps for market that afternoon.

Playing cards is a vehicle for learning about both self and other through concrete action and evidence, acting as an effective way of breaking the un-knowability of people's thoughts. Playing a game like *bom* is yet more useful, as it involves a high turnover of revelations due to its mechanical speed.[7] The many rounds, one after another, the assessment which this implies and the speed by which decisions are made and turns taken, make *bom* a fast game. When the game ends with the 'bomb' card and players are forced to count the value of their cards, it is astounding how fast this is done (cf. Pickles 2009). *Bom* is favoured for this as it is considered easy, exciting and fast, as against other, slower and more thoughtful games. Because of its speed and the rapid opening and curtailing of opportunities to pull the game towards you, *bom* is an ideal way to occupy time while keeping losses at a minimum. The rounds come thick and fast, and the people playing feel thoroughly tested. Unsurprisingly then, *bom* is associated with the young, as they are considered the most quick-witted and hungry for opportunities to test themselves; card games played between children were almost always *bom*.

Earlier I mentioned the marketeer Charlie's son, a boy of thirteen, leaving the game as we joined it. In the mornings, games of *bom*, which may last the full day, often begin among a group of children, playing for fun or for

10 toea (the lowest denomination in circulation). Restless adults would join until a critical number were able to dictate the size of stake and push the children out. This is how the game described above began, when Charlie's son Dominic had finished what might be thought of as his psychic warm-up for the day, and had gone to find money and prospects elsewhere in the faster-moving areas of the settlement, hoping to be sent to buy betel nut or other marketable things for a fee. In a way, what we have been watching is an aftermath, the real action has gone elsewhere. Those who remain are creating and resolving small monetary transactions to fill their hours, and at the same time to gain some measure of control over the range of possible futures. As one creates and engages with little transactions and uncertainties, one gains insight into, and prefigures, those larger transactions which preoccupy one's thoughts, creating future certainty in the act of dealing with present uncertainty (see da Col 2012).

Acknowledgements

The people of Goroka will continue to shape my future, for which I am thankful. In 2013 I learnt that the chapter's primary character Charlie died shortly after I left Goroka in 2010, so this is for him. Adam Reed gave insightful comments and suggestions on a first draft, C. N.-C. renewed it, Will Rollason took it further and three reviewers made it stronger. The research was funded by the UK Economic and Social Research Council and the Royal Anthropological Institute of Great Britain and Northern Ireland through an Emslie Horniman Scholarship, and supported by the University of St Andrews, University of Goroka, and the National Research Institute of Papua New Guinea. An earlier draft won the David Riches Medal for Anthropological Research at St Andrews.

Notes

1. For those accounts that take Papua New Guinean gambling as their primary subject matter, see the special issue of *Oceania* 58 (1987), as well as Laycock (1966, 1967), Brandewie (1967), Zimmer (1986), Mitchell (1988), Hayano (1989) and Mosko (2012). In another Pacific context, see Alexeyeff (2011).
2. Anthropologists readily admit that gambling repeatedly at any magnitude often has long-term effects on its regular participants (see Schüll 2012), and I therefore see no reason to rehearse that argument here. Geertz meanwhile famously championed the idea that high wagers can be read (in juxtaposition against low ones) as high-cultural forms, to be read as texts (Geertz 1973). Such an approach should write *bom* off as an inconsequential 'shallow' affair (ibid.: 431). Bom also lacks the house edge that so often leads well-meaning people to conclude that a game is exploitative, and so in keeping with the overall volume,

I believe this would be the wrong time to engage with occidental attempts at rationalising the 'irrational' actions of bettors through cultural relativism.

3. Bom is also known as a craze that is likely to be replaced by a new form of gambling in the near future because the kinds of thought that lead people toward *bom* cause those same people to become bored and invent it's replacement (Pickles 2012). I am therefore conscious that the model I put forth is not one that reproduces itself, but deliberately spells its own end (see Pickles 2013a).
4. There are 100 toea to 1 kina, the currency of Papua New Guinea. At the time of fieldwork (April 2009 to June 2010), £1 was equivalent to between 3.5 and 4 kina.
5. This figure derives from a survey of 201 households in Kaunsil Kem devised by myself and conducted by my field assistant Loui Ipatu in January 2010.
6. For similar examples of redefinition in another context, see Swancutt (2012: 64–65).
7. For more detail on how *bom*'s form engenders Gorokan concerns during gameplay, see Pickles (2012).

References

Alexeyeff, K. 2011. Bingo and Budgets: Gambling with Global Capital in the Cook Islands. In Mary Patterson and Martha Macintyre (eds), *Managing Modernity in the Western Pacific*, pp.201–30. St Lucia: University of Queensland Press.

Bentham, J. 1882. *The Theory of Legislation*. London: Trubner.

Brandewie, E. 1967. Lucky: Additional Reflections on a Native Card Game in New Guinea. *Oceania* 38(1): 44–50.

Caillois, R. 1958. *Man, Play, and Games*, trans. M. Barash. New York: Free Press.

Crook, T. 2007. *Exchanging Skin: Anthropological Knowledge, Secrecy and Bolivip, Papua New Guinea*. London: Oxford University Press.

da Col, G. 2012. Introduction: Natural Philosophies of Fortune-luck, Vitality, and Uncontrolled Relatedness. *Social Analysis* (special issue) 56(1): 1–23.

da Col, G., and C. Humphrey. 2012. Introduction: Subjects of Luck-contingency, Morality, and the Anticipation of Everyday Life. *Social Analysis* (special issue) 56(2): 1–18.

Geertz, C. 1973. *The Interpretation of Cultures*. New York: Basic Books.

Graeber, D. 2012. The Sword, the Sponge, and the Paradox of Performativity: Some Observations on Fate, Luck, Financial Chicanery, and the Limits of Human Knowledge. *Social Analysis* 56(1): 25–42.

Guyer, J.I. 2007. Prophecy and the Near Future: Thoughts on Macroeconomic, Evangelical, and Punctuated Time. *American Ethnologist* 34(3): 409–21.

Hayano, D.M. 1989. Like Eating Money: Card Gambling in a Papua New Guinea Highlands Village. *Journal of Gambling Studies* 5(3): 231–45.

Laycock, D.C. 1966. Three Native Card Games of New Guinea and Their European Ancestors. *Oceania* 37(1): 49–53.

_______ 1967. Three More New Guinean Card Games, and a Note on 'Lucky'. *Oceania* 38(1): 51–55.

Mimica, J. 2006. Dreams, *Laki*, and Mourning: A Psychoanalytic Ethnography of the Yagwoia 'Inner Feminine', Part II: Soul and the Oneiro-dynamics of Luck. *Oceania* 76(2): 113–31.

Minnegal, M. 2009. The Time is Right: Waiting, Reciprocity and Sociality. In G. Hage (ed.), *Waiting*, pp.89–96. Victoria: Melbourne University Press.

Mitchell, W.E. 1988. The Defeat of Hierarchy: Gambling as Exchange in a Sepik Society. *American Ethnologist* 15(4): 638–57.

Miyazaki, H. 2004. *The Method of Hope: Anthropology, Philosophy and Fijian Knowledge*. Stanford: Stanford University Press.

Mosko, M.S. 2012. Laki Charms: 'Luck' and Personal Agency in North Mekeo Social Change. *Social Analysis* 56(2): 19–38.

Munn, N.D. 1986. *The Fame of Gawa: A Symbolic Study of Value Transformation in a Massim (Papua New Guinea) Society*. Durham: Duke University Press.

_______ 1992. The Cultural Anthropology of Time: A Critical Essay. *Annual Review of Anthropology* 21: 93–123.

NSO. 2002. Eastern Highlands Provincial Report 2000 National Census. Port Moresby: Papua New Guinea National Statistics Office

Pickles, A.J. 2009. Part and Whole Numbers: an 'Enumerative' Reinterpretation of the Cambridge Anthropological Expedition to Torres Straits and its Subjects. *Oceania* 79(3): 293–315.

_______ 2012. The Pattern Changes Changes: Gambling Value in Highland Papua New Guinea. PhD diss. St Andrews: University of St Andrews.

_______ 2013a. Pocket Calculator: A Humdrum 'Obviator' in Papua New Guinea? *Journal of the Royal Anthropological Institute* 19(3): 510–26.

_______ 2013b. 'One-Man One-Man': How Slot-machines facilitate Papua New Guineans' Shifting Relations to Each Other. In R. Cassidy, C. Loussouarn and A. Pisac (eds), *Qualitative Research in Gambling: Exploring the Production and Consumption of Risk*. Oxford: Routledge.

_______ 2014a. Introduction: Gambling as Analytic in Melanesia. *Oceania*, under review.

_______ 2014b. '*Bom* Bombed *Kwin*': How Two Card Games Model *Kula*, Moka, and Goroka. *Oceania*, under review.

Read, K.E. 1959. Leadership and Consensus in a New Guinea Society. *American Anthropologist* 61(3): 425–36.

_______ 1965. *The High Valley*. New York: Columbia University Press.

Reed, A. 2011. Hope on Remand. *Journal of the Royal Anthropological Institute* 17(3): 527–44.

Robbins, J. 2001. Secrecy and the Sense of an Ending: Narrative, Time, and Everyday Millenarianism in Papua New Guinea and in Christian Fundamentalism. *Comparative Studies in Society and History* 43(3): 525–51.

Robbins, J., and A. Rumsey. 2008. Introduction: Cultural and Linguistic Anthropology and the Opacity of Other Minds. *Anthropology Quarterly* 81(2): 407–20.

Schüll, N.D. 2012. *Addiction by Design: Machine Gambling in Las Vegas*. Princeton: Princeton University Press.

Stasch, R. 2008. Knowing Minds is a Matter of Authority: Political Dimensions of Opacity Statements in Korowai Moral Psychology. *Anthropology Quarterly* 81(2): 443–53.

Strathern, M. 1992. The Decomposition of an Event. *Cultural Anthropology* 7(2): 244–54.

Swancutt, K. 2012. Fame, Fate-fortune, and Tokens of Value among the Nuosu of Southwest China. *Social Analysis* 56(2): 56–72.

Wagner, R. 1978. *Lethal Speech: Daribi Myth as Symbolic Obviation.* Ithaca, NY: Cornell University Press.

——— 1986. *Symbols that Stand for Themselves.* Chicago: University of Chicago Press.

——— 1991. The Fractal Person. In M. Godelier and M. Strathern (eds), *Big Men and Great Men: Personifications of Power in Melanesia* pp.159–73. Cambridge: Cambridge University Press.

Zimmer, L.J. 1986. Card Playing among the Gende: A System for Keeping Money and Social Relationships Alive. *Oceania* 56: 245–63.

——— 1987. Playing at Being Men. *Oceania* 58: 22–37.

5

The Future of Christian Critique

Lost Tribes Discourses in Papua New Guinean Publics

Courtney Handman

Secular discourses usually imagine Christianity to be anchored permanently in the past. That is to say, from a secular perspective religion is the domain of tradition, bearing down upon innovation through the scriptural limits placed on rational debate (e.g. Mill 1978; or, more recently, Dawkins 2008). Every defence that says, 'because the Bible says so' is a further retreat from the horizon of potential change that is the supposed calling card of secular modernity. The fact that Protestantism so easily turns to internal critiques and denominational schisms only solidifies for secularists the fruitlessness of religious discourses that have to remain faithful to scriptural traditions. And yet, Protestant Christians themselves often figure their lives very pointedly in terms of the future's Christian possibilities of redemption and reunion with God. Moreover, what seem from secular perspectives to be nit-picking complaints about the legalities of ritual practice can be from schismatic Christian perspectives globally important debates about the path to salvation. As I argue here and elsewhere (Handman 2012), Christianity in many places appears as a powerful discourse of critique, whether that is a critique of tradition, culture, politics or even Christianity itself. This critical sensibility lays out a 'space of openness' (Introduction, this volume) about the future, even when the debate itself is about the morality of the past.

Guhu-Samane communities of the Waria Valley (Morobe Province, Papua New Guinea) are engaged in just these kinds of debates, often in the form of seemingly endless denominational disputes about the proper form of Christian worship or the moral coding of 'custom'. From this field of finely constituted differences, there is however one area of overlap among all the denominations. A wide range of Guhu-Samane Christians toy with the idea that the ethnic group as a whole is related to the ancient Israelites, that is, they think they might be one of the Lost Tribes of Israel. It is actually more of a hypothesis right now that people are working on, since claims of Semitic origin are often expressed as questions to themselves. Features of the local landscape and of language are often discussed as signs of Hebrew roots, material traces of a past that connects contemporary Guhu-Samane with the Israelites of old. While people seem to be in no rush to answer these questions one way or another, the hypothesis frames Guhu-Samane Christianity, making its mark on everyday religious practice.

Within the Waria Valley and in Papua New Guinea more broadly I argue that this discourse of 'lostness' is becoming a way for people to organise and recognise one another as Christians engaged in critical discourses of evaluation. In much of the writing about Christianity in anthropology, authors tend to focus on one of two moments: First, people tend to talk about the highly individualising moments when people renounce their kin and their pasts. This is something that Joel Robbins (2004, 2007), for example, has discussed in great detail.[1] But, anthropologists also tend to see Christianity as a way to make other kinds of social relations, be they partible (Mosko 2010), political (O'Neill 2010) or spiritual (Luhrmann 2004).[2] However, I think this either/or version of Christianity can oversimplify contemporary Christian conditions, at least for Guhu-Samane, since one of the things that drives local denominational battles is the process of critique itself: of seeing others making certain kinds of social relations, of arguing that these are not the proper social relations for Christianity, and then creating a new denomination in which a different set of relations is formed. These critical moves are oriented to the creation of a future that will ideally be able to establish a moral form of Christian practice. From the sect-makers' perspective, they are casting off old relations. From the point of view of people in other churches, the members of a new sect simply make new kinds of social relations. This premise of critique has long been a central part of the missiological practices in places like Papua New Guinea (Handman 2007). 'Look at your culture!' missionaries say, 'judge it, compare it', or in Tok Pisin, '*skelim!*' What I want to argue here is that recognising oneself as a member of the Lost Tribes is a way of establishing a future orientation to this process of critique: of knowing that one is lost and in need of being found in the future. As Dundon (2011) discusses with respect to similar Lost Tribes discourses in the Gogodala area of Papua New Guinea, these global discourses are becoming increasingly central to local conceptualisations of Christianity.

As I will discuss in the latter half of this chapter, Lost Tribes discourses are starting to be seen in a number of places across Papua New Guinea, and, moreover, are starting to be seen even in contexts of national electoral politics. Not simply a set of diverse and disparate groups each hitting upon this connection in ignorance of others, the Lost Tribes discourses apparent in Papua New Guinea are starting to be seen as ways of recognising others who are similarly engaged in a moral discourse of critique of the past and a turn towards new possibilities of unity for the future.

While this social formation would seem to share characteristics with the model of nationalism made popular by Benedict Anderson (1991), Lost Tribes discourses are, I argue, quite different. In Anderson's model, nationalism spread across the globe in the nineteenth and twentieth centuries because of its uniquely modular form. That is, nationalisms share a desire to manifest specific national pasts and traditions similar to but nevertheless distinct from those that other nations have. A group demands its own nation-state because it has a particular history and set of traditions, just like other nations have their own history and set of traditions.

But for groups that organise themselves around Lost Tribes imaginaries, the goal is not to be unique but to share a relationship to Israelites that others could have as well. Lost Tribes discourses that work to guide moral transformations constitute a kind of future governed by a connection to the past that is specifically not modular in Anderson's sense of the term. Robbins (1998) argues that Papua New Guinea has what can be called a 'negative nationalism', one that is predicated on a shared sense of inferiority which can still be seen in Andersonian terms, even if it is not the celebratory sense of nationalism usually implied by the term. I am arguing here, though, that there is an emerging discourse of critique based on the image of the Lost Tribes that creates an open-ended invitation to addressees to celebrate the 'not yet'. Lost Tribes critiques hold out the possibility that there is a kind of moral reform of Papua New Guinea soon to be materialized. Placing oneself within that critical process is the crucial distinction, one that (hopefully, or ideally) trumps ethnic, linguistic or denominational differences that have long been seen as problematic to forming a national consciousness.

Lost Tribes discourses therefore are at odds with the standard Andersonian nationalisms that were particularly important in the post-independence eras of Pacific nations when national politicians developed theories of the 'Melanesian Way', as in Bernard Narakobi's formulation of postcolonial Papua New Guinea, or the 'Pacific Way' developed in Fiji (Lawson 2010). As I will discuss in more detail in the second half of this chapter, Lost Tribes discourses that specifically invoke and look to become a part of another nation-state – the contemporary state of Israel – subvert the particularities of specifically 'Melanesian' national politics that have dominated post-independence governance.

At the same time, this transformation in the basis of moral unity presents what are by now well-known problems for liberal democracies, and modernisation theories more generally (see Habermas 1991). Lost Tribes critiques are not based on the secular proceduralism of rational critical debate. While Papua New Guinea's constitution states that it is a Christian nation, and while government meetings often begin with prayer, there has been a particularly strong move in recent years towards political discourses based upon Christian ethics, of which Lost Tribes discourses are a part. Led in large part by Talal Asad's (2003) recent work, many scholars are rethinking the nature of secularism that has been assumed to be at the heart of liberal democracies across the world, particularly as religious discourses are more and more frequently becoming the basis for public sphere and counter-public formations (see Gifford 1998; Hirschkind 2006; Meyer and Moors 2006; Marshall 2009). The level of specific Christian interventions in national Papua New Guinea politics might still be relatively low, as Eves (2008) discusses. However, Christian and related discourses, like those employing Lost Tribes imagery, are becoming the basis on which people in Papua New Guinea are starting to recognise one another as having similar critical goals about their political and moral futures.

Genealogical Thinking in Christian Communities: The Lost Tribes

Christianity is both historically and geographically rooted in the Middle East of 2,000 years ago at the same time that it is argued to be a universal religion by most if not all of its adherents. In the first moments of New World missionisation, church leaders anxiously debated the historical particularity of the inception and spread of Christianity through the then-known world. Were the Indians of the New World kept from the historical spread of Christianity because of historical accident, or because they were not human? Was the universality of Jesus' redemptive work applicable to those who had never heard of it before?

As discussed by Tzvetan Todorov, quite a few early church leaders answered these questions by creating a genealogically based middle road. Noting many similarities in ritual and language, Bartolomé de las Casas and fellow Spanish missionaries compared the others of Europe – the Jews – to the recently discovered others of the New World – the Indians

(Todorov 1999). Could the Indians actually be Jews, the original convert society? Working from Biblical clues that had been honed through long-standing interest among Europeans, the Indians became descendants of the Lost Tribes of Israel. Positing a Jewish origin for New World Indians established a genealogical and historical link to the Old World that put Indians squarely within the realm of the human, while the fact that they were 'lost' accounted for why they had not heard of Jesus. The Lost Tribes hypothesis created a unity for humanity that nevertheless depended upon a sense of geographical and genealogical distance.

The story of the Lost Tribes as discussed in the Bible can be summarised as follows: The twelve tribes of Israel were divided into a northern kingdom of ten tribes and a southern kingdom of two. When Assyrian kings invaded the northern kingdom (in 732 and 721 BC) they carried these ten tribes into exile (2 Kgs. 17). These are the ten 'lost' tribes, which later became important in the prophetic books (such as Isaiah and Jeremiah) in which the reunion with the Lost Tribes would be a harbinger of the final redemption of Israel. References to them are scarce in the Bible, although these sources were later augmented with various 'sightings' of and correspondence with the Lost Tribes in early European history (Parfitt 2002).

The Lost Tribes hypothesis about the New World Indians was based on resemblances that the missionaries saw between Indians and Jews, although the sense of resemblance between the two populations needs to be qualified. Missionaries working in the Americas consistently found the rituals of cleanliness (such as separating women during menstruation), the guttural sounds of indigenous languages and the dark skin and large noses of the populations to be indicators of Jewish descent (see Eilberg-Schwartz 1990; Parfitt 2002). The resemblances found in these cases were signs in search of a causal linkage, which would position Indians firmly in the 'capable of conversion' category. At the same time, proof against the Lost Tribes hypothesis could take the same form as proof for it. Parfitt summarises a portion of an argument against the Lost Tribes hypothesis as follows: 'In addition there were many things the Indians did that the Jews patently did not: no Jew for instance would eat unclean meat, whereas the Indians would eat anything; no Jew would marry a whore but all Indian women were whores' (Parfitt 2002: 76). Damned if you do, damned if you don't.

This semiotic hunting and pecking for evidence of Israelite-ness occurred across the globe as Europeans came into contact with new peoples, and Lost Tribes hypotheses existed for Asia, Africa, North America, South America and Oceania. Moreover, these discourses were often taken up by local populations themselves, as is the case in Papua New Guinea.

Lost Tribes in the Waria Valley

In 2004, between my initial trip to the Waria and my later return for fieldwork, a Jew for Jesus named Gabriel came to visit the Guhu-Samane, a rural Papua New Guinean community in Morobe Province, for a few days to lead church services.[3] When Gabriel preached to the assembled crowd of Christians, he did so wearing the paraphernalia of an adult male Jew in prayer (a kippah, tefillin and prayer shawl), and he spoke to Guhu-Samane about the right way for them to pray and be Christian. The following account of Gabriel's trip comes entirely from conversations I had with Guhu-Samane Christians who participated in it, since, as I noted above, I was not present for these events.

First, Gabriel identified himself and the source of his authority. He is a Jew from the family of Jesus, about which people understood him to be saying that his 'clan line' (which locally refers to a matrilineal genealogy) includes Jesus. Next, he praised the dance group that had performed earlier, which used Christianised 'traditional' songs that had been sung to drum accompaniment. But then he changed his tone. Guitars, he said, are specifically the property and the tradition of his group, white people. Drums and the decorations worn in dances are the property and the tradition of the Guhu-Samane, black people. Drums and other aspects of traditional culture are God's blessings upon the Guhu-Samane, and those blessings should continue to be used today. Moreover, to use guitars as Guhu-Samane often do in church is to steal the blessings from his group, from white peoples' traditions. Just as Gabriel prays to Jesus as a Jewish man with Jewish paraphernalia of prayer, so too the Guhu-Samane should pray to Jesus as culturally Guhu-Samane people using their traditional garb and instruments.

When I arrived a few months later, and throughout my time in the Waria Valley, Guhu-Samane often brought up Gabriel's visit and his message about the role of culture in contemporary Christian life. In the highly charged environment of local denominational differences and contestation about the role of culture in Christianity, Gabriel's sermon was a bombshell. Some churches celebrate the use of drums and traditional songs in church services; others have banned drums entirely in favour of guitars, and others still have precise ways of calculating the appropriate mixture of 'tradition' and Christianity. For those who celebrate the use of drums in church services, Gabriel became an important figure of authority, while those who disagreed with him developed extended Pauline counter-arguments with which to defeat his claims.

By asserting a genealogical link to Jesus, Gabriel created for Guhu-Samane a slippage between Jews of today and the 'ancient Israelites', as they are often referred to in Christian literature, of the Old and New Testaments. As a Jew, Gabriel seems to Guhu-Samane to inhabit multiple historical times at the same moment, living in (or having a connection to) the past as well as the present. This slippage between ancient and contemporary must also be looked at in terms of Gabriel's racial categorisations. Able to say 'we, the white people', Gabriel presents the Guhu-Samane with something that they have probably experienced rarely, if ever before: a white man of means and stature who nevertheless seems to have 'tradition', some funny clothes, and a meaningful relationship to his ancestors. Here is a model of conversion that is alluded to in missions literature: a way to be both 'traditional' and 'modern;' part of an old culture (Jewish) at the same time that one is part of a new religion (being 'for Jesus'). So while he specifically told people not to try to imitate him or 'his people's traditions', the people who related this story to me all reflected on the correctness of his synthesis of traditions and Christianity. That is, the idea of being properly modern seemed to hinge on getting this synthesis right.

As is common across Papua New Guinea (see Knauft 2002a, 2002b), many Guhu-Samane sharply feel that they are living in a modern world only in the most defective sense of the term. The constant lament about a lack of development is one expression of that feeling. The local aspirations for development and questions about what is known in the national lingua franca Tok Pisin as *kastom* ('custom') reveal a sense that at best they are living within the letter of modernity, not its spirit. Not so Jews for Jesus. For Guhu-Samane, Jewish people seem to have a culture that at least at one point had the sanction of God (they are the 'chosen people' as most Guhu-Samane know). The Jewish context was the one out of which Jesus came to spread the Good News. And, at least for someone like Gabriel, Jews are able to recognise God's later revelation, and thereby be recognised by God as well. Having accepted Jesus, Jews for Jesus enter into universality, but do so authentically, with tefillin and kippah firmly attached. The challenge thrown down by this visit, quite overtly, was whether the Guhu-Samane could do the same, with drums and local musical styles in the place of leather boxes and skull caps.

However, several of my interlocutors saw the challenge differently. For them, they hope that their culture is sufficiently 'like' the Ancient Jewish form that they can eventually become 'good Christians' like some of the Jews did, people who do not fight or have social divisions like denominations. This is not, then, a celebratory reformulation of specifically Guhu-Samane traditions that could be thought of as a micro-nationalist movement (see Worsley 1968; May 1982) in an Andersonian vein. Guhu-Samane are, instead, trying to constitute themselves in terms of another culture. More specifically, they are trying to constitute themselves in terms of another culture that promises a future transformation into a different group altogether: from Guhu-Samane to Ancient Israelite to modern Christian.

This stance can be seen by looking at an all-week tent revival (locally called a 'crusade') that occurred in the Waria Valley in 2005. On entering the main crusade grounds, the first thing that I noticed was the series of flag poles that stood in front of the raised stage. On the left and right hand sides were flag poles flying the Morobe provincial flag and the Papua New Guinea national flag. In the middle, however, flying higher than either of these two, was the Israeli flag (Figure 5.1). The man running the crusade received the flag when he donated money to a group that helps the Israeli nation defend itself. As he said, all Christians have a duty to defend Israel. He was not interested in making claims that the Guhu-Samane were one of the Lost Tribes, at least not in the meetings I had with him or in the sermons he delivered at the crusade. However, he was interested in proclaiming a kind of spiritual brotherhood with and a relation of debt to the Jews in Israel. Thus, even though no specific genealogical relation to the Ancient Jews was argued here, connections to Israel were standard, un-remarked-on facets of local Christianity. As with many Christians in the US and around the world, a general feeling of sympathy for and spiritual relation to the Jews is felt by the Guhu-Samane Christian community.

Figure 5.1
2005 Crusade in the Waria Valley with Israeli flag. Photograph by Courtney Handman.

However, some take this relation a bit further than just a spiritual brotherhood, suggesting a specific likeness to the Ancient Israelites. For these Guhu-Samane, the Guhu-Samane people 'have' culture in the same way that the Ancient Jews 'had' culture – taboos, rites, odd decorations – and do so in a way that distinguishes them from the colonial Australians (or anthropological Americans) who seemed to not have such things. Missionaries across Papua New Guinea ratify this sensibility, and some even publish booklets in local languages that ask people to draw comparisons between their own Papua New Guinean cultures and Ancient Jewish cultures. Do you have the levirate? How are menstruating women treated? This comparison is pervasive in contemporary missionary literature, from training documents for native language Bible translators (Handman 2007) to theological texts on cross-cultural missionisation (Kraft 1979).

Some other Guhu-Samane take this relation to its logical limit, positing a direct line of descent or transmission from the Ancient Jews to the Guhu-Samane. The first introduction to this form of the Lost Tribes hypothesis that I had was when one of my consultants explained why an interior land-based group would have words for canoe, paddle or various species of fish. He told me that the exact origins of the Guhu-Samane are unknown, but that he had narrowed things down to some probable locations across the sea. At first my consultant thought that the Guhu-Samane would have come from Africa, since their skin is black like Africans. However, he had heard that Africans used to worship fetishes, and he said that the Guhu-Samane had never done so. Instead, he suggested either India or, in another conversation, Palestine or Egypt.

Moreover, there were some lexical correspondences that he found intriguing. One of the lineages within the Basi clan is called Pita Basi, and one man in the village where I was living had Pita as his given name. 'Pita' is also the spelling used in the Tok Pisin Bible for the apostle Peter. He could also identify that the name Peter derives from Petros, and he suggested that Pita did as well (the conflation of Greek language and Israelite identity will be discussed more below). This seemed to him to be positive proof towards Jewish origin, rather than an Indian one. Over the next year or so, this story was repeated to me on many occasions as an important sign of a link to the Jews of the Bible. Later, this same consultant would tell me the myth in which a ship travels up the river valley, and that the remains of the boat could still be seen when he was a child. 'Perhaps this was Noah's boat?' he asked.

A while later I was visited by one of this consultant's affines, a man who lives several days' walk away. He had made the trip up to the middle Waria to conduct some business, but he had specifically gone out of his way to come to my house and ask me to visit him in his village at some point. He was anxious to have me come down to his village because he said there were some rocks up on the mountains above it that I would be interested in seeing as an anthropologist. These rocks had some kind of writing on them and he wanted me to bring my camera to take a photo. He could identify that the writing was not Roman script; it was Greek, Hebrew or perhaps Egyptian hieroglyphics – he wasn't sure. He insisted on my visit and felt that this would be essential for any anthropological investigation that would detail the origin and history of the Guhu-Samane since it would point to biblical origins in the Middle East.

Later in my stay I was visiting some villages upstream from my home, and I was told of a myth in which the characters crossed the length of the entire valley, and the mythic action ended up close to the present-day town of Wau. This myth was unique for several reasons, including the fact that it involved a cow, an animal introduced to Papua New Guinea during the colonial era. The action ended with one of the main characters dying and being entombed in a rocky cave of the Chapman Range of mountains. The large rocks that formed the entrance to the tomb were covered in Hebrew writing. People shook their heads in awe and amazement at this, while one of the storytellers suggested Hebrew origins for this culture hero.

The specific pieces of evidence for the Lost Tribes hypothesis did not add up to very much, and it would be easy to discount them if it were not for the fact that people seemed so engrossed by the stories, and spent so much time circulating them widely. The evidence forms a series of potential similarities which people are trying to order into a chain of relation. As with the Lost Tribes hypotheses in the New World, the corpus of evidence is a series of relations of likeness: If *x* looks like or sounds like *y*, then perhaps *x* is *y*. If 'Pita' sounds like 'Peter', then perhaps it is because it is Peter/Petros and not a local name. To use terms from C.S. Peirce, people are engaged in a process of 'abductive reasoning', or hypothesis making, where potential icons are placed in an indexical chain of causal meaning (see Lee 1997). Such moments of abductive reasoning and speculation have been discussed by a number of authors working across Papua New Guinea (e.g. Battaglia 1990: 8–11; Munn 1990; Merlan and Rumsey 1991: 225), although doing so in terms of traditional cultural forms rather than Christian ones.

Lost Tribes in Papua New Guinea

Quite a few ethnic groups in Papua New Guinea claim an Israelite connection. In 2003, Tudor Parfitt, a geneticist from the School of Oriental and African Studies at the University of London came to Papua New Guinea at the request of the Gogodala community and their Pentecostal Australian missionaries to conduct DNA testing on individuals.[4] Parfitt had made a big splash a few years earlier by demonstrating that an African group called the Lemba had genetic markers usually indicative of Jewish heritage. The hope was that similar markers could be found among the Gogodala. The missionaries first had the idea because of certain Gogodala phenotypic facial features (such as big noses), and after hearing about Parfitt's Lemba research the missionaries thought that there might be an opportunity to concretise these surface similarities.

A few years later, a Papua New Guinean geo-scientist named Samuel Were, who works in the mineral resources industry but who has had divine visions of and revelations from God, wrote a book called *Bine Mene: Connecting the Hebrews* (2006), which claims a connection between his ethnic group, the Bine, and Ancient Israelites. Officially launched and effusively praised by the governor-general of Papua New Guinea, the book formalises a similar set of connections that circulated orally among Guhu-Samane.

Like Guhu-Samane, Were also identifies a connection to Petros, and adds a whole list of Greek–Bine and Hebrew–Bine similarities. What kind of connection is this, then, if it can include historical relations to two different languages from completely different language families? In an obvious sense, a strict genetic relation is unlikely to say the least. But more importantly, what kinds of Ancient Israelites are these different Papua New Guinean actors hoping to create connections to? The connection is not really to the Lost Tribes, if that means the tribes who were lost in 700 BC. Rather, the connection is to the Israelites who were living near the eastern Mediterranean shore at the time that Jesus was alive; the Jews who would be a part of the trading world in which Koiné Greek was commonly spoken as a lingua franca; the Jews who would be converted to Christianity. It is a sacred ethnicity of future transformation: the Papua New Guinean sense of the Lost Tribes is that the connection makes one's group not only the chosen, but the chosen who can be changed through future processes of Christian critique.

Lost Tribes discourses thus seem to share quite a bit with Pauline forms of evangelism that take it as axiomatic that critique of one's own culture is an important part of the transformation into Christianity. Mosaic Law has to be amended to accord with the new revelation, as Paul suggests when he argues that Gentile converts do not need to be circumcised (see Gal. 3; 1 Cor. 7). Among Guhu-Samane, people likewise used Pauline arguments to critique traditional practices, arguing that, for example, pig sacrifice is no longer moral after Jesus' revelation and redemption of mankind as the 'last sacrifice'. At the same time, though, Paul himself was not always consistent in his missiological strategy. In 1 Cor. 9: 20, for example, Paul seems to suggest that critique cannot be so radical, and that space must be left for traditional cultures to perdure, even if some changes must be made.[5] This ambiguity in Paul's statements about critique are mobilised today to support different denominational perspectives on Guhu-Samane 'tradition'. But even with this ambiguity, the outcome seems to be the same. To the extent that local people can place themselves within this biblical history of Jewish/Christian cultural criticism (a primary focus of Acts 15, for example, when the Council of Jerusalem discusses the role of Mosaic Law for followers of Jesus), then local people can work to create a moral Christian future.

With this in mind, two aspects of the Lost Tribes hypothesis are important to Guhu-Samane (and perhaps other Papua New Guinean ethnic groups). First, if they are Ancient Jews then they are a people, a unity. Local traditions of mytho-history vacillate between moments of unity and division in the Guhu-Samane past, but the Lost Tribes hypothesis would seem to offer a definitive, sacred statement of initial Judeo-Christian unity. Second, if they are a people with a culture like the Ancient Jews, or even are descendants of the Ancient Jews themselves, then through Christian culture critique they can be Christians. In other words, if they critique their culture the way the apostle Paul seemed to critique his own Jewish culture, then they too might become 'really' Christian. As with any of the kinship genealogies with which Guhu-Samane engage, relatedness offers a set of possibilities for recognition from others imagined in terms of roads which traverse different domains. In the present, when Guhu-Samane have each individually made their choices to belong to one church or another, the potentiality of Christian commitment gives way to a social reality of denominational division and antagonism. But within the temporal frame of the Lost Tribes hypothesis, Guhu-Samane figure themselves in this sociocentric genealogy as united in their genealogically based potential to be Christian.

In addition to the Gogodala, Bine and Guhu-Samane examples, Lost Tribes discourses have been noted for Engans (Jacka 2005), Mt Hageners (Parfitt 2002: 175), Fijians (Kaplan 1990), Solomon Islanders (Burt 1994) and Biaks (Rutherford 2003), to name just a few nearby Melanesian groups. In fact, they are common across the world. But more than simply being a phenomenon comparable across ethnographic sites – for anthropologists to wonder how Ten Lost Tribes became 800 Papua New Guinean ethnic groups – the Lost Tribes discourse appears to be an incipient form of political organisation in Papua New Guinean politics.[6] That is, taking up the mantle of being 'lost' is a sign to others of being engaged in a process of critique that has not yet produced one's desired results. Being 'lost' means living in a world of potential transformation that has not happened yet, of being divided by ethnic, cultural and denominational schisms without having the unity of the Ancient Jews, or, even better, what many think of as the universal unity of Christianity. That is, the quest for modernity or development is itself understood in terms of this critical engagement with finding a moral relationship between Christianity and some form of tradition. In contrast to Knauft's (2002b) discussion of the Gebusi desire for modernity being a product of modernity itself, Lost Tribes discourses frame modern longing in Christian terms. Lost Tribes discourses seem then to be a way that Papua New Guineans are able to recognise others who are engaged in critical projects of their own. Even if these critical projects produce denominational differences at the local level, in their Lost Tribes form of critical hope (see Miyazaki 2006a, 2006b), they are able to produce a form of connection, and one that is visible across ethnic boundaries.

Lost Tribes of the Nation

Lost Tribes discourses are then an emerging basis for a kind of Christian public sphere in Papua New Guinea. Take for example the Mapai Levites Party, which first fielded candidates during the 2007 parliamentary elections. The name Mapai comes from an abbreviation of the original Israeli Labour Party formed by David Ben Gurion, the Mifleget Poalei Eretz Israel (Party of the Workers of the Land of Israel), and the Mapai Levites slogan is 'Mapai Levites Party (Papua New Guinea-Israeli Labour Party, Serving People)'. The Papua New Guinea Mapai Levites also invoke the tribe of 'Levi' in their party name, and note that the Levites were priests who were set apart to fight religious battles; that is, Levites were engaged in critique. As they say in their promotional material, 'Historically, the Levites are known for being fierce, unyielding and ruthless in matters when relating to God's Covenant. They have no regards for anybody or anything. If the issue involved desecration of the holy things of God, [then] no amount of odds will deter them from exacting divine justice'.[7] Here are political actors trying to rally together others in a determined critique and unification of Papua New Guinea society. Nevertheless, their political platform has a number of different foci that aim at both reform and restoration. Thus, the Mapai Levites hoped to institute a rural kibbutz system, develop an import substitution program and have mandatory Bible teaching in school, yet also preserve traditional wisdom.

The Mapai Levites Party represents a new turn in Papua New Guinea politics away from post-independence projects of self-sufficiency through the celebration of what is generally called 'the Melanesian Way'. A term originally coined by Bernard Narakobi to describe the local form of governance to be practised in postcolonial Papua New Guinea, the Solomon Islands, Fiji, New Caledonia and Vanuatu, 'the Melanesian Way' would be based on the principles of consensus and local knowledge that were seen as part of regional traditional culture. 'It is unnecessary for us to be perfect Englishmen or Americans if we know who we are' (Narakobi 1983: 9). Narakobi's vision was for a region that could find unity in tradition, a stance taken in opposition to the colonial gaze that saw only a democracy-denying variety of languages and cultures.

> We should spring from our cultural values to forge ahead in a world that is moving more and more towards a confused uniformity, monotony and insensitivity to the fine, subtle and sublime beauty of diversity. It is the simplistic imperialist who seeks uniformity as a technique to command obedience while portraying Papua New Guinea as a land of division, of disunity, of 700 languages and thousands of cultures. Some have even dared to call it a land of chaos. These are arguments of defeat and despair, betraying an inability to transcend one's cultural conditioning. (ibid.: 7)

In contrast to the colonizer's chaos of diversity or the globalising trend of 'confused uniformity', the Melanesian Way would be able to establish consensus in traditional 'person to person' (ibid.: 6) forms of interaction, even if this would now take place at the level of the nation-state rather than the village.

As Lawson (2010) argues, this and cognate calls for a 'Pacific Way' were anti-colonial positions, but ones that have had the effect of entrenching a leadership elite that has established its own forms of hegemonic power. For many voters in recent elections, the Melanesian Way is starting to be synonymous with the failures of the contemporary Papua New Guinean nation-state, as Eves (2008) and others have noted. Instead of 'Melanesian' leaders, much contemporary political discourse demands that politicians be 'good Christians' first.

However, there has not been a simple transfer of legitimating force from local tradition to Christian morality. That is, there is still considerable disagreement about how to bring Christianity into the political sphere. In the 2007 elections, for example, many criticised the Electoral Commission for holding elections on a Saturday in provinces like Morobe and the Southern Highlands with a large population of Seventh-Day Adventists (SDA). SDA members hold Saturday as the Sabbath, and they felt that it would be impossible for them to vote on the Sabbath. In letters to the editors of the major newspapers, writers debated if polling should be moved to another day to accommodate SDA members. Likewise, while many churches encourage young men to stand for elected office in provincial or national governments, they also feel it is necessary to expel or otherwise demote those same men during the time that they are engaging in the world of electoral politics (see Eves 2008). Christian churches and missions have long been an important part of colonial and postcolonial politics in Papua New Guinea. In rural areas colonial missions and contemporary churches have been or are the government for all intents and purposes, providing many of the health and education services available to communities. But local people nevertheless see a difference between these activities and governance as such. For members of both mainline churches and their evangelical cousins, politics and religion remain somewhat separate domains of social life and people are unsure how this boundary should be treated.

The Mapai Levites Party thus seems to represent a new turn towards an integration of these two domains. Israelite perspectives provide the basis for a political platform in an unambiguous way. The leader of the party, Paul Kamakande, is an itinerant evangelical preacher who sees his political work to create a kibbutz system of moral labour as an extension of his spiritual work. But this movement towards the integration of religious discourse in electoral politics does more than just upset the categories of secular liberal democracy. It also disrupts the specifically Melanesian basis of post-independence politics that Narakobi and many others long championed. As one author in a letter to the editor of the *National Newspaper* put it, 'ISRAEL is now in PNG! I wonder if it sounds good to attach a name of another sovereign nation to a PNG political party. Basing your policies on platforms is OK with me but on a name? Don't tarnish PNG politics with this name'.[8] Not only has another sovereign nation become the moral centre of the Mapai Levites Party, but in doing so the Mapai Levites displace Melanesia as a unifying force. Unity, for the Mapai Levites, comes from the different ways in which people work to create indexical connections to Israelites, contemporary or ancient, rather than from their local traditions. Or, in the forms used by Guhu-Samane and other Papua New Guinean groups, local traditions only become legitimate places for moral unification given a capacity to draw indexical connections to Israel. Critique within a political process is used to magnify and reify these indexical connections. Mapai Levites see the brutal force of Levite priests ('ruthless in matters when relating to God's Covenant') as the proper basis of political critique in a quest to create a moral Christian future.

One can see this conflict between the Israelite and Melanesian forms of political unity even in the logos used to identify political parties. In the Mapai logo there is a flag of Papua New Guinea amended to hold a menorah, the sign of Judaism, rather than the constellation of the Southern Cross and the bird of paradise that otherwise are the official symbols of Papua New Guinea and its place in a political world dominated by Australia and New Zealand (which also have the Southern Cross on their flags). Following Zech. 4, cited on the logo, it also depicts olive branches and a container of oil. It also includes a phrase about the origin of all actions ('Not by might nor by power, but by God's spirit') which comes from Zech. 4: 6. In contrast is the Melanesian Alliance Party logo: a traditional Papua New Guinean with handheld drum, native body coverings and decorations, and a coconut tree near the sea shore: here is the old model of adaptation that asked that indigenous culture be used to look towards a new horizon of independence that would unify society. Surrounding this traditional character are slogans from the independence era, using the two colonial lingua francas originally imagined as the languages through which to unite an ethnically disparate people, Tok Pisin and Hiri Motu (although note that they cannot even decide on a language). In the two languages it says 'we ourselves' or 'just us', meaning 'we can do it on our own!' – a message of self-empowerment. The Mapai Levites in contrast find in God a vengeful power with which to tear down the desecrations that post-independence society has brought. Rather than traditional culture being the warrant for authentic modernity, Lost Tribes discourses and Israelite models of critique are instead the warrant for future moral transformations.

Conclusion

In this chapter I have tried to demonstrate how critique is used in a somewhat paradoxical way to foster unity. And indeed, critique does develop and exacerbate divisions, creating the need for more critical efforts at unification. This process of Christian schism includes not only Guhu-Samane denominationalism but also that found in numerous other contexts of particularly Pentecostal Christianity (Wishlade 1965; Errington and Gewertz 1995; Meyer 1999; Jebens 2006). Guhu-Samane have been able to find a multiplicity of models of unity in their engagements with Christianity. One important model for unity is the Pauline interpretation of Judaism, which was potentially redeemable if Jews could throw off their cultural rules, like circumcision. Indeed, not only is this a model, as I have shown it is now a reality – Guhu-Samane and other Papua New Guinean groups are making themselves into the Ancient Jews. The Lost Tribes model puts the possibility of unity into sacred discourse: even if unity is not working out now, we can hope that it still might work out in the future. It is in this mode of the potential that unity seems achievable. Above and beyond denominational confrontations about the morality of traditional culture, Guhu-Samane people from all different denominations think about the possibilities of the Lost Tribes connection.

Unfortunately for the Mapai Levites Party, none of the sixteen candidates that they fielded in the 2007 parliamentary elections won a seat. The Lost Tribes discourse is, as I noted, an emerging form of political mobilisation. Nevertheless, this project of Christian critique, which seems to create so many denominational divisions at the level of the ethnic group, produces a platform from which to organise with others at a supra-ethnic level. Christianity – even with its many denominational divisions – is not hindering the formation of a public and a way to organise, as it is so often depicted as doing in secularist Western discourses, but it is actually producing a way for people to recognise one another across ethnic, linguistic and denominational boundaries. Critical Christianity as encapsulated by Lost Tribes discourses, at either the ethnic or national levels, establishes the basis on which hope for transformation can be grounded. Being lost will hopefully allow people to one day be found.

Notes

1. See also Marshall (2009) on the negative identity that limits the possibilities of a born-again theological political community in Nigeria.
2. Note, however, that Robbins (2004) also discusses the social formations of Urapmin Christians in the final chapters of his book.
3. The 'Jews for Jesus' organisation performs outreach to Jews to have them recognise Jesus as the Messiah. Although it works at an international level, it began in the early 1970s in San Francisco and was part of the counter-cultural movement that produced a number of new forms of religious practice. Although many other Jews dispute this, Jews for Jesus do not consider themselves to be Christians, nor do they consider themselves to have converted.
4. See Dundon (2011) for an analysis of this event.
5. 'To the Jews I became like a Jew, to win the Jews. To those under the law I became like one under the law (though I myself am not under the law), so as to win those under the law' (1 Cor. 9: 20, New International version).
6. Compare Worsley's (1968) arguments about the proto-nationalist bent of cargo cult activities.
7. John Barker (personal communication). As someone recently pointed out to me, Ben Gurion's Mapai Party was a specifically secular one. The pairing of the Mapai name with that of Jewish priests is thus a particular innovation on the part of these Papua New Guinean actors.
8. 'Don't Tarnish PNG Politics', *National Newspaper*, 6 December 2007.

References

Anderson, B. 1991. *Imagined Communities* rev. edn. London: Verso.

Asad, T. 2003. *Formations of the Secular: Christianity, Islam, Modernity*. Stanford: Stanford University Press.

Battaglia, D. 1990. *On the Bones of the Serpent*. Chicago: University of Chicago Press.

Burt, B. 1994. *Tradition and Christianity: the Colonial Transformation of a Solomon Islands Society*. Chur: Harwood Academic Publishers.

Dawkins, R. 2008. *The God Delusion*. New York: Houghton Mifflin Harcourt.

Dundon, A. 2011. DNA, Israel and the Ancestors: Substantiating Connections through Christianity in Papua New Guinea. *Asia Pacific Journal of Anthropology* 12(1): 29–43.

Eilberg-Schwartz, H. 1990. *The Savage in Judaism*. Bloomington: Indiana University Press.

Errington, F., and D. Gewertz. 1995. *Articulating Change in the 'Last Unknown'.* Boulder, CO: Westview Press.

Eves, R. 2008. Cultivating Christian Civil Society: Fundamentalist Christianity, Politics, and Governance in Papua New Guinea. State, Society, and Governance in Melanesia Discussion Papers No. 8. Canberra: Australia National University.

Habermas, J. 1991. *The Structural Transformation of the Public Sphere*, trans. T. Burger. Cambridge, MA: MIT Press.

Handman, C. 2007. Access to the Soul: Native Language and Authenticity in Papua New Guinea Bible Translation. In M. Makihara and B.B. Schieffelin (eds), *Consequences of Contact: Language Ideologies and Sociocultural Transformations in Pacific Societies*, pp.166–88. Oxford: Oxford University Press.

_______ 2010. Events of Translation: Intertextuality and Christian Ethno-theologies of Change among Guhu-Samane, Papua New Guinea. *American Anthropologist* 112(4): 576–88.

_______ 2012. Mediating Denominational Disputes: Land Claims and the Sound of Christian Critique in the Waria Valley, Papua New Guinea. In M. Tomlisonand D. McDougal, (eds), *Christian Politics in Oceania*, pp.22–48. New York: Berghahn.

Hirschkind, C. 2006. *The Ethical Soundscape: Cassette Sermons and Islamic Counterpublics*. New York: Columbia University Press.

Gifford, P. 1998. *African Christianity: Its Public Role.* Bloomington: Indiana University Press.

Jacka, J. 2005. Emplacement and Millennial Expectations in an Era of Development and Globalization: Heaven and the Appeal of Christianity for the Ipili. *American Anthropologist* 107(4): 643–53.

Jebens, H. 2006. *Pathways to Heaven: Contesting Mainline and Fundamentalist Christianity in Papua New Guinea.* New York: Berghahn.

Kaplan, M. 1990. Meaning, Agency, and Colonial History: Navosavakadua and the 'Tuka' Movement in Fiji. *American Ethnologist* 17(1): 3–22.

Knauft, B. 2002a. *Exchanging the Past.* Chicago: University of Chicago Press.

_______ 2002b. Trials of the Oxymodern: Public Practice at Nomad Station. In B. Knauft (ed.), *Critically Modern: Alternatives, Alterities, Anthropologies*, pp.1–55. Bloomington: Indiana University Press.

Kraft, C. 1979. *Christianity in Culture.* Maryknoll, NY: Orbis Books.

Lawson, S. 2010. Post-colonialism, Neo-colonialism and the 'Pacific Way': A Critique of (Un)Critical Approaches. State, Society, and Governance in Melanesia discussion paper No. 4. Canberra: Australia National University.

Lee, B. 1997. *Talking Heads.* Durham, NC: Duke University Press.

Luhrmann, T. 2004. Metakinesis: How God Becomes Intimate in Contemporary US Christianity. *American Anthropologist* 106(3): 518–28.

Marshall, R. 2009. *Political Spiritualities: The Pentecostal Revolution in Nigeria.* Chicago: University of Chicago Press.

May, R.J. (ed). 1982. *Micronationalist Movements in Papua New Guinea.* Canberra: Research School of Pacific Studies, Australian National University.

Merlan, F., and A. Rumsey. 1991. *Ku Waru: Language and Segmentary Politics in the Western Nebilyer Valley, Papua New Guinea.* Cambridge: Cambridge University Press.

Meyer, B. 1999. *Translating the Devil: Religion and Modernity among the Ewe in Ghana.* Trenton, NJ: Africa World Press.

Meyer, B., and A. Moors (eds). 2006. *Religion, Media, and the Public Sphere.* Bloomington: Indiana University Press.

Mill, J.S. 1978 [1859]. *On Liberty.* Indianapolis: Hackett Publishing.

Miyazaki, H. 2006a. Economy of Dreams: Hope in Global Capitalism and Its Critiques. *Cultural Anthropology* 21(2): 147–72.

_______ 2006b. *The Method of Hope: Anthropology, Philosophy and Fijian Knowledge.* Stanford: Stanford University Press.

Mosko, M. 2010. Partible Penitents: Dividual Personhood and Christian Practice in Melanesia and the West. *Journal of the Royal Anthropological Institute* 16(2): 215–40.

Munn, N. 1990. Constructing Regional Worlds in Experience: Kula Exchange, Witchcraft and Gawan Local Events. *Man* 25(1): 1–17.

Narakobi, B. 1983. *The Melanesian Way.* Boroko: Institute of Papua New Guinea Studies.

O'Neill, K. 2010. *City of God: Christian Citizenship in Postwar Guatemala.* Berkeley: University of California Press.

Parfitt, T. 2002. *The Lost Tribes of Israel: The History of a Myth.* London: Weidenfeld and Nicolson.

Robbins, J. 1998. On Reading 'World News': Apocalyptic Narrative, Negative Nationalism and Transnational Christianity in a Papua New Guinea Society. *Social Analysis* 42(2): 103–30.

_______ 2004. *Becoming Sinners: Christianity and Moral Torment in a Papua New Guinea Society.* Berkeley: University of California Press.

_______ 2007. Continuity Thinking and the Problem of Christian Culture: Belief, Times and the Anthropology of Christianity. *Current Anthropology* 48(1): 5–38.

Rutherford, D. 2003. *Raiding the Land of the Foreigners.* Princeton: Princeton University Press.

Todorov, T. 1999. *The Conquest of America: The Question of the Other.* New York: Harper and Row.

Were, S. 2006. *Bine Mene: Connecting the Hebrews.* Port Moresby: Voice of the Tora'a Mene Ministry.

Wishlade, R.L. 1965. *Sectarianism in Southern Nyasaland.* London: Published for the International African Institute by the Oxford University Press.

Worsley, P. 1968. *The Trumpet Shall Sound: A Study of 'Cargo' Cults in Melanesia.* New York: Schocken Books.

6

A Cursed Past and a Prosperous Future in Vanuatu

A Comparison of Different Conceptions of Self and Healing

Annelin Eriksen

In this chapter I discuss a widespread concern about curses in Vanuatu. The point of departure is a story about a curse caused by the volcanic eruption in west Ambrym in 1913. I compare two different solutions to this curse, one emphasising social community and the other emphasising individual repentance. In dealing with their 'cursed past', people imagine a different future. Looking at conceptualisations and imaginations of the future becomes a methodological avenue into understanding local ideas without taking either cultural continuity or change for granted.

Port Vila, the capital of Vanuatu in the south-west Pacific, has become the scene of a rapidly expanding number of Pentecostal churches. The number of different church organisations has increased from about five to fifty in less than a decade (see Eriksen and Andrew 2010). These churches both originate locally as independent denominations, as well being local branches of international (often US or Australian) churches.[1] These new churches all share the belief in the importance of being 'born-again' and the power of healing through the Holy Spirit. The extreme growth of these churches has brought about a number of changes in people's everyday life, whether one is a member of one of them or not. Some of these changes are easily observable: the new churches are very visible on the urban scene; campaigning in the streets, in front of supermarkets, or in the market hall during the busy lunch hours. Here they recruit both passers-by and among the many women who regularly spend their full days in the marketplace selling vegetables and fruit. These churches are also taking over the medical scene. Whereas a decade ago one would usually consult a doctor or a nurse at the hospital or at a health clinic when sickness occurred (and if this did not help, perhaps a 'kleva' [traditional healer] with some traditional or 'herbal' medicine), today people might first go to the healers in the many Pentecostal churches. Even non-members often consult the healers in the new churches, in spite of being 'faithful' to the 'old' Presbyterian or Anglican churches. Some of these healers have gained a reputation well beyond Port Vila, and in the many villages around the archipelago people are receiving spiritual 'treatment' over the telephone.

However, in spite of becoming used to evangelical preachers on street corners and visiting charismatic healers, there are still a number of people who are not members of these new churches. This is my point of departure in this chapter. How is this difference between adherents to 'old' and 'new' churches played out, and how fundamental is it? The first part of this question is first and foremost sociological: who joins the new churches? Having initially done work on north Ambrym (see Eriksen 2008) and then in Port Vila (see Eriksen 2009), I have observed a generational and gender difference between older men and younger men and women,[2] the latter are often more interested in the new churches. The issue I want to address in this essay however is not so much these sociological differences in church membership as much as the significance of them. If the new churches bring about not only change at the level of social practice but also at the level of fundamental cultural values (Robbins 2004), then we need to look at how this process of change unfolds, and how it relates to these different social groups. Thus, this chapter addresses the debate on how to understand the relationship between cultural continuity and cultural change by introducing the aspect of social differentiation.

The question of cultural continuity and cultural change is of course not a novel one for anthropologists, but the focus of this volume on the future has an interesting and novel take on the 'problem'. When dealing with people's visions for the future, attention is shifted away from the relation of the present to the past to an imagined future. Looking at conceptualisations and imaginations of the future becomes a methodological avenue into understanding local ideas without taking either continuity or change for granted. The way in which the future is imagined reveals core cultural values. However, these core cultural values might not necessarily be imagined in uniform ways. As Rollason points out in the Introduction to this volume, that people can act in accordance with past practices and ideas does not mean that they must or necessarily always do so. In some cases people do, in others they do not. The question is: What are the circumstances in which they do not imagine the future as a matter of continuing the present? In which case, do people envision radical breaks with the present in order to imagine a future? Robbins (2005) and Sahlins (2005) have argued that when people experience a sense of extreme worthlessness in the encounter with a new concept, when people cannot make sense of events taking place, people might develop a form of inferiority complex on behalf of their established cultural categories. This form of humiliation might in some cases lead to radical breaks with the past and the embracing of totally new perspectives and values. Might this idea of humiliation, however, be differently perceived in relation to differently positioned social groups? If younger people fundamentally challenge the older people's perspective on the world, might this not also involve a fundamental humiliation of their world-view?

In this chapter I deal with two very different conceptions of the future among people from the same village. Although radically different in terms of perspectives on the future, both of these 'visions' are fundamentally linked to ideas of a Christian morality. One of them, however, involves the expansion of an established cultural logic, the other involves a radical break.

The Curse

When I returned to Port Vila in December 2009 to conduct five months of fieldwork, following up on a project I initially started in 2006 on new religious movements, I was struck by a new turn in religious discourse. Rose Andrew, a long time Ambrym friend who had helped me in 2006 with my research into new Pentecostal churches, informed me on the very first day I met her, 'There is a new development that you really have to understand in order to write about the new churches'. She told me that people have realised that they are cursed, and have been so ever since they drove the first white men, the missionaries, off their islands. She reminded me that in most places in Vanuatu, missionaries were met with great hostility upon their first arrival. The missionary John Williams's experience in Erromango in 1839 is perhaps most well known. Williams, along with his companion James Harris, were clubbed to death and reportedly eaten. In 2009 a grand forgiveness ceremony was conducted on Erromango where the descendants of John Williams received gifts and apologies from the people of the island. This ceremony was widely publicised, both in national newspapers and the international media.[3] I told Rose that I had heard about this forgiveness ceremony, and that I had heard that people on Erromango had felt a curse being lifted as they asked for forgiveness. 'You will experience', she said, 'that everywhere we go and whoever we talk to, we will hear about the fatal impact of the curse that has been following us since the first encounter with *waetman* [white men]'.

Rose was indeed right. Much of our interviews with healers in the new Pentecostal churches often centred on the concept of the curse. We also heard about the experience of living under a curse from a number of different persons. I will first present an outline of what a curse is as it was explained to me. I then present two stories about the effect of the curse today, both of them being from Ambrym, where I conducted my initial fieldwork in 1995 and in 1999. These stories present similar ideas about the cause of the curse, but very different ideas concerning how to heal it. At the close of the chapter I will suggest how one might understand these different solutions and how they reflect different perspectives on the future, one involving the humiliation of the other.

What is a Curse?

Dora, an experienced healer in the Bible Church, one of the new Pentecostal churches in Port Vila, explained to me what a curse is. Almost all sickness and deaths that are not natural (as examples of natural sickness she mentions colds and flu) are the result of different kinds of curse or black magic or sorcery (*su* or *posen*) (Rio 2010). Curses, unlike black magic, are self inflicted or, potentially, inherited. As an example of a typical symptom of a curse, Dora mentioned asthma. Sometimes asthma runs in the family and is thus an example of a curse that is inherited, but sometimes asthma might occur suddenly, as it did once when an old man in Dora's village on Tongoa had problems breathing one evening. He was sitting next to the fire and was suffocating. People called out for Dora, because she had a reputation for being a great healer. As she arrived, people told her that it was most likely the smoke from the fire that was making it hard for the old man to breathe. Dora did not agree. She claimed the cause was asthma, and she told the old man that the only way for him to get well was to admit to the original sin for which he was being punished. She told the old man to search in his past for wrongdoings that might be causing the curse. The man, realising that his only chance to be healed was the revelation of a secret he had hidden for many years, told the story of how as a young man he had accidentally shot and killed one of his friends, but never admitted his fault. However, as he realised that this was the cause of his breathing problems, he publicly admitted to having committed this crime. Afterwards, according to Dora, he had no problems breathing any more.

Curses cause not only physical sickness. Madness is commonly recognised to be a result of a curse. Madness, like asthma, can run in the family, or it can occur suddenly. When it runs in a family it is as a result of a sin committed by an ancestor who has died without repenting. The descendants therefore have to carry the burden of the curse. Often they do not even know that they are cursed. We were told that as a healer Dora can discover these curses through visions she receives from God.

The cause of the curse is always quite clear. The agent behind the curse, however, is always very ambiguous. When asking Dora whether the curses were inflicted by God or people, she responded immediately that only God had the power to bless and to curse, but that God would never himself curse anyone. God is good, she replied. However, curses are only lifted through divine intervention. Thus, curses are caused by immoral actions and can only be lifted through sincere repentance.

Sometimes a curse might cause misfortune and misery too. In several of the conversations we had with not only healers but also ordinary members of many of the new healing churches in Port Vila, we were told that a curse might be the very cause of Vanuatu's lack of development. We were told by a pastor in one of the healing churches (the Praise and Worship Ministry) that the prime minister had asked for forgiveness for the way people in Vanuatu had behaved in their first encounters with the missionaries in a grand, public ceremony of forgiveness. This had taken place a couple of years ago, but the pastor was not convinced that this was enough. It is not enough that the prime minister does it: everyone should ask for forgiveness, he said. Rose told us that this was exactly what her plans were: she wanted to ask for forgiveness for a sin committed by one of her forefathers at the time of the first missionaries, and to lift a curse that had brought misery and misfortune to her family every since.

Rose's Story

Having lived on Ambrym for a period in 1995 and in 1999, and having spent a lot of time with Ambrym friends and family in Port Vila on visits in 2000 and 2006, I was familiar with the situation on north Ambrym: the conflicts which have caused the breakdown of several development projects (see Eriksen 2008), the many land disputes, the problems the volcano causes when it occasionally spreads ashes, destroys crops and spoils drinking water. I was also familiar with the story of Rose's family, who had arrived in north Ambrym after the volcanic eruption in west Ambrym in 1913.

Dip Point in west Ambrym was initially intended as a main centre in the archipelago. Dr Lamb, working on behalf of the New Zealand Presbyterian Mission, set up a hospital in 1895, a majestic building with two wings, a male ward and a female ward. It was 'a splendid up to date hospital of 52 beds' (Don 1918: 57). One of the reasons for setting up Dip Point as the headquarters for the mission was the heathen population in the area: 'The great bulk of the heathen population are in the neighbourhood', wrote Reverend Don in 1918 (ibid.: 56). Another reason, he outlines, was the 'invariable success of such Mission [*sic*] wherever they have been tried' (ibid.: 56). The newly established Condominium government also developed plans for settlements and an administrative centre at Dip Point. It was thus imagined as the main colonial centre and perhaps future capital.

However, not everyone was pleased about these plans. There were different opinions among the local population in west Ambrym about the significance of this development. To some extent these differences followed the division between *kastom* and *skul* (see Jolly 1995), where the converts who had joined the Presbyterian mission (the *skul*) supported the plans, whereas the *kastom*-oriented 'traditionalists' who were sceptical of the white men's interventions opposed them. Rose's great grandfather, Lingmal, was a man of *kastom*. He did not approve of the mission's work in west Ambrym. Lingmal had great powers, not only because of his career in the secret male society, the *Namange* (Patterson 1981; Rio 2007), but also because of his magical skills, with which he could affect the volcano.

In spite of the missionaries' strong belief in the mission's success, and in spite of their talk about trust in God, during the night of 6 December 1913 the volcano erupted, and 'tracks of red-hot lava could be seen like the tail of a serpent' (Don 1918: 61). The volcanic eruption completely destroyed the hospital, including the 50 beds, the operating room, the doctor's residence, the assistants house, the nurses cottage, the boathouses, the concrete tanks and a large new church (ibid.: 61). The village and gardens were also destroyed, and several people lost their houses. Many people fled the island by canoe, seeking refuge either in north Ambrym or in west Malekula.

Lingmal was of course instantly blamed. People assumed that he was using his powers to get rid of the white man and effectively stop their plans for the region. When people tell this story today, both descendants of Lingmal (Rose, for instance) and others will point out that the volcanic eruption was without doubt Lingmal's doing. In other words, the cause of the eruption is generally agreed upon: Lingmal had used his powers to stop the white man as well as 'development'.

In this, Lingmal thoroughly succeeded. Every plan to develop west Ambrym as the capital of the New Hebrides was irrevocably buried. Lingmal's family settled in Ranon, in north Ambrym. When I arrived with my husband and child in 1995, we were told both by Rose's father Billy, who lodged us, and by other villagers, that the members of Billy's family were 'refugees' in Ranon, and not really *manples* ('of the place'). After having stayed with the family for some months, and having visited some of their relatives who had moved back to west Ambrym, we were told the story of

Lingmal, and we were also told that Billy and his brothers, some of them still living in west Ambrym, were still afraid that there were some who might want to avenge Lingmal's deed. They were worried that there were villagers who had lost relatives and property during the eruption in 1913 and who could be poisoning them, or who could spoil their garden crops with sorcery or harm them in some other way.

However, I was not aware of the connection between this event and the circulation of the concept of the curse. Rose, who had moved from Ambrym to Port Vila more than a decade before, pointed out to me one day that her kin group had done all they could in order to succeed in life, but there was too much sickness, death and misfortune. She explained how her brothers were prone to spend all their income on drinking and gambling, and how they were more familiar with the kava bar than their own home. She also pointed out that when her youngest brother had moved back to Ambrym from the capital a couple of years back and tried to set up a farming project, too many people had asked him for favours and for money, which would make it hard for the project to succeed. Her youngest sister died in her teens, reportedly eaten by a shark just off the beach at Ranon. Her mother had a stroke last year, leaving her crippled, and the wife of the eldest brother ran away from her family and now lives on Santo, in north Vanuatu. Rose's list of the numerous misfortunes that had hit her family went on and on. Her explanation however, is interesting and similar to several other stories we were told. The reason for the misfortune is a curse, and this has prevented success in financial projects, and has caused bad luck, sickness and death in every generation. The curse was caused by Lingmal's opposition to the missionaries, and the role he played in causing the volcanic eruption in 1913.

The Concept of Healing

Before returning to Rose's solution to the curse that has haunted her family for generations, the concept of Christian healing in this context has to be analysed. As was outlined above, it was a widely held belief in the new healing churches that a curse is always the result of a person's actions. It is either self-inflicted through immoral acts, or it is passed on to you from your ancestors. A curse thus needs to be consciously removed through redemption and salvation. According to Dora, the healer mentioned above, it is only the individual who, through prayer, can achieve redemption and salvation. In order to make the implications of this clear I will briefly mention the unfolding of certain events in Port Vila in March 2010.

Rose had mentioned to us that William (a pseudonym), one of her classificatory sons from Ambrym who had been working on cargo ships for a couple of years and now lived in Port Vila, was sick. We knew him and his brothers well from our time on Ambrym and wanted to visit. We found him in his home in one of the squatter areas outside the main city centre, where he lived with his wife, from the Banks Islands, and three small children. He was lying on his sleeping mat. He did not recognise us, which was not surprising since we had not seen him for a number of years. It was much more surprising that he did not recognise Rose, whom he had seen often and who had been a close neighbour and relative on Ambrym. 'He talks as if he is crazy (*Hemi toktok kranke*), his wife complained. He had been confused and in a state of delirium for a couple of days, she told us. He had been hospitalised a year ago for some months after his body had started swelling up. At Vila Central Hospital they had been unable to find anything that could be causing his sickness, and he had been sent home. He was fine for a couple of months, but then the sickness, which at first had been affecting his body through swelling, started to affect his head. 'It is going to his head now' (*I go long hed blong hem nao*), his wife stated. He had lost his mind and was only occasionally conscious of where he was and who the people around him were, we were told. We offered to take him to a doctor, but his wife, along with Rose, were certain there was nothing a doctor could do. They had not found anything the last time and would not find anything now. He was much better off being taken care of by his family, they explained.

A couple of days later, the reason for the lack of interest in taking him to a doctor became clearer. We were called up one morning by Rose's brother, who told us that William was now dying. We had to bring his 'mother' Rose to him quickly. We were surprised by the escalation of his sickness. When we arrived at his home with Rose, we found him lying unconscious on his sleeping mat, eyes rolled back. He was breathing and occasionally making some unclear sounds. His family and relatives were sitting around him, massaging him and praying. 'It is all we can do now', his mother's brother told us. Once more we offered to take him to the hospital. 'There is no point', we were told. 'It is too late. He is already dying'. His mother's brother explained to us that when they had prayed for him the day before he had had a brief but clear moment:. 'As we were saying "Amen"', his mother's brother said, 'William looked at us and said "Thank you". We understood that these were his last words (*last toktok blong hem*), and that he was saying goodbye'. Realising our confusion and our wish to bring him some medical assistance, his uncle tried to explain the situation to us. 'You understand', he said, 'that in order to be healed you need to be conscious. Look at my wife', he pointed to his skinny but strong wife who had been operated on for cancer six times over the last three years. 'The doctor says there is nothing more to do for her, that she will die. But look at her – she is getting stronger'. He argued that it was because of their prayer. 'We pray every day, morning and night, and God is healing her', he said. In William's uncle's opinion, God was healing her because his wife had consciously sought his salvation. He explained to us that William had committed many sins over the last couple of years: drinking kava and alcohol, smoking marijuana, committing adultery, and misusing money that was not his. He had caused his own curse. Rose explained it further by saying: 'God has given him a challenge, he is testing him. William has to repent and to ask for forgiveness. However, William cannot redeem himself, because his mind is not straight'. If his mind had been clear, his uncle explained, he could have asked for healing.

As we can deduct from this case, the healing of a curse can only take place through individual consciousness. Thus, the only path to salvation and the lifting of a curse requires the individual's willingness to repent. William, having lost consciousness, was beyond healing. Thus, for Rose to achieve healing for herself and her family, she needs to make every individual aware of their role. The only way to deal with the curse from the volcanic eruption of 1913, according to Rose, is through prayer, redemption and salvation. Her plan was to visit her father and mother, then her father's brothers and their wives, and her own brothers, and pray together with them in their homes. First, they have to become aware of the situation. They have to realise the original sin (the volcanic eruption) and the inheritance of this sin, and then they have to be able to repent.

It is thus clear that for people in the many new Pentecostal healing churches in Port Vila, before one can receive healing and forgiveness from a curse, one has to be conscious of God's power and his presence, and thus become born-again in a Christian faith. This is a matter of individual consciousness. Healing thus comes from the ability of the individual to be conscious of God. 'I have to raise their level of awareness (*leftemap level blong olgeta*)', Rose said. She was worried that their long-standing habit of living immorally would make them unable to become conscious of God and his power to lift the curse. Thus, only through a conscious act of realising the nature of the original sin and the fatal impact of this on the descendants of Lingmal can healing take place.

'White Men' and the Curse

When living in Port Vila from December 2009 until May 2010, we had a lot of visitors from Ambrym who were spending weeks or months in Port Vila, either selling cash crops (mostly kava) or selling carvings to tourists in the market or to art dealers from Noumea. One of the friends who visited us was Jimmy, an old man from a small village uphill from Ranon – the village to which Rose's ancestors had migrated after the volcanic eruption in 1913. Jimmy had been one of our regular conversation partners during our time on Ambrym, and we knew about his interest in documenting Ambrym *kastom*. Jimmy was worried about the lack of development on Ambrym. He explained that everything was deteriorating. The local council had internal problems. They were busier arguing against each other than thinking about bringing development to the island, he told us. Jimmy also pointed to the curse that still affected Ambrym: the volcanic eruption that drove the *waetman* ('white man') away and put a curse on the island. This, he said, is making it hard for Ambrym to develop.

Jimmy, unlike Rose, saw this as a matter of concern for everyone on Ambrym. Whereas Rose connected the volcanic eruption to her own family's situation, Jimmy connected it to the lack of development on Ambrym as a whole. Jimmy was very concrete on how the curse works: the curse makes it impossible to attract *waetman*, money and business, he said. It was *waetmen* who were originally chased away from the island, and the curse still makes it impossible for *waetmen* to return to Ambrym. He pointed out that ever since Lingmal drove the missionaries at Dip Point off the island, no *waetman* has ever successfully settled or established a business. Even the plantation manager in Ranon was driven off the island in 1980 as Vanuatu was achieving independence. Jimmy told us that he had defended the plantation owner, Mitchell, at the time arguing that his business was helping people and developing the island. However, there were others who were more aggressive, and Mitchell had left and never returned. The same thing happened when two American Peace Corps workers were stationed in north Ambrym. The chief who was looking after them ended up quarrelling with them, and they left the village. 'Even you', he said, pointing to my husband and myself, 'you got sick on the island, and now you mostly stay in Port Vila. It is the curse from the volcano, which makes it impossible for *waetman* to settle on Ambrym'. The implication of this is, according to Jimmy, that there is no development. *Waetmen* and development are fundamentally linked in Jimmy's mind.

Jimmy, in the same way as Rose, had a strategy for lifting the curse, and so enabling development. However, Jimmy's plan was different. Jimmy had for a long time been compiling a record of *kastom* on Ambrym in two large books he always carried with him. We were shown these books, but never allowed to read them. They were secret. We had helped him some years back with money for equipment and travel expenses, and in return he briefly showed us the content of his work. The books contain all known genealogies and all rank-taking on Ambrym. These are based on interviews with chiefs and high-ranking men, some of them now dead. He had started his work in the late 1960s, when he returned to Ambrym after his secondary education in the capital. His idea was that when everything was written and all history was known there would be no reason for dispute and conflicts anymore. Many of the conflicts today on Ambrym are about access to land and knowledge, based on genealogical connections and rank-taking. Jimmy pointed out to us that unity was the key to development and to the attraction of *waetman*, money and business to Ambrym again. First they have to achieve unity, and then they can all pray together in one church and ask for forgiveness for the volcanic eruption. He told us that currently all church denominations on Ambrym have their own forgiveness ceremonies – but these will not work, he claimed. His point was that in order for these forgiveness ceremonies to be effective people had to be unified. He explained this further by saying that there are two powers in the world: darkness and light. The power of darkness creates conflict; the power of the light creates unity. Because of the curse, people are still in the dark on Ambrym, he explained. Ambrym *kastom* is also in darkness. 'People have not realised that our *kastom* is already in the Bible', he argued. He explained that he had checked and that everything in his newly compiled book on Ambrym *kastom* was correct according to the book of Genesis.

Jimmy's project, as he sees it, is to bring *kastom* into the light. In other words, he wants to write it down and make it known, and thus make people see that *kastom* is not opposed to the Bible. This, he thinks, will end all conflicts. He will then be able to lift the curse through a unified church. Furthermore, he has an important business and government scheme, which will be successful once unity is achieved. He has already established a 'company', the 'Larum', which will encompass all of Ambrym and everyone on the island.[4] It is a company which will attract foreign investment and *waetmen*. His primary idea is to establish a new kind of government wherein local people will govern themselves, independently of the state. Furthermore, they will exploit the power of the volcano and build a factory on the volcanic mountain. This will be a cement factory and enable people to build permanent houses. One of the central goals for the company is exactly this: the construction of permanent houses of cement for everyone on Ambrym. This will be the manifestation of a new era of development on the island.

Thus, Jimmy's solution to the curse affecting Ambrym is quite different from the one Rose envisions. They both agree on the cause of the problem: the curse due to Lingmal and the volcanic eruption. However, whereas Rose, from a Pentecostal perspective, focuses solely on the role of individual consciousness in the process of healing, Jimmy imagines creating a new social movement for the same purpose. Jimmy has received the signatures of all the chiefs of north and west Ambrym, which he proudly showed us in the document he has created to officially represent 'Larum', his Ambrym business and government movement.[5] For Jimmy, the process of lifting the curse is twofold: First, the *kastom* of Ambrym needs to be recognised as Christian and therefore morally good. This will be achieved through 'awareness' (a term he himself uses): everyone must learn that *kastom* does not prevent them from being good Christians. Secondly, when this knowledge is achieved, everyone can acknowledge the importance of his books of *kastom*, and through this a new unity will be achieved. Then, as a last step in this process, they will ask for forgiveness. When the curse is lifted, business and money will again find its way to Ambrym. The 'Larum' movement can only be realised after the curse has been lifted.

A Comparison

Thus, we have two very different stories of how to lift the curse that affects Ambrym: one emphasising the role of individual consciousness, and the other emphasising social unity. This unity is achieved through the act of giving back to people on Ambrym books containing the truth about *kastom*. By handing over the books to the chiefs on Ambrym in a grand ceremony to take place in the near future, the focus will be put on the history of ceremonial activity, of rituals and rank-taking. Jimmy's goal is the elicitation of this relational cosmos from his books. When it is all laid out, when everyone knows where they have rights and which ranks they have access to, the relational cosmology will be settled once and for all. This will create unity and enable the 'Larum' movement. This is Jimmy's vision for the future.

Thus, Jimmy envisions a kind of social healing, whereas Rose's focus is on individual healing. However, while neither of them would disagree about the importance of the other's project, they would disagree on which one has primacy. Rose would argue that social healing and the creation of a new business and form of government on Ambrym is not possible before individual healing has been achieved. For Jimmy, however, his work and the creation of a new social whole encompassed by his 'Larum' movement are primary. Jimmy pointed out several times that the work the churches are doing on Ambrym today, where they each organise prayer meetings to lift the curse, is without effect. Unity is primary.

I have thus presented two different perspectives on the future self, one emphasising the individual, in particular individual consciousness, and the other emphasising the cosmos of social relations, represented in *kastom*. Although both focus on 'healing the past' in order to create a new future, they vary greatly in their cosmological conception of this future. The emphasis that younger generations of Pentecostal Christians puts on individual responsibility is fundamental to their Christian cosmology. In a Christian worldview, as portrayed in Genesis, humanity itself, in the shape of Adam, is responsible for the most fundamental curse and the most original sin of all: the disobeying of God's rule. Evil, as pointed out by Ricoeur (cited in Sahlins 1996: 396), is perceived as inherent in man; it is not, as in other mythologies, a matter of historical development, of accident or of a trickster god or ancestral hero (ibid.: 396). Thus it is the free will of humanity that is the cause of the curse on humanity. Rose, in her elaboration of the necessity of healing, points to exactly this: the individual will to repent and individual consciousness. The individual is the location of evil, and is also the location of possible redemption. The solution to the Ambrym curse is thus parallel to the Christian solution to Adam's original sin and the original curse. The Ambrym curse is an extension of the biblical one.

For Jimmy, connection with the Bible is found at another cosmological level. Although the name of the 'Larum' movement remains secret until it is officially launched, the official document of the movement (authored by Jimmy and written by his computer-skilled daughter) was to be distributed to chiefs and important people (mostly men) on Ambrym. One of the central passages of the document reads as follows:

> [the 'Larum' movement] believes that the God Creator Our Father clearly demonstrates to us how we must develop this world in order for him to develop us. He created everything before He created man in his taboo image and He gave man all creations so that man could use them to develop himself. Our Taboo God Papa demonstrated very clearly that everything that He created with his conscience and intelligence that He gave to man also came with a responsibility and duty: to develop HUMAN BEING, which is His unique creation that he made in his taboo image. We can read about God's way of thinking in Genesis 1: 29–30.[6]

The particular focus is on Genesis and God creating man in his image. Jimmy's concern is not with the Fall but with the Creation. Here, I think, is the root to a fundamental difference. The curse, in Jimmy's world-view, is not a matter of individual responsibility. The curse on Ambrym is not a continuation of the Fall. Rather, the curse can be dealt with through the realisation of the divine nature of Ambrym people and thus Ambrym *kastom*, which is further underlined in the following paragraph of his document: 'Kastom ownership only follows the right that God of History gave to our ancestors before and leading up until today'.

Jimmy's focus is not on the distance between humanity and God (created by the Fall). Rather, his focus is on the continuation of God into humanity and their *kastom*. Therefore, in his official 'Larum' document, he also outlines the origin myth of the Ambrym volcano. This myth is told by people from Jimmy's village, as they are the ones who can control the volcano. They possess magical stones, buried (for now) in the ground. These stones can disturb the volcano and make it erupt. This is of course an essential component in Jimmy's plan for the volcanic mountain: only with knowledge of *kastom* can the potentially destructive energy of the volcano be turned into something productive.[7] In the origin story, Jimmy's ancestors find a bundle of bananas in their garden.[8] They eventually bring it back to the village, but the banana starts making a noise; then it glows and moves. Because of the noise, people in the village bring the banana into the interior of the island. They bury it on Marum Mountain, where the volcano is today. Here the banana has dug a huge hole in the ground, and it still makes noise and lights up occasionally. However, because it was the people of Jimmy's village who originally found the bundle of bananas, they are also the ones who can control the activity of the volcano and banana today. The magical stones they use are stones that were thrown out by the banana as it dug the hole in the ground during its first night in the village. In Jimmy's account of the origin myth of the volcano, he points out that it was God who lit the light of the banana. God did this at the same time as he also lit another light, the burning bush described in Exodus 3: 1–21. The encounter between Jimmy's ancestors and the burning bundle of bananas is therefore parallel to the encounter between Moses and the burning bush. Significant passages in the Bible are located in the Ambrym landscape, and significant biblical events are connected to Ambrym mythology. Here we can see how Ambrym cosmology as a totalising structure internalises narratives from the Bible and makes them meaningful in relation to an existing cultural logic, in a process similar to that which Michael Scott has described as ethno-theology (Scott 2005: 102).[9] It is the continuation between Ambrym mythology and biblical narratives which is the focus.

This focus on continuation, however, is challenged by a different perspective. The difference between Rose, as a representative of the young and mobile generation, and Jimmy, a representative (and perhaps currently the most outspoken and active representative) of older *kastom* men, is not a difference between a world-view based on Christian cosmology and one based on a pre-Christian one. As should be apparent, the two solutions to the curse are thoroughly based on the Bible. Nevertheless, they are fundamentally different. Rose's focus is on radical breaks. She emphasises discontinuities: between God and humanity (as inherently evil), and between the present and the future. Rose emphasises the primacy of individual conscience, while Jimmy emphasises the primacy of *kastom* as the shared property of everyone on Ambrym, as well as *kastom* as the representation of a relational cosmos with a new potential (as embodied by the 'Larum' movement). Here we can thus see the contours of a cultural change: the younger generation challenging the worldview of the older generation.

The Process of Cultural Change

Recent Melanesianist anthropology has questioned the extent to which Christianity as a cultural system imports the value of the individual (Robbins 2004; Scott 2005; Hirsch 2008; MacDougall 2009; Mosko 2010).

I have shown in this chapter how this form of cultural change involves a complex social process. Humiliation of established cultural categories in new and challenging situations must be analysed with a view to how different social positions play out. Change is never neutral. People are differently positioned in this process. In the Ambrym case, people seem to easily agree on their shared past but not on their future. Thus, focusing on the future gives us a perspective on difference, and this difference might be the key to an understanding of how cultural change takes place. When Jimmy argues for the importance of handing over his books about *kastom* to the people of Ambrym he is also arguing for the fundamental value of relationships, of sharing *kastom*. When Rose argues that before social healing can take place everyone must repent their sins on an individual basis, she is arguing for the fundamental value of the individual. As should be clear from my ethnography, the primacy of the individual in healing processes takes a particular form; it is the individual will and individual consciousness which takes centre stage. This does not mean, however, that the level of the social, of relationships, is not important. Rose and other Pentecostal Christians will point out that individual will and the capacity for repentance is the first step on the road to a social process of healing. What I am pointing to is not so much a difference between the individual on the one hand and the social on the other, but rather to a difference in the evaluation of which one of them is primary and which secondary for a healing of the past and an imagined future.

Let us take their imagined futures a step forward. If Rose's plan works out, if she convinces people about the importance of her project (of 'raising their level of awareness'), this implies the possible humiliation of Jimmy and other followers of *kastom* on Ambrym. As I have argued elsewhere (Eriksen 2005, 2008), the power of followers of *kastom* has long been in decline on Ambrym. The ceremonial and ritual contexts wherein in the past they could achieve fame and glory, and where they could display their knowledge and management of different kinds of *kastom* as magical knowledge, knowledge about artefacts and so on, are rare nowadays. Jimmy's plan to arrange a big ceremony is to some extent a plan to reassert the importance of the kinds of ceremonial arenas where 'big' men can meet. If Jimmy should succeed in his plan, it would mean the revitalisation of these kinds of arenas for men who seek to become representatives of social unity through *kastom*. Men in the past who became known for their high rank in the *Namange* (the secret male society) or for their achievements in other kinds of ritual activities (see Patterson 1981) often became the symbol of the relational cosmos in which they were involved. Tainmal, for instance, a well-known follower of *kastom* from Ambrym who interacted with the colonial authorities in the 1950s and 1960s, almost became iconic for north Ambrym as a whole; he was not only a *kastom* man, he was the *kastom* man who knew everything and thus represented the whole. His son Tofor also gained the same position in the national arena, becoming well known for magical abilities, even managing, according to rumours on Ambrym, to get his own private house when he was arrested for murder in the 1970s. Here he could cook his own meals and eat and sleep by himself. The other prisoners were afraid of him and his skills. This fear was also expressed during our first stay on Ambrym when people there would point him out to us and say, 'When you see him, get off the path, let him pass, do not look at him or speak to him'. He was portrayed as almost a holy man. He was, however, the last holy man. He was a man of importance, because of his ability to represent the cosmos of relations (Eriksen 2008; see also Rio 2011).

Today, no one can be compared to Tainmal or Tofor. No one can manage and represent *kastom* the way these great men of the past could. Jimmy, however, might aspire to. But he wants to achieve this position in a new way. He brings along the knowledge and power of *kastom*, but he brings it forward in a completely new context, in the planned ceremony for all Ambrym chiefs and his new 'Larum' movement. His plans for the future involve setting up ceremonial arenas different from the ones from the past (such as the *Namange*), but which would enhance the same values. The ceremony he plans will make it possible for men of *kastom* to display their ability to represent the cosmos of relations, the history of rank-taking, of genealogies, of attachment to land and place. Jimmy underlines that his plan for revitalising *kastom* will also involve bringing *kastom* into the light, uniting *kastom* and Christianity. If Christianity has been the main reason for the disappearance of several arenas for displaying knowledge of *kastom* on Ambrym (see Eriksen 2005, 2008), then his plan for unifying *kastom* and Christianity implies an important change: a neo-*kastom* encompassing Christianity. It shows how, in the words of Jimmy, everything according to *kastom* is already described in the Bible. This neo-*kastom* can potentially revive the *kastom* man. It can bring him out of the shadow in which he has been for the last decades.

This is not the position adopted by Rose and others of her generation. Younger women and men move more frequently to town (see Lindstrom 2011). Once there, they stay for longer periods. In town they are exposed to a larger degree than at home to the more radical forms of Christianity, such as Pentecostalism. Jimmy represents the older generation – one which is based on the island, which goes to town on shorter trips and which retains membership of the older, Presbyterian Church. He represents the remains of *kastom* authority. If Rose should gain support for her view, not only for her own project of countering Ambrym's curse but for the way in which one should go about removing curses in general, it would imply a further marginalisation of the *kastom* 'way', and thus the further marginalisation of the value of relationships and collective ceremonial arenas. Her solution to the curse involves making the value of the individual, in particular individual consciousness and the ability to be repent and redeem oneself, a fundamental value.

Here we can see the contours of how cultural change takes place. Although they both have embraced Christianity, the older man imagines a future which does not radically break with the established notion of a relational cosmos. The younger woman cannot see a future without individual conversion and repentance. Only the future will show how this process unfolds, whose plan will gain momentum, and whose plan will not.

Notes

1. In 2006 and 2010 I did a survey for the Vanuatu Cultural Centre on the new churches (Eriksen and Andrew 2010), looking at church numbers, recording brief histories and key persons. Today there are about fifty churches in Port Vila alone, most of them independent Pentecostal churches, or churches with some informal ties to an overseas funding organisation.
2. Older men are often those with more access to *kastom* and they play significant roles in village communities. Younger men and women are more mobile (see Eriksen 2008). The latter group often go to town to work on a more permanent basis than the older generation (see Lindstrom 2011). To some extent, the younger generation has been more interested in the new churches. This was constantly emphasised in conversations I had with church founders and pastors during my more recent periods of fieldwork. Young people make up the core of the congregation of new churches. When asked about this, younger people point out that the new churches are more fun, the services are livelier and there are musical instruments available (some of the churches invest considerable sums of money in electric guitars, keyboards and drum kits). Some of the material I collected during interviews in 2010 indicated that women join the new churches at a higher rate than men, in turn recruiting their husbands and kin. This gender difference in conversion to Pentecostal churches is also well documented in other regions (Garrard-Burnett and Stoll 1993).
3. For example, Radio Australia interviewed Ralph Regenvanu, the director of the Vanuatu Cultural Centre.
4. Regarding the planned company, at this stage Jimmy wanted its name to be secret. It is a very potent name, connected to Ambrym *kastom*. 'Larum' is therefore not the real name of his new movement.
5. To some extent, the 'Larum' movement resembles what in the literature has been described as cargo movements (e.g. Lindstrom 1990, 1993; Lattas 1998,

2006). It is a movement uniting people beyond previous divisions, creating a vision of future richness and success based on a new organisation and a new kind of government. Jimmy might thus be in the initial phase of the creation of a cargo movement. Jimmy is a well-respected and even feared man on Ambrym, having a reputation for sorcery. However, whether his plan for a prosperous future is a success depends on his political ability to gain allies for his project on Ambrym. But, as has been pointed out by others (e.g. Lindstrom 1993), cargo movements are never really about cargo and never really about a future of richness. They are almost always about creating a new unity and a new spirit of government.

6. All quotations from this document are translated from Bislama.
7. See also Patterson (2002) for the relationship between Ambrym mythologies and the dynamics of place, both on and beyond Ambrym.
8. See Eriksen (2008) for details of the mythology.
9. 'These ethno-theologies evaluate indigenous ideas and practices in relation to those of Christianity and situate ancestral identities and histories within biblical history' (Scott 2005: 102).

References

Don, A. 1918. *Light in the Dark Isles*. Foreign Missions Committee, Presbyterian Church New Zealand

Eriksen, A. 2005 The Gender of the Church in Melanesia. Conflicts and Social Wholes on Ambrym. *Oceania* 75(3): 284–300.

_______ 2008. *Gender, Christianity and Change: An Analysis of Social Movements in North Ambrym*. Aldershot: Ashgate.

_______ 2009. New Life: Pentecostalism as Social Critique in Vanuatu. *Ethnos* 74: 175–98.

Eriksen, A., and R. Andrew. 2010. 'Churches in Port Vila'. Survey report. Port Vila: Vanuatu Cultural Centre.

Garrard-Burnett, V., and D. Stoll. 1993. *Rethinking Protestantism in Latin America*. Philadelphia: Temple University Press.

Hirsch, E. 2008. God or Tidibe? Melanesian Christianity and the Problem of Wholes. *Ethnos* 73(2): 141–62.

Jolly, M. 1995. *Women of the Place: Kastom, Colonialism and Gender in Vanuatu*. Philadelphia: Harwood Academic Publishers.

Lattas, A. 1998. *Cultures of Secrecy: Re-inventing Race in Bush Kaliai Cargo Cults*. Madison: University of Wisconsin Press.

_______ 2006. The Utopian Promise of Government. *Journal of the Royal Anthropological Institute* 12(1): 129–50.

Lindstrom, L. 1990. *Knowledge and Power in a South Pacific Society*. Washington: Smithsonian Institution Press.

——— 1993. *Cargo Cult: Strange Stories of Desire from Melanesia and Beyond.* Honolulu: University of Hawaii Press.

——— 2011. Urbane Tannese: Local Perspectives on Settlement Life in Port Vila. Unpublished paper presented at 'Urban Life in Melanesia' workshop, Bergen, October 2010.

MacDougall, D. 2009. Christianity, Relationality and the Material Limits of Individualism: Reflections on Robbins's Becoming Sinners. *Asia Pacific Journal of Anthropology* 10(1): 1–19.

Mosko, M. 2010. Partible Penitents: Dividual Personhood and Christian Practice in Melanesia and the West. *Journal of the Royal Anthropological Institute* 16(2): 215–40.

Patterson, M. 1981. Slings and Arrows: Rituals of Status Acquisition in North Ambrym. In M. Allen (ed.), *Vanuatu: Politics, Economics and Ritual in Island Melanesia*, pp.189–236. Sydney: Academic Press.

——— 2002. Moving Histories: An Analysis of the Dynamics of Place in North Ambrym, Vanuatu. *Australian Journal of Anthropology* 13(2): 200–18.

Rio, K. 2007. *The Power of Perspective.* Oxford: Berghahn.

——— 2010. Handling Sorcery in a State System of Law: Magic, Violence and Kastom in Vanuatu. *Oceania* 80(2): 183–97.

——— 2011. High Chief, Waetman and the Codification of Ritual Objects in Vanuatu. In E. Hviding and K. Rio (eds), *Made in Oceania: Social Movements, Cultural Heritage and the State in the Pacific*, pp.223–53. Oxford: Sean Kingston Publishing.

Robbins, J. 2004. *Becoming Sinners: Christianity and Moral Torment in a Papua New Guinea Society.* Berkley: University of California Press.

——— 2005. Humiliation and Transformation: Marshall Sahlins and the Study of Cultural Change in Melanesia. In J. Robbins and H. Wardlow (eds), *The Making of Global and Local Modernities in Melanesia*, pp.3–22. Aldershot: Ashgate.

——— 1996. The Sadness of Sweetness: The Native Anthropology of Western Cosmology. *Current Anthropology* 37(3): 395–428.

——— 2005 [1992]. The Economics of Developman in the Pacific. In J. Robbins and H. Wardlow (eds), *The Making of Global and Local Modernities in Melanesia*, pp.23–42. Aldershot: Ashgate.

Scott, M. 2005. 'I Was Like Abraham': Notes on the Anthropology of Christianity from the Solomon Islands. *Ethnos* 70(1): 101–25.

7

Chiefs for the Future?

Roles of Traditional Titleholders in the Cook Islands

Arno Pascht

> Cook Islands traditional leaders can choose the path of becoming figureheads only, and therefore irrelevant to the general population. Or they can show leadership, by speaking out on important issues … People do not just give you respect, you have to earn it. This means making public statements, either supportive or critical, about policies that affect our Cook Islands people, and topics that affect them. Traditional leaders have to get savvy and educated; groom the next generation to have the same future-facing outlook; obtain the necessary modern tools to become effective – then act like leaders of our people.[1]

In this chapter I will deal with the future of Cook Islands' society. In doing so I will concentrate on one aspect: the role of holders of traditional titles or 'chiefs'.[2] Although I will also address views of Cook Islanders who do not have a title, I will focus on the perspective of the titleholders themselves. The question I shall investigate is: What roles do titleholders in the Cook Islands see for themselves in the future of the society of the Cook Islands? How do they act in the present to bring about this future?[3] I will start with a short sketch of the pre-colonial system of titleholders, and then outline the changes in the missionary and Protectorate period before I concentrate on the views of titleholders about their role today and in the future. My ideas are based on fieldwork in 2000/1 and 2009, mainly on Rarotonga, so I will concentrate on this island.

Before I start with the actual topic, I will sketch some general issues about the Cook Islands and Rarotonga. Rarotonga is the main island of the South Pacific state of the Cook Islands, itself comprised of fifteen islands. The northern group of islands consists exclusively of atolls, whereas the islands of the southern group are with one exception raised coral and volcanic islands. Rarotonga is part of the southern group and a volcanic island. The government and an international airport are located on Rarotonga, and the greater part of the resident population of the Cook Islands live here: the last census from 2006 counted about 10,000 people,[4] whereas only 5,000 lived in the other so called 'outer islands'. The estimated number for the year 2009 is about 13,000.[5] Past trends have seen population decrease on the outer islands, whereas the population of Rarotonga has remained nearly stable. On Rarotonga, about 80 per cent of the population denoted themselves as 'Cook Islands Maori', about 10 percent as 'Part Cook Islands Maori'.[6] Rarotonga is, at 67.1 square kilometres, the biggest island of the state.

The Cook Islands are an independent state that is in so-called 'free association' with New Zealand. Among other things, this means that Cook Islanders automatically have New Zealand citizenship. Accordingly, many Cook Islanders use this opportunity and move for certain periods or permanently to New Zealand. A secondary effect of this high mobility and migration rate is that people from other islands migrate to Rarotonga, so that a high percentage of non-Rarotongans live on the island today.

'Chiefs' in the Past

In order to understand the situation today it is important to look at the social and political organisation that existed on Rarotonga before, or at the moment of the first arrival of Europeans, and how it has changed over the last two centuries – according to today's state of knowledge. In the following paragraphs I summarise research about the history of social and political groups as well as the meaning of titles, and the roles titleholders or 'chiefs' had at the time of first European contact with the Cook Islands.

Ron Crocombe developed a lineage-based model of Rarotongan society (Crocombe 1964). Although it has been repeatedly criticised, many aspects of it are still important. Crocombe describes Rarotongan society in the past as a system of segmentary descent groups (ibid.: 25–37). By using the lineage model as a basic structure, descent and kinship became prominent principles in his description. In fact they did play a role, and Rarotongans recognised those persons who were descended via male or female links as a social category: descendants of a common ancestor. However, cognatic descent groups were not the functional units in economic, political and religious respect for all the levels Crocombe described. So the most important territorial and political units on Rarotonga in pre-colonial times were not descent groups but the *tapere*. The *tapere* were identified with descent groups that were named after an ancestor.[7] The inhabitants of a *tapere* were named *matakeinanga*. They consisted of members of the descent group and others, for example those who had been permitted to use land of the *tapere*. Each descent group owned a named title (*tā'onga*) – for example, an *ariki* or a *mata'iapo* title. The holders of titles had the highest status in Rarotongan society. Holders of titles normally had a leading role in minor and major descent groups, and in the *matakeinanga* as a whole. Holders of *ariki* titles usually achieved a leading role in a confederation of a number of *tapere*, a *vaka*. At least since the arrival of European missionaries, three *vaka* have existed on Rarotonga (Pascht 2006: 143–48).

The three categories of chiefs – or more precisely categories of titles or title names – that are mentioned by most authors still exist today. I will concentrate on these three: *ariki*, *mata'iapo*, and *rangatira*. *Ariki* in the past had a very high status. They were seen to have close connections to gods, and thus to have more *mana*[8] than holders of titles of other categories (Sissons 1989: 333; Campbell 2002: 229). Because of their status, *ariki* were immediate heads of descent groups (*ngāti*). Additionally, they were, at the time of the first European contact, heads of the confederations of sub-districts on Rarotonga. *Mata'iapo*, the second category or class of title, also had a high status, and were also heads of descent groups (*ngāti*). Although they were to a high degree independent, *mata'iapo* were usually associated with a distinct *ariki*. The third important title category was that of a *rangatira*. The status of *rangatira* was below that of *ariki* and *mata'iapo*, and *rangatira* were always associated with and subordinated to an *ariki* or *mata'iapo*.[9] The title names were hereditary. Although the ideal probably involved the passing on of a title to the eldest son, there were many instances of other lines of succession – such as to the younger brother. Most probably there was a great deal of variation among the different descent groups on Rarotonga concerning the succession, competence and power particular titleholders had. Although the notion prevailed that they inherited *mana* from their ancestors, the actual amount of power different titleholders held depended to a large part on their personal qualities and their achievements; importantly, their power over people outside their immediate descent group and their relation to other titleholders was not something static but depended on personal achievement (Baltaxe 1975: 93–94; Campbell 2002: 236–37; Pascht 2006: 1455–48). This view contrasts with Crocombe's model (Crocombe 1964: 27), which is rather static and hierarchical.

Information about the tasks of 'chiefs' in the time before the arrival of Europeans is not very detailed. Leaders of social groups had leading functions in agriculture and other fields of work. They might control access to resources (especially land and crops) with a so called *ra'ui*, a prohibition that is shown by a physical sign. Crocombe also mentions their role as arbitrators, especially in cases of land disputes, but there were also other methods of conflict management (ibid.: 23–24). They also played a role when land issues such as allocation had to be decided. In the case when a branch of a descent group or an extended family had no descendants, the titleholder would reallocate the land of this group after 'consulting other members of the group' (ibid.: 39). Negotiations between groups in cases of conflict and leadership in war were other tasks of 'chiefs'. An important function was to represent the whole group before the gods (Gilson and Crocombe 1980: 9–10), or better, to mediate between men and gods and to conduct or legitimise rituals for the gods. This was an important reason for their power (Campbell 2002: 229; see also Sissons 1989: 333).

In common with other authors (Gilson 1955, 1980; Crocombe 1964; Scott 1991), Campbell stresses the increase in power of *ariki* in the nineteenth century. He shows that the influence of European missionaries and colonial officials was not the only reason for changes in Rarotongan society, and that this increase in the *ariki*'s power began before the arrival of the missionaries (Campbell 2002: 230–34). His very important point, which he contrasts with Crocombe's model, is that the social and political structure of pre-contact Rarotonga was characterised in some important respects by fluidity and flexibility: 'Traditional power relations were not monolithic structures predicated on invariable laws of genealogical precedence ... The relationships between mata'iapo or rangatira, and between them and the ariki, were negotiated and renegotiated on a case by case basis' (ibid.: 237). Not until the beginning of the twentieth century, when the Cook Islands became a colony of New Zealand, did the power of the *ariki* in the political system of the new state decline.

The Changing Role of Titleholders since Independence

Today, six *ariki* titles are recognised on Rarotonga: Tinomana Ariki, Pa Ariki, Kainuku Ariki, Makea Nui Ariki, Makea Karika Ariki and Makea Vakatini Ariki. *Ariki* title names are today seen as the most prestigious and highest ranking. Second in rank and prestige are the *mata'iapo*, and third the *rangatira*.[10] When considering the roles of titleholders today and in the future I will distinguish three levels: the national level, the local or village level and the family level. In the rest of the chapter I will focus on the national level, but first I will briefly touch on the other levels. At the family level, the importance of titleholders is very diverse, depending on the specific family and the particular holder of the title. Whereas in a number of cases titleholders are very influential – especially regarding land matters – other families hardly consult their titleholder at all. At the local level, titleholders participate in local political bodies, and thus have a certain influence on particular local political issues.

For the national level I begin with the history of the relationship between titleholders and national politics in the Cook Islands after self-government was established in 1965. The role of chiefs must also be seen in connection with a more general national and regional discourse and politics regarding 'modernity' versus 'tradition' and 'custom'. Jeffrey Sissons (1999: 16) distinguishes four phases of the postcolonial period of the Cook Islands: modernist party nationalism from 1965 to 1974; traditionalisation from 1974 to 1978; the abandonment of tradition as a state responsibility from 1978 to 1988; and a second traditionalisation from 1988 to 1999, the time Sissons was writing.

Sissons argues that for the first decade of self-government, the administration took an approach to nationalism that stressed the notion of 'progress' (ibid.: 19). This did not mean that the titleholders did not have a role in the new state. The first premier, Albert Henry, even declared the *ariki*, *mata'iapo* and *rangatira* to be the 'backbone' of the nation. Accordingly, *ariki* were, on the one hand, included in the nation state: the government legislated for a national body named the House of Arikis, and a respective act was included in the constitution (ibid.: 61). Although it seems to have been the intention of the government to define the role of the House of Arikis in a similar manner to the British House of Lords – a second chamber of Parliament – and to give one *ariki* the role of the Queen's representative,[11] the outcome was that the House of Arikis received a mere consultative role, so that they were actually excluded from political power (ibid.: 64–65). The House comprises the *ariki* of Rarotonga and one *ariki* as a representative of each of the other islands. The House of Arikis has the power to comment on matters that Parliament submits to it, or it can on its own initiative make recommendations on issues concerning customs or traditions.[12] Thus it has predominantly a symbolic role – mainly as hosts, honoured dignitaries and official speakers at ceremonial occasions, such as during royal visits or annual celebrations of the Constitution (ibid.: 63). The House of Arikis tried nevertheless to influence policy-making and legislation during this period, but was unsuccessful (ibid.: 66). Proposals by the *ariki* to extend their power, especially concerning land and local government, were rejected (ibid.: 68).

This does not mean that 'tradition' did not play a role in this period at the state level. One important example of a 'tradition' that was supported by the government was dancing: 'Dancing youth embodied the nation's future and the modernist values of unity and 'progress' … The dance competitions served both to unite and differentiate the more localized identities as parts of a whole' (ibid.: 56–57). Over the next five-year period, the focus of the government on 'tradition' and 'culture' was extended, and finally also included chiefs – but rather the *mata'iapo* and *rangatira* than *ariki*. A state Cultural Development Division (CDD) was established that provided a link between cultural and national development. A diversity of customs were designated 'local culture' by the CDD, whose work involved collecting and recording traditional history and other forms of traditional knowledge (ibid.: 74). Similarly, efforts were made to include 'culture' in curricula for primary schools and colleges (ibid.: 76). In 1972, the House of Arikis Act was amended in order to create a new national body of chiefs consisting of *mata'iapo* and *rangatira*. Sissons stresses that this body was sympathetic to the ruling Cook Islands Party. They 'upheld the cultural heritage of an ancient nation' (ibid.: 80–81). The new body, named Koutu Nui, comprised *mata'iapo*, *rangatira* and *kavana* (a title category of the island of Mangaia). It can also make recommendations to parliament.[13]

In 1978 the new government abandoned the cultural projects of the previous government and emphasised the economic development of the country (ibid.: 84). The CDD was closed in 1980, the government limited the sponsoring of cultural performances and the privatisation of dance was encouraged (ibid.: 87–89). Although Premier Thomas Davis intended to give the House of Arikis more powers in the legislative process, he was not successful because even his party colleagues voted against it. The result was that the emphasis was again on the symbolic role of the *ariki* (ibid.: 94). The Koutu Nui lost its minor political role as consultative body, but was not abolished. Sissons writes that this did not mean that the *mata'iapo* and *rangatira* lost their status at the local level. He mentions the increase of investiture ceremonies during this period, which he ascribes to the local continuation and intensification of the revival of tradition that had been enhanced by the former government and supported at a regional level by the South Pacific Commission and the Maori cultural renaissance in New Zealand. Sissons does not dwell on the detailed role and tasks of the titleholders at the family level (ibid.: 95).

After 1989, when the Cook Islands Party won the election, 'culture' and 'tradition' were again seen as state issues. A Ministry of Cultural Development with a considerable budget was established (ibid.: 100), dance was sponsored and sailing with traditional canoes was encouraged. The highlight of these developments was the Festival of Pacific Arts that took place on Rarotonga in 1992 (ibid.: 108). These activities also supported the role of chiefs at an informal local level or in specific situations. But his did not mean that their official political power increased at the same time (ibid.: 114), and the role of the House of Arikis did not change considerably. The Koutu Nui, inactive over the previous ten years, was reconvened in 1988, but it was unable to extend its competences concerning local or national government (ibid.: 116).

According to present day Cook Islands' state law, titleholders still only play a minor role in the political system of the state. At the national level, their most important functions relate to the above mentioned House of Arikis and the Koutu Nui. Both still exist and have retained their consultative role. Apart from this official political role, titleholders are engaged at various levels in situations that are connected with ceremonies where they act as representatives of the family, the district, the whole island or even the nation. *Ariki* represented their districts, for example, when each *ariki*, held aloft in their traditional palanquin by their warriors, carried the torch for the Olympic Games that took place in Sydney in 2000. Additionally, visits by important guests are events in which chiefs invariably play a central role, such as the visit of Kiingi Tuheitia, the New Zealand Maori King, in 2009. When he came to Rarotonga, the titleholders of the districts of the island received and hosted him on various occasions. Another important example of the representative role of titleholders at the national level is the annual celebrations of the Constitution (*Te Maeva Nui*), which comprise mainly of a competition between dance teams from all the islands of the Cook group. In 2009, the president of the House of Arikis was one of the opening speakers at the celebrations, and the president of the Koutu Nui was on this occasion present on the stage together with the president of the Cook Islands Churches, the deputy prime minister and other important people. Other occasions when titleholders play an important representative role at the state level are visits of state dignitaries, such as the prime minister of New Zealand. Titleholders are usually present at official welcoming ceremonies and so on, and they actively organise meals and celebrations for the guests. Although this role is not defined in the present constitution or in other state laws, titleholders are seen as an important part of such events and act as an integral part of the modern nation-state of the Cook Islands in this context.

Titleholders and Political Power

A view that is reiterated in the discourse regarding titleholders on Rarotonga is that they do not have political power or even influence today, or that their influence is declining. 'I think the power and the importance of the *ariki* is diminishing', said a Rarotongan to me – and I often heard similar views. As mentioned above, politicians are often seen as the new decision-makers, a role that it is thought titleholders had in pre-European times. On the other hand, two points were often mentioned when I talked to Rarotongans that contradict or relativise this view, at least partly.

The first is that politicians are not connected to land. Power or *mana* on Rarotonga today still is closely associated with land. Land is associated with a title and the families to which it belongs. 'The government has no control over land. This is where the power lies for the titleholders', said one *mata'iapo*. He added that in the end the land can never be sold and that the land, as well as the title, belongs to the tribe.[14]

The second point relates to the nature of the democratic political process. Elected politicians are seen as representing their political party and its members, but not of all the people. Because of this, their legitimacy – although it is acknowledged that they are democratically elected – is not always fully accepted. Moreover, the fact that politicians hold office for only a few years is in contrast to titleholders, whose office is held for life. The continuity of the latter is positively valued, whereas the vicissitudes of the political system of the state is seen as negative.

The question of whether titleholders should have more power in the political system of the state did not elicit consistent answers among my Rarotongan interlocutors. Several of them expressed doubts about the necessary competence of titleholders. On the other hand, some concrete options were expressed. The most important was the wish that one of the *ariki* should become head of state. As stated above, this has been promised to the titleholders in the past but has never been realised (Sissons 1999: 65).

An event that took place on 12 July 2008 dramatises the tense relationship between titleholders and the state regarding issues of political power, and shows some of the tasks titleholders see for themselves in the present and future. On this day, a proclamation was announced by a majority of members of the House of Arikis, 'which seeks to abolish parliament, cut off ties with the Queen, and vest executive power in the ui ariki'.[15] To be more specific, the proclamation of the *ariki* attacked the government, which in their opinion had not recognised the status and *mana* of the *ariki*.[16] They declared that 'all the country's natural resources in the air, land and sea be vested in the hands of the ui ariki',[17] and that they no longer recognised Parliament, the Crown or ties to the Queen. They further demanded that all treaties and agreements made with other countries be no longer recognised, and that legislative and executive power be transferred to the *ariki* 'to look after the interests of the country and the people'.[18] The majority of the *ariki* who were members of the House of Arikis at the time signed this proclamation.

What led the *ariki* to this dramatic proclamation? It appears that Bruce Ruatapu Mita, described as a 'New Zealand Maori sovereignty campaigner',[19] met several times with the *ariki* of the Cook Islands prior to the proclamation. The *Cook Islands News* states that 'Mita has been promising traditional leaders millions of dollars if they claim ownership of the country's manganese nodules' that were found on the seabed in the Exclusive Economic Zone of the Cook Islands.[20] In several conversations with Cook Islanders, the potential money for manganese nodules was said to be responsible for the proclamation. But I was also told that the *ariki* suspected members of the government of using profits from the exploitation of seabed resources for their own ends rather than for the benefit of the people. In other conversations, as well as in newspaper articles, it became clear that one significant reason for the proclamation was the *ariki*'s disappointment regarding the government's treatment of them, and of the limited influence that they have on political decisions and processes. In one newspaper article, the journalist Noeline Brown suggested that, 'the Proclamation is their [the *ariki*'s] making a stand and to reclaim the mana and high standing that is their rightful heritage'.[21] Pa Ariki, the holder of one of the highest titles of Rarotonga reinforces this view in an article in the *Cook Islands News*: 'If it chose to do so, government could do much to support the ui ariki [...] Our [the holders of ariki-titles] days as rulers are long-gone but in our office as ariki we embody centuries of culture and tradition. Today, more than ever, that culture and tradition is under threat'. Pa Ariki asks what political party could hope to win an election without promising to cherish their culture. She also writes: 'Government needs to know that for this reason, if no other, we are as much players in the future of the Cook Islands as we are guardians of its past'. Pa Ariki suggests that the *ariki* should come together and work to persuade the government that their house is not a relic from the nineteenth century. She stresses that 'in fact we are at the heart of Cook Islands society and that our house should be part of a strategy of taking Cook Islands culture, tradition and custom confidently into the twenty first century'.[22]

However, less than two weeks after the proclamation, the House of Arikis met and the participating members reaffirmed their allegiance to the Queen, and distanced themselves from the proclamation.[23] Whereas the majority of the *ariki* of the Cook Islands today do not support the 2008 proclamation, a small number of *ariki* over a year later still upheld their claims,[24] and continue to do so today. The other members of the House of Arikis decided to take the opportunity to apologise to the Queen's representative. The request to apologise in order to qualify again as a member of the House of Arikis was even codified in state law.[25]

The incident of the 2008 proclamation suggests that some or most *ariki*, at least over the last decades, had become very dissatisfied with their relation to the government and the conduct of politicians. While other factors may have played a role, this is the most plausible reason for why the normally rather passive House of Arikis was willing to allow an outside activist to push them into such a drastic move. They saw a chance to repay the government for its disregard of them and to reposition themselves in order to accrue more power and influence.

The Actions and Influence of Titleholders

Do Cook Islander titleholders act as 'chiefly bureaucrats', to use Lindstrom and White's term, acting mainly as middleman and mediators of the state? Or do they aim to be a 'chiefly opposition' who as heads of communities represent the 'common identity and aspirations of that community' (Lindstrom and White 1997a: 16) towards state institutions? The relationship between titleholders and the state in the Cook Islands is a complex and ambiguous one. What the Koutu Nui does, a titleholder explained to me, 'is neither for nor against [the government]. We just look at the issues and we [tell the] government what we think'. Because their position as defined in legislation is weak with respect to political power, titleholders are on the one hand dependent on the approval of the government if they want to be included in regular political decision-making processes. On the other hand, they have influence of their own. As one politician who is also a *rangatira* put it: 'For politicians they [titleholders] are a power base, they are pressure groups ... for politicians maintaining a good working relationship with titleholders, with the Koutu Nui, with the Ui Ariki is a plus ... Politicians who are not popular with the Koutu Nui and the House of Ariki will be disadvantaged'. While their formal constitutional role may be limited, this politician stresses the pressure which they can nevertheless bring to bear on governments and politicians owing to their widely respected authority. The idea that titleholders represent the interests of 'the people' means that they in some instances have to play the role of government opponents, while also involving themselves, on occasion, as middlemen. Elements of both of Lindstrom and White's ideal types can thus be found in the Cook Islands.

Titleholders in the Cook Islands creatively employ different methods in order to exert influence on social and political processes, and to realise their vision of the future. In practice, titleholders seldom make use of their statutory powers, and when they do they are rarely successful. Titleholders instead experiment with and have already found other ways to get involved in political decision-making processes, and be heard by state politicians. One of these ways is the participation of titleholders from the Koutu Nui in government committees. The Cook Islands government has recently made moves to involve titleholders in diverse bodies. For example, the president of the Koutu Nui was chair of the immigration review committee, and acted as a representative on the seabed minerals committee. A titleholder who is at the same time working for the Cook Islands government said: 'Most government agencies actually recognise the important role, the emerging important role that the Koutu Nui is playing'. Indeed, politicians can use this participation strategically: 'Government can say to overseas agencies: "We are consulting with the … traditional leaders through their national bodies, the House of Ariki, Koutu Nui". That impresses overseas agencies'.

In addition to the role defined by law and their participation in government committees and events, titleholders also employ alternative ways and forms of action: the Koutu Nui especially has initiated and accomplished projects on its own or in cooperation with other entities. The use of 'traditional' methods of restricting the harvesting or exploitation of natural resources provides one example of this: the *ra'ui* prohibition is now widely used to support conservation efforts. A second instance is a recent 'community visioning project'. The background to this kind of activity is varied. The members of the Koutu Nui see themselves as an active body that realises things. 'We are the people who do the work', as the secretary of the Koutu Nui told me, a view stressed in several conversations I had with members of the Koutu Nui. In contrast, the House of Arikis is seen as a body of 'figureheads' where matters are discussed rather than acted on – although I also heard people complain that in practice the Koutu Nui is more a 'talking forum' than an 'action forum'.

A second aspect of the Koutu Nui's aim of being involved in developing projects is that some members see it as an interest or pressure group, rather in the manner of contemporary non-governmental organisations (NGOs). Members of the Koutu Nui have recognised that it is possible for them to be acknowledged at both the national level by the government and at the international level by development agencies as relevant actors by adopting concepts, topics and formal aspects of NGOs. Some members have experience in participating in events such as international conferences, and they may have adopted some principles and views from them. A third motive for taking an 'active role' in projects is that members of the Koutu Nui realise that their advisory work in government committees goes largely unnoticed by the public, whereas in projects they become considerably more visible.

Titles Today and in the Future

In order to understand more about the importance and meaning of titles and their holders, additional aspects of Cook Islands life have to be considered. When I asked Rarotongans if they see a renaissance or a demise of titleholders, the answers varied considerably. Statements I heard during my fieldwork ranged from, 'the title in our family doesn't bother me … [T]he titles will disappear because nobody is interested in taking them', to 'I think [the titles] need to be retained … because it's our cultural identity'. (Both statements are from people who at the time did not have a title.) While it is true that a number of titles are presently unoccupied, there are also many serious conflicts about who is the rightful successor to a title. A number of titles are thus vacant, or in other cases more than one person claims to be the actual titleholder, leading to disputes within families. The ideal that family members support a titleholder is in reality thus not met in a number of cases.

The high number of conflicts over succession to a title hints at the fact that the role of titleholders in Rarotongan society has a certain relevance. The question arises: In which respect are they are relevant, and what causes people to argue about the titles? *Ariki* titles in particular are connected with prestige, privileges and in some cases with considerable amounts of land. Thus self-interest and personal strategic considerations are likely to play a role in these conflicts.

Prestige and material benefit are of much less significance for *mata'iapo* and *rangatira* titles. Nevertheless, many conflicts take place over succession to these titles, whereas others are vacant because family members are not interested in being invested with them. This reflects the diversity within classes of titles: the influence as well as prestige of titles varies considerably from one family to another.

In keeping with this diversity, contemporary Cook Island titleholders have positioned themselves differently with regard to untitled people. This is consonant with the kingly/populist distinction that Marcus (1989) has proposed for Polynesian societies. Whereas they are seen as ordinary persons, approachable in everyday life, and it is expected that they are role models for everyone, titleholders have in certain contexts consciously or unconsciously distanced themselves from people without a title. For example, *ariki* are carried on a palanquin during certain ceremonies; they and other high ranking titleholders have special areas and seats during public events. People without titles often do not know what the House of Arikis or the Koutu Nui are doing. So although their status is not mystified, they are in some respect socially distant to people without a title.

Titleholders are expected to behave properly, and they should act as role models – it is, for example, expected that they do not get drunk in public. Rarotongans like to gossip about examples where this ideal was not adhered to by titleholders. It is also expected that titleholders possess leadership qualities. Influence on the family level depends to a high degree on these factors. Without knowledge of history and land, genealogy and 'proper' behaviour, the chief's ability to perform tasks that are connected with titleholders at the family level – like settling conflicts or influencing land matters – is limited.

Does the Importance of Titleholders Lie in the Past or the Future?

A view that was explained to me in similar form by several members of the intellectual stratum of Rarotongan society can be illustrated by a historical sequence that Makiuti Tongia, the former secretary of the Ministry of Cultural Development presented in a speech. He partitioned the history of the Cook Islands into four phases, and identified in each case the crucial actors or influences behind the main developments of the Cook Islands. In the first, the pre-colonial period, 'chiefs' played the most important role in society. This was followed by a period where missionaries and the Church were central. The next period, the contemporary one, is determined by politicians. They are seen as the decision-makers regarding central trends in the life of the Cook Islands. The future is seen as being dominated by a modern capitalist economy. In this sequence titleholders are thus not relevant to today's main developments. Tongia said in conversation that he saw the role of titleholders today as a mainly ceremonial one, with only little political power. Titleholders in this view are seen mainly as hallmarks of the remote past, present only as a memory, a reminder of history. This does not mean that they do not have any significance for the present and future, but they do not have significance as active shapers of that future.

On the one hand, Tongia can be seen as a typical representative of a more 'modernist' view, in which economic development plays an important role in the future of the Cook Islands as a state in which titleholders are not involved. On the other hand, this does not mean the total exclusion of 'tradition' from the modern world. In his capacity as secretary of the Ministry of Cultural Development, for example, Tongia tried an innovative way of reviving – or (re)inventing – various 'traditions' that were not connected with titles.

In contrast to the view expressed by Makiuti Tongia, there are a number of titleholders who see themselves as an important part of the present and future of the Cook Islands, and it is these to which I now turn. The majority of titleholders I spoke with saw a renaissance of the importance of titles and of 'traditions' generally. 'Tradition, customs have become important again. [People] have realised it is something beautiful … [W]e still have our traditions and yet we are still very Westernized as well', said one *rangatira*. An important example in this regard is that in the mid 1980s the investiture of titleholders on *marae* was reinvented.[26] 'I wanted to re-establish our identity', said Te Tika Mataiapo when she talked about her investiture in 1985. She had insisted that it take place on a *marae*. Today *marae* have become the usual site for investiture ceremonies that before took place in other sites like graveyards. Whereas *marae* were previously sometimes forgotten or at least not used, they regained the function of an essential part of the investiture ceremony. The Koutu Nui is planning a publication where *marae* will be documented, including photographs and historical information. *Marae* are now seen as being closely associated with a title, land, a family and history. The intention is to secure knowledge about *marae* for future generations.

All the titleholders I spoke with were very conscious of the importance of the political and legal order of the contemporary Cook Islands. Nevertheless, they saw an essential and legitimate role for titleholders. Two main aspects are important. First, the above-mentioned formalisation of the House of Arikis and the Koutu Nui through parliamentary acts was a topic that was stressed in the majority of conversations I had with titleholders. It is seen as a very important foundation for their future role, and titleholders stressed that they see it as a very important aspect in comparison with some countries where traditional chiefs do not have this kind of legitimacy. Their inclusion in the constitution and in state laws is seen as an important basis for ensuring the future role of titleholders in the Cook Islands.

Second, although legitimation by state law is seen today as most important, legitimation by 'tradition' also plays an important role. Here, knowledge about the origin and history of a title and family, including associated lands, is central. Ideally, a titleholder should be able to trace his genealogy at least to a titleholder that was invested by Tangiia and Karika. According to oral tradition, these two culture heroes came twenty-eight generations ago with their followers to Rarotonga. Although the island was already settled, they gained a very powerful position. They erected *marae* on the whole island, and they invested their sons with *ariki* titles and their followers with *mata'iapo* titles. They divided the land of the island into pieces (*tapere*) and gave them to the holders of the titles for their families. Thus they established the spatial and political order of Rarotonga that was found when the first missionaries came. These land divisions and titles are present today. A titleholder should ideally know where their *marae* is.

When I asked about tasks and roles titleholders think to be important in the present and future, the following aspects were routinely mentioned. When I talked to titleholders about their tasks and their roles at the family level, I heard many times the view that titleholders are responsible for the well-being of the people and that titleholders should act to ensure this. One *mata'iapo* explained that she feels responsible for the fair allocation of land, whereby every member of the family is allotted enough to prevent conflicts within the family. This notion resembles the Polynesian principle of *aro'a* that Richard Feinberg (2002) identifies as one of the basic values of Oceania, although this word is not currently used explicitly in this context, and its use is not documented in the past.[27] However, the titleholders' tasks that I describe below – especially 'representation' towards government as well as 'care for traditions and customs' – are closely related to this principle.

The formal or symbolic representation – or perhaps better, embodiment – of the family, its origin, genealogy, history and lands vis-à-vis outsiders is a capacity of 'chiefs' that is clearly important today. It is realised, as shown above, mainly through their presence – and this presence has its focus in ceremonies and feasts where titleholders are invited as guests. Of importance here is the way titleholders act as representatives during meetings with guests who visit the island or the country. I often encountered this view: 'If we did away with them all [the titleholders] and we get a country like Samoa ... and they [distinguished guests] come here and they need to be welcomed, to be just welcomed by a government official to me is – then what – where is the people? So it's good to have *ariki*, they can host them'. The point here is that, embodying custom in the form of family, land and history, titleholders stand for the people in a way an elected politician or a bureaucrat could not. The capacity of titleholders to host foreign dignitaries in the name of the people is very significant for the way Cook Islanders understand their own social and political order and their relationships to the wider world.

A third task of titleholders is care for traditions, the land and the environment, so that knowledge is not lost in the future. 'We are the custodians of land, traditions and customs ... [W]e also feel very responsible as titleholders to our environment', the president of the Koutu Nui stressed. Such 'traditions' include a number of fields of knowledge, for instance investiture ceremonies, performing arts, medicine and language. So, for example, the Koutu Nui supports or participates in activities that promote these 'traditions'. This topic was discussed at the annual conference of the Koutu Nui in 2006, which had the theme 'The Way Forward'. A part of the conference involved talking about reviving and preserving 'Cook Islands Maori culture, custom and traditions'.[28] The issue was topical, as not only the Koutu Nui but also other Cook Islanders – especially teachers – complain that 'Cook Islands culture' is taught in schools on only a limited scale (Braukmann 2010).

Another project of the Koutu Nui that is a good example of the role of titleholders as 'custodians of tradition' is a cooperative venture between the University of the South Pacific and the Koutu Nui in which traditional crafts like the production of *tapa* (bark cloth) are revived and documented on film. Similarly, titleholders have been involved in the introduction of *ra'ui* (prohibitions) in the Rarotongan lagoon as a means of protecting the marine environment. The *ra'ui* involves a complete ban on fishing and collecting of marine life. It was initiated in 1998 and established by the Koutu Nui in cooperation with the government (Hoffmann 2002). Along with a 'tradition' involving a ban on harvesting marine resources, the *ra'ui* represents a 'traditional' undertaking focused on care for the environment. The aim of the *ra'ui* is to ensure that the lagoon is not over-fished, and that marine life can recover and be available in the future. The *ra'ui* makes clear that the lagoon is not only important as a food resource but is also an attraction for tourists who expect a rich variety of marine life when snorkelling there. The *ra'ui* and other activities – such as the involvement of the Koutu Nui in climate change issues – show that these are not simply reiterations of a static tradition and a continuation of the past, but definite projects aimed at securing a specific future.[29]

Another role of titleholders that should be mentioned is that of their embodiment of a family, and thus as foci for identification for individuals. Cook Islanders in general and titleholders specifically often mentioned the role 'chiefs' play in the 'identity' of people, and that it is important to secure this sense of 'identity' for the future. A member of the Koutu Nui explained that one of her most important concerns is the re-establishment of the identity of Cook Islanders, something which in her eyes they have lost. As an example she mentioned Cook Island teenagers who live in New Zealand.

A final task titleholders see as important is representing the interests of their families or more generally 'the people' vis-à-vis the government. In this respect I encountered different views. One is that titleholders should act as a sort of opposition. A titleholder and member of the Koutu Nui explained to me that they can be a 'dissenting voice', acting as a 'watchdog' and doing 'advocacy work'. On the other hand, the same titleholder told me that the Cook Islands ultimately have a democratic system where Members of Parliament should be approached and backed in order to represent interests. An example of this 'advocacy work' – or of acting as a sort of 'civil society' body – is the 'community visioning' project that the Koutu Nui conducted in 2009. The purpose of the project is stated in the report that was written by two members of the Koutu Nui:

> There was some concern among *Koutu Nui* members that there had not been adequate consultation with communities prior to the launch of the National Sustainable Development Plan 2007–2010 ('Te Kaveinga Nui') in January 2007. It was felt that the views of communities, particularly in the Outer Islands, needed to be sought and articulated. The aim was that the *Koutu Nui* community visioning project would combine the traditional village meeting consultations with modern participatory decision-making practices to record the views and aspirations of the communities on the main sectors of sustainable development. (Ingram and Browne 2009: 6)

Funds for this project were provided by UNESCO, and community meetings were conducted from July to November 2009. Topics discussed regarding sustainable development were the governance sector, the social sector, the environmental sector and the economic sector, with the cultural sector added by the Koutu Nui (ibid.: 7). The report detailing these meetings was finally presented to the prime minister. The topics taken up by the Koutu Nui here show that titleholders are familiar with concepts and ideas of international development discourse. In using them, they engage themselves as important actors in political processes shaping the future at a national level and beyond.

Conclusion

At the beginning of this chapter I asked: What roles do titleholders in the Cook Islands see for themselves in the future of the society of the Cook Islands? How do they act in the present to bring about this future? I have shown that today diverse notions about the future of titleholders coexist and play a role in the Cook Islands. In order to realise their visions of the future, titleholders themselves act within a complex field constituted by relations between 'tradition', state law, national politics and transnational factors.[30] Whereas the legal and political system of the state is acknowledged widely, 'traditional' notions and practices that have their roots in the legal and political order of the pre-colonial Cook Islands and that are transmitted at the family level also possess validity in certain contexts and situations. In order to create their future, titleholders make recourse to these 'past' concepts. But they also use concepts and ideas from other contexts (such as international politics), as well as fashioning their own ideas and concepts in order to achieve their goals. So, on the one hand they actively commit themselves to creating continuity with the past, which is seen as an important basis of chiefly authority and legitimacy. In so doing they aspire to (re)creating a role for themselves that is endowed in the future with political influence and power. On the other hand, titleholders are aware that 'the old system' doesn't exist anymore – and the majority of them do not intend to re-establish it. On the contrary, titleholders undertook a number of moves to transform and rebuild their existing roles in new ways, and to give them new contents. In order to secure the continuity of the institution of the 'titleholder' or 'chief' in changing political, economic and cultural contexts, they invent new forms of action, meanings and so on. Although they revert to the past in various ways, titleholders' vision of the future is very distinct from that past. I have shown some of the tasks that titleholders regard as important for the future. A good example in my view is the proposal of some titleholders that they assume the role of 'watchdog' and 'pressure group', and that their activity be seen as 'advocacy work', all this in combination with such things as environmental protection and sustainable development, idioms which they draw from a broader, transnational arena. These notions did not exist in the past as there was no state or central government. Another topic is identification. The need for 'identity' is not seen as emblematic of the past, but an issue of the present and the future. In the view of titleholders, it can be strengthened or recreated for people by disseminating lost knowledge about titles, land, *marae*, family history and so on, because these things embody the belonging of individuals to a group and a place of origin. In this respect, titleholders represent the past and the future for many Rarotongans. In line with the perspective adopted by Will Rollason in the Introduction to this volume, I have shown some of the actions that Cook Islands titleholders have undertaken to secure their futures. They are grounded in a vision that is connected to the past and the present, but also envisages distinctive projects for shaping Cook Island society in the future.

Notes

1. I. Ingram (personal communication, 31 July 2010).
2. The words 'titleholder' and '(traditional) chief' are used as synonyms in the Cook Islands in many contexts. I follow this convention here. Whereas Cook Islanders stress that before the arrival of Europeans only men were allowed to hold a title, today it is possible for men and women to hold them.
3. Chiefs do not only play an important role in modern societies in Oceania (see e.g. Lindstrom and White 1997b). In other parts of the world, such as Africa, chiefs and chiefdoms have persisted, and they have even gained new political, cultural and social powers (see e.g. Krämer 2009).
4. Figures from: http://www.stats.gov.ck/Statistics/CensusSurveys/census06/Cen06-Tab2.pdf, last accessed 10 May 2011.
5. Figures from: http://www.stats.gov.ck/Statistics/Demography/demognav.htm, last accessed 10 May 2011.
6. Figures from: http://www.stats.gov.ck/Statistics/CensusSurveys/census06/Cen06-Tab2.pdf, last accessed 10 May 2011.
7. The prefix *ngāti* was used to denote the descendants of a common ancestor – e.g. Ngāti Karika are the descendants of Karika.
8. *Mana* is usually translated as 'power'. Shore specifies in his discussion of this important concept that for 'Polynesians, *mana* manifests the power of the gods in the human world' (Shore 1989: 164).
9. Baltaxe (1975) states that *rangatira* were titles of a different kind altogether.
10. The list of title names and holders of the Koutu Nui contains 75 *mata'iapo* and 153 *rangatira* for Rarotonga (Koutu Nui 1999).
11. As the Cook Islands form part of the Commonwealth, the Queen of the United Kingdom serves as titular head of state.

12. See the Constitution of the Cook Islands and the House of Arikis Act (1966).
13. See the House of Arikis Amendment Act (1972).
14. In fact land cannot be sold in the Cook Islands. More precisely, this means in legal terms that the alienation of land in fee simple and for a longer period than sixty years is prohibited; the only exemption is an alienation to the Crown for public purposes (Cook Islands Act 1915, §. 468, 469).
15. *Cook Islands News*, 13 May 2008. The *ui ariki* is the totality of the *ariki*.
16. *Cook Islands News*, 13 May 2008; *Cook Islands Herald*, 11 June 2008.
17. *Cook Islands News*, 13 May 2008.
18. *Cook Islands News*, 13 May 2008.
19. *Cook Islands News*, 7 June 2008.
20. *Cook Islands News*, 7 June 2008.
21. *Cook Islands Herald*, 11 June 2008.
22. *Cook Islands News*, 23 June 2008.
23. *Cook Islands News*, 21 June 2008.
24. *Cook Islands Times*, 21 July 2009.
25. See the House of Arikis Amendment Act (2008).
26. In the pre-colonial era, *marae* were important structural elements in Rarotongan society. *Marae* were ceremonial places that were connected with titles (*tā'onga*), land and gods. Every descent group possessed its own *marae* that was used for important ceremonies of this group – e.g. for investitures of title holders.
27. The term *aro'a* can be translated variously as, 'Kindness, sympathy, sorrow (for [somebody] in trouble), love (i.e. divine love, or loving kindness, not love between sexes…)' (Buse and Taringa 1995: 77).
28. *Cook Islands News*, 1 July 2006.
29. Another example with environmental implications is the plan of the Koutu Nui to promote organic agriculture in the Cook Islands, with the aim that the whole country will ultimately grow all its food organically.
30. See e.g. my discussion of legal pluralism concerning land rights (Pascht 2006).

References

Baltaxe, J.B. 1975. The Transformation of the Rangatira: A Case of the European Reinterpretation of Rarotongan Social Organisation. PhD diss. Urbana: University of Illinois.

Braukmann, F. 2010. Vom *ta'unga* zum Grundschullehrer: Das Bildungssystem von Rarotonga auf dem Weg in die Emanzipation. Unpublished manuscript.

Buse, J., and R. Taringa. 1995. *Cook Islands Maori Dictionary*. Rarotonga: Ministry of Education, Government of the Cook Islands.

Campbell, M. 2002. History in Prehistory. The Oral Traditions of the Rarotongan Land Court Records. *Journal of Pacific History* 37(2): 221–38.

Crocombe, R. 1964. *Land Tenure in the Cook Islands*. Melbourne: Oxford University Press.

Feinberg, R. 2002. Elements of Leadership in Oceania. *Anthropological Forum* 12(1): 9–44.

Gilson, R. 1955. The Background of New Zealand's Early Land Policy in Rarotonga. *Journal of the Polynesian Society* 64(3): 267–80.

——— 1980. *The Cook Islands 1820–1950*, ed. R. Crocombe. Wellington: Victoria University Press; Suva: Institute of Pacific Studies of the University of the South Pacific.

Hoffmann, T.C. 2002. The Reimplementation of the Ra'ui: Coral Reef Management in Rarotonga, Cook Islands. *Coastal Management* 30: 401–18.

Ingram, I., and N. Browne. 2009. Shadow Report Submitted by Koutu Nui O Te Kuki Airangi to the Office of the Prime Mminister on Review of Te Kaveinga Nui (The National Sustainable Development Plan) 2011–2015. Unpublished manuscript. Rarotonga. Koutu Nui.

Koutu Nui. 1999. Akapapaanga Ingoa Mataiapo/Rangatira no te Kuki Airani. Unpublished manuscript.

Krämer, M. 2009. Vom administrativen zum konkurrenziellen Häuptlingtum. Anmerkungen zur Legitimität und Transformation neotraditionaler Herrschaft in Namibia und KwaZulu-Natal, Südafrika. *Sociologus* 59(2): 173–98.

Lindstrom, L., and G.M. White. 1997a. Introduction: Chiefs Today. In L. Lindstrom and G.M. White (eds), *Chiefs Today: Traditional Pacific Leadership and the Postcolonial State*, pp.211–29. Stanford: Stanford University Press.

——— (eds). 1997b. *Chiefs Today: Traditional Pacific Leadership and the Postcolonial State.* Stanford: Stanford University Press.

Marcus, G.E. 1989. Chieftainship. In A. Howard and R. Borofsky (eds), *Developments in Polynesian Ethnology*, pp.175–209. Honolulu: University of Hawaii Press.

Pascht, A. 2006. Das Erbe Tangiias und Karikas: Landrechte auf Rarotonga. PhD diss. Bayreuth: University of Bayreuth.

Scott, D. 1991. *Years of the Pooh-Bah: A Cook Islands History.* Auckland: Hodder and Stoughton.

Shore, B. 1989. *Mana and Tapu.* In A. Howard and R. Borofsky (eds), *Developments in Polynesian Ethnology*, pp.175–209. Honolulu: University of Hawaii Press.

Sissons, J. 1989. The Seasonality of Power: The Rarotongan Legend of Tangiia. *Journal of the Polynesian Society* 98: 331–47.

——— 1999. *Nation and Destination: Creating Cook Islands Identity.* Suva, Rarotonga: Institute of South Pacific Studies, University of the South Pacific.

8

A Coup-less Future for Fiji?

Between Rhetoric and Political Reality

Dominik Schieder

In November 1986, during his memorable visit to the Fiji Islands, the late Pope John Paul II coined Fiji's famous tourist slogan 'Fiji – the way the world should be' (Scarr 1988: 6), as a recognition of the fact that the multi-ethnic country's communities lived in peace and harmony. Fiji was, according to the Pope, 'a symbol of hope for the world' (quoted in Garrett 1997: 400). Less than half a year later, however, John Paul II's vision of a peaceful Fiji was dramatically challenged by the country's first military coup d'état, followed closely by another one in September 1987. A civilian putsch supported by members of an elite military unit was staged in May 2000, and in December 2006 a third military coup took place. In less than two decades, Fiji had acquired the image of a country where legitimate governments where violently overthrown, and people began speaking about the existence of a 'coup culture' in the islands.

On 14 May 1987, Lt.-Col. Sitiveni Rabuka entered Fiji's Parliament with a group of soldiers, specifically trained for the purpose of ousting the country's coalition government, formed by the Fiji Labour Party and the National Federation Party. Rabuka and his forces staged a second coup on 28 September that year. His aim seemed to be quite clear: the coups had been staged in order to safeguard indigenous Fijian political privileges endangered by the election of a multi-ethnic government which, the coup protagonists argued, was dominated by Indians.

Thirteen years later, ethnic divisions seemed to have led to another political crisis when a group of heavily armed indigenous Fijians, led by the part-European George Speight, stormed Parliament in May 2000. This time, their proclaimed aim was to secure once and for all the paramountcy of Fijian interests threatened by the electoral victory of the Fiji Labour Party and its Indo-Fijian leader Mahendra Chaudhry. Chaudhry acted as Fiji's first prime minister of Indian origin after the 1999 general elections until the 2000 coup. While Speight and the other coup perpetrators eventually triggered events that saw the removal of Chaudhry's coalition government, they were unsuccessful in their attempt to secure a place in Fijian politics after the coup. After a period of uncertainty they were arrested by the Fijian military commanded by Frank (Josaia Voreqe) Bainimarama. However, political turmoil did not come to an end.

In the years following the 2000 coup, ongoing power struggles between Fiji's military and Fiji's politicians remained a source of political instability.[1] This was evident in the difficult relationship between Commodore Bainimarama and Laisenia Qarase, who was appointed caretaker prime minister in the wake of the coup by the military command in order to lead Fiji out of its socio-economic crisis. More specifically, the origins of the uneasy relationship between Qarase's politicians and Bainimarama's army were related to the government's decision to implement several policies which aimed to reconcile Fiji's multi-ethnic communities by absolving some of the protagonists of the 2000 putsch attempt. For his part, Bainimarama challenged the government-drafted Reconciliation, Tolerance and Unity Bill which aimed to reconcile the victims and perpetrators of the 2000 putsch. Bainimarama strongly opposed the bill because of its tendency to serve as a *carte blanche* for future coup perpetrators. In the end, the military went so far as to intervene in the 2006 general elections by openly endorsing a number of candidates who contested the elections in opposition to Qarase's Soqosoqo ni Duavata ni Lewenivanua party. Bainimarama's failure to disempower Qarase through awareness campaigns aimed at educating the public about his ethno-nationalist and despotic agenda led to numerous open threats by the military commander that a coup would be staged if his demands were not fulfilled.

Eventually, on 5 December 2006, the military takeover took place. It was staged by Bainimarama and his followers in the name of good governance and nation-building and was described as a clean-up campaign against favouritism, nepotism and the racism which, according to Bainimarama, had dominated Fiji's politics for far too long.[2] Speaking to the United Nations General Assembly in 2007, Bainimarama justified his takeover thusly:

> It was with the utmost of reluctance that Fiji's Military, under my leadership, removed the former government from power in December 2006. There have been critics of this decision. In response to this criticism I say this. Fiji has a coup culture – a history of civilian or military coups executed in the interests of a few and based on nationalism, racism and greed. To remove this coup culture and to commit to democracy and the rule of law, policies which promote racial supremacy, and further the interests of economic and social elites, must be removed once and for all. Racism, elitism and disrespect for the law are undemocratic.[3]

The 2006 military takeover had the potential to change Fiji's political landscape. Unlike earlier coups, which had a reactionary nature (and were staged, according to the perpetrators themselves, to counter Indo-Fijian political ambitions), the Bainimarama takeover was envisaged as a reform-oriented clean-up campaign (Schieder 2012b: 48). Since the coup, the Bainimarama regime has initiated policies such as the People's Charter for Change, Peace and Progress to strengthen Fiji's ongoing project of nation-building.[4] Furthermore, after his takeover, Bainimarama promised to introduce a new constitution and to hold elections in 2009. He also established the Independent Commission against Corruption. Based on these and other promising reforms, many citizens of Fiji placed hope in the Bainimarama coup and a future Fiji free of racism, nepotism and corruption, as well as of the coup perpetrators of 1987 and 2000.

However, thus far the political rhetoric of the regime has not led to any significant changes. Although the Bainimarama government implemented a new constitution in September 2013 which will serve as a foundation for elections in 2014, critics claim that the steps taken by the interim government since December 2006 contradict its own rhetoric. They specifically refer to numerous instances of human-rights violations which have been recorded since 2006 in order to silence coup opponents, the draconic implementation of the Media Industry Development Decree,[5] which ultimately led to a clampdown on the freedom of the press, and numerous instances of diplomats and academics being expelled from the country (Bhim 2011). Finally, the inclusion of notable former coup perpetrators in the interim government, the abrogation of Fiji's constitution in April 2009, and the extended deferral of Bainimarama's promise to implement a new constitution and to hold elections left most people in Fiji in a state of uncertainty and disillusionment about their future.

This chapter aims to understand how political elites envisage Fiji's future in general and their own futures in particular by focusing on elite political agents,[6] their agencies[7] and the socio-cultural divisions[8] which underlay the actions of Fiji's political protagonists. I discuss, for example, the contradictions between Bainimarama's political rhetoric, which promotes a coup-free future for Fiji, and the actual political actions of the military government, which clearly contradict their promises. In order to make sense of the contradictions between the political rhetoric and actions of the current Fijian government, the chapter discusses in detail a central theme of local political discourse: the notion of 'coup culture', taking into consideration its historical origins and how it is used in discussions about Fiji's political crisis. I argue that this concept is a valuable tool for understanding the gap between political rhetoric and political action which characterises contemporary Fijian politics. More importantly, a focus on the notion of coup culture shifts the emphasis from social structures and divisions to individual political actors, and fully acknowledges their agency in shaping Fiji's present.

Research has usually explained Fiji's long-lasting socio-political instability by emphasising ethnic divisions and conflicts (e.g. Scarr 1988) or class divisions and forces (e.g. Robertson and Tamanisau 1988; Sutherland 1992) as the main reasons behind the coups of 1987 and 2000. Some scholars have attempted to shed light on the events of 1987 and 2000 by focusing on intra-Fijian divisions and rivalries (Fraenkel 2000; Tuimaleali'ifano 2000, 2007), although they do acknowledge the plurality of causes which underlie Fiji's political instability. These studies, however, do not pay attention to the agency of political actors and the ways in which this agency binds together all the centrifugal forces which are usually recognised as the reasons behind Fiji's coups.

To put it differently, although some authors (e.g. Lal 1992) rightly acknowledge the complex nature of Fiji's political dilemma, their works do not offer an in-depth analysis of political elitism, coup culture and its future implications. Such an analysis is, however, necessary to understand and explain the nature of the coups. More importantly, it adopts an emic perspective on a political landscape which in the past has been far too often validated through the narrow lens of Western political models. These models fail to capture non-Western political actors' innovative and resourceful political thought and action that, while built on established political ideas and concepts, can be rethought and adapted to contemporary local political settings, and therefore shape very specific political currents and futures.

Fiji's ethnic, intra-ethnic and class divisions alone cannot explain its socio-political problems, and approaches which ignore the agency of political actors only lead to misinterpretations of the political rhetoric of Fiji's current leaders. I argue that Fiji's political situation is best explained by using an ethno-historical and especially comprehensive analysis which brings these explanations together, highlighting both the complexity of the Fijian situation and the ability of various political actors to navigate political discourse and action.

In this respect, a future-oriented perspective on the politics of history, culture and tradition is particularly fruitful. Following Martha Kaplan, I call for a 'dialogical account of colonial and postcolonial [Fijian] history' (Kaplan 2004: 59), and by extension Fijian postcolonial future(s). Fiji's political future, as well as the agency of those political protagonists who determine it, can only be understood if we approach the past, tradition and cultural values not as causes of political thought and action in and of themselves but as potential bases for highly innovative and situational political projects. Fijian political projects certainly build both on an imagined and lived or experienced past, and we have to understand the political strategies and agendas of Fiji's coup protagonists in order to overcome simplistic depictions which portray Fiji's current political conflicts as a result of its multi-ethnic social structure.

Thus, while the Bainimarama government continues to promise a future for Fiji free of ethnic tensions and coups, its genuine interest in pursuing this agenda needs to be fundamentally challenged because ending the coup culture would contravene the regime's own political ambitions. Therefore, talking about the existence of a coup culture in Fiji has become a project for Fiji's current political establishment, and it helps them negotiate their own future in various ways, which the present chapter will highlight.

In what follows I first discuss the origins and usage of the notion of coup culture in Fiji, and go on to critically examine the main elements of this political discourse, namely inter-ethnic, intra-ethnic and class divisions, and evaluate them against the actions of the military regime. In the last two sections I show how Fiji's coup protagonists make use of these elements in an innovative and highly contextualised way, and I consider the implications of the gap between political rhetoric and action for Fiji's future.

Fiji's Coup Culture

Shortly after the 2006 military takeover, the term 'coup culture' became part of the political, public and academic discourse which sought to explain Fiji's long-lasting political instability (cf. Schieder 2012b: 47–51). Interestingly, the use of the term coup culture is confined almost exclusively to the Fijian context.[9] According to my own observations, this concept originated in the way Fiji's coups were perceived and described by politicians, scholars and laymen alike. In this sense, talking about the existence of a coup culture in Fiji is a reflection of local understandings and articulations of the country's long-lasting socio-political instability. For example, Sitiveni Rabuka revealed to me his own perspective on coup culture: 'I accept that people blame me for introducing the coup as a solution to an unacceptable political situation. It became a "culture" when others like Speight and Bainimarama followed suit!'[10]

Other useful insights on Fiji's coup culture are offered by Sandra Tarte and Steven Ratuva. Following Rabuka, Tarte summarises Fiji's coup culture as 'a pattern of instability that is repeatedly being played out' (Tarte 2009: 409). She also emphasises the fact that the coups of 1987, 2000 and 2006 shared significant parallels, including the rhetoric of the coup perpetrators that Fiji was not ready for democracy, the numerous human consequences of the coups (the clampdown on the freedom of speech and the freedom of assembly), the negative economic fallout and the exposure of racial, class, regional and political divisions within Fijian society (ibid.: 411–13). Steven Ratuva reaches similar conclusions. The term coup culture, according to Ratuva, has to be understood by taking into account a number of inter-related aspects. The repeated usurpation of state authority by Fiji's coup protagonists not only made the coups a part of Fiji's political culture, but led in turn to a number of social consequences such as the normalisation of a coup language and the development of a state of mind which reflects the characteristics of life in a coup environment. Furthermore, Ratuva points out that, while military men carried out the coups, one needs to be aware of other protagonists, such as politicians and businessmen, as well as community and church leaders, who were involved in planning and coordinating the coups and who pursued personal political and economic interests (Ratuva 2008).

Ratuva's reference to a group of coup protagonists is supported by Ratu Joni Madrawiwi's perspective on the dominant figures in Fijian politics. According to Ratu Joni, a Fijian paramount chief and former vice-president ousted from office during the December 2006 coup, Fiji's coup protagonists consist of a network of Fijian chiefs, party politicians, religious leaders, military men, businessmen, diplomats, lawyers and judges of various ethnic backgrounds whose connections to each other are not just political. Ratu Joni describes Fiji's political landscape as a playground of established and influential networks and dynasties represented in key institutions such as the military, political parties and in many key economic sectors. For him, it is not exceptional that individuals who describe themselves as close friends or relatives have varying religious or denominational preferences, belong to different political parties or have differing opinions and attitudes towards the coup culture and its implications.[11]

In sum, what Fiji's postcolonial coup protagonists have in common is that they are the most visible figures and leaders of political projects. They come from diverse ethnic, class and regional backgrounds, and they draw on a certain form of legitimacy, as well as charisma and leadership, in order to implement their projects and set themselves apart from their followers.

Using these arguments as a starting point, I suggest that the term coup culture is of great conceptual value in understanding Fiji's long-term political instability because it offers a local perspective on the manifold forces that have dramatically shaped Fiji's postcolonial history. The notion of coup culture is particularly relevant if understood as a local rhetorical device used by Fiji's political protagonists to make sense of the country's ongoing political instability. It encapsulates the long-term historical and structural interrelations of the coups and, by extension, cultural change and cultural stasis. It does not limit the coups to discrete, non-related, contemporary political alternatives for the usurpation of state authority and political power, but allows us to explore Fiji's socio-political instability as a historical, multi-layered phenomenon which has undergone significant changes over the last few decades without ultimately losing its overall make up. In order to understand the historical dimension of the coup culture, we need to remember that Fiji's recent history was significantly shaped by colonial policies, such as the practices of indirect rule and divide and rule, or the system of indentured labour migration. Thus, Fiji's colonial and even its pre-colonial history have to be taken into account if we wish to understand the interconnected nature of its coups and, especially, coups as potential strategies for the future of Fiji's political elites.

Talking about the existence of a coup culture in Fiji represents an integral part of Fijian political discourse. This discourse is shaped by a number of significant socio-cultural forces and, most importantly, by its protagonists. The centrifugal forces I refer to can be summarised as inter-ethnic, intra-ethnic and class-based divisions. As indicated above, it is exactly the complex interplay of these forces exploited by Fiji's coup protagonists to advance their political aims that makes the coup culture such a complex and multi-layered phenomenon. In what follows, I discuss the historical forces that have shaped this coup culture. The division of the discussion into sections is entirely for analytical reasons. While it is necessary to present a historical overview of these factors and forces, it should be kept in mind that the coup culture does not stem from pre-existing and pre-conceived ethnic, regional or class divisions alone. Rather, the coup culture must be understood in the light of the political strategies and aims of the current political actors who navigate discourses on ethnicity, class and tradition, and therefore constantly reinvent and recontextualise the coup culture without challenging its fundamental framework.

Inter-ethnic Tensions: Fijian Ethno-nationalism and Coup Culture

Predominant Descriptions of Fiji's Socio-political Instability

The dominant explanation of Fiji's socio-political instability is based on a critical evaluation of the multi-ethnic composition of its society. Following a simplistic model that characterises societies with a multi-ethnic make-up as 'plural' (Furnivall 1948), Fiji's indigenous Fijians, Indo-Fijians and other population groups are supposedly living next to, not with, each other as a result of the country's colonial history (e.g. Scarr 1988; Fraenkel 2006).

The Fiji Islands were incorporated into the British Empire as a Crown Colony in October 1874. This marked the end of several efforts to establish a domestic government in the settler town of Levuka, run by local Europeans and chiefs from the most powerful Fijian chiefdoms located in the eastern coastal areas. Fiji's first governor, Sir Arthur H. Gordon, together with his advisor and future governor, Sir John Bates Thurston, were instrumental in establishing Fiji's political and economic future (Legge 1958). Their decision to declare inalienable communally owned, indigenous Fijian land has survived until today. As a result, nowadays more than 80 per cent of the archipelago's landmass is owned by local Fijian communities, while other ethnic communities, especially Indo-Fijians, depend on a complex system of land-leasing. Similarly, Gordon and Thurston decided to protect the political rights of the indigenous population by introducing a system of indirect rule with a separate Native Fijian Administration. This system was aimed at ruling Fijians through Fijians by relying on chiefs from the eastern regions of the archipelago. In consequence, Fiji's early colonial years witnessed the birth of a new class of colonial Fijian leaders who dominated Fijian politics from the late nineteenth until the turn of the twentieth century. The third decision taken by Gordon was to import labourers from South Asia for the colonial plantation economy. This eventually led to the formation of a supposedly bifurcated society in Fiji. Until the 1990s, Fijians and Indo-Fijians made up more than 90 per cent of the country's population, while also forming two population groups almost equal in size.[12] Gordon's vision of an exceptional colony meant, in essence, that Indo-Fijians were not entitled to the same political status as indigenous Fijians. The colonial takeover thus facilitated the cementing of a doctrine of Fijian paramountcy, at the expense of other population groups (Lawson 1991: 58).

In fact it can be argued that until Fiji's 1997 constitution was implemented, Indo-Fijians were politically marginalised. The political imbalance which characterised twentieth-century Fiji can indeed be traced to the country's colonial legacy. However, it is not Fiji's colonial heritage itself that shapes Fijian politics, but the way it is deployed and re-articulated by leading political agents. While the initial purpose of Gordon's promise was to protect Fijians from European settler exploitation, the doctrine of Fijian political paramountcy was also employed by Fijian and European leaders to counter Indian struggles for social, political and economic equality (Lawson 2004). Although never formally codified in any of Fiji's constitutions, this doctrine became a powerful tool for Fiji's coup protagonists, and was used to safeguard indigenous Fijian and, most importantly, the coup protagonists' own political rights and privileges (Schieder 2012b: 53).

Taking Fiji's colonial heritage into consideration, it can be argued that the 1987 coups were highly motivated by an ethno-nationalist agenda, and staged in the name of the paramountcy of Fijian interests. Thirteen years later, coup-maker George Speight and his group of soldiers and civilians claimed to fight for indigenous Fijian rights, which were threatened after the election of Mahendra Chaudhry and his Labour Party-dominated government. The ethno-nationalist Taukei Movement, which was formed in the wake of the 1987 general elections and had featured prominently in Rabuka's takeover, played a prominent role in Speight's putsch as well.[13] Even Bainimarama's ongoing clean-up campaign heavily draws on a rhetoric of race and ethnic identity, this time however in order to counter ethno-nationalism and racism. In summary, ethnicity has been employed by all of Fiji's coup protagonists: in 1987 and 2000 to paint the image of a political future exclusively shaped by indigenous Fijian rights and privileges, and in 2006 in the name of nation-building and good governance.

While I do not question the fact that these common descriptions of Fiji's coup culture have a certain degree of legitimacy, I argue that in order to understand Fiji's socio-political instability and its future prospects we need to critically engage with the relevance of ethnic divisions and conflicts by considering other potential causes of political instability as well.

(De-)Constructing Ethnic Fijian Identity

Among the other forces which generate political instability in Fiji are significant intra-ethnic divisions. As I pointed out above, ethnic Fijians and militant Fijian ethno-nationalists are significant outcomes of Fiji's colonial past, yet they only partially cover intra-ethnic frictions and tensions. In other words, Fijians form a rather heterogeneous community, and their identity as a social group with a collective agenda is highly situational. This becomes particularly obvious when ordinary Fijians are being politically mobilised by Fijian coup protagonists before, during or after election campaigns. This means that in order to understand the strategies employed by Fiji's political actors we need to carefully deconstruct ethnic identities in Fiji.

The term 'indigenous Fijian' refers to the descendants of the initial settlers of the archipelago, who migrated to the islands between 1500 BC and the sixteenth century AD, and lived in scattered hamlets across the island group. According to Rechtman (1992), more complex social and local groups evolved during the next centuries. These developments were triggered mainly because of increasing conflicts over political power and resources. Despite efforts towards political centralisation made by certain Fijian chiefdoms in the eighteenth and nineteenth centuries, it was only after Fiji was incorporated into the British Empire that Fijians were unified for colonial administrative purposes. In short, contemporary Fijian identity and language is a colonial product that was achieved by imposing an eastern Fijian social structure and language over the entire archipelago. Similarly, the common language, nowadays referred to as Standard Fijian, based on a pre-European lingua franca (Standard Fijian), missionary Fijian (Old High Fijian) and a number of dialects (Bau, Bua, Lau), was established only after the arrival of Europeans (Geraghty 1983). Yet, both in the Fijian and Indo-Fijian case, several centrifugal forces are at work which undermine the idea of two separated and homogeneous ethnic groups facing each other.[14] These include differences of a regional, linguistic and religious nature.

My observations based on fieldwork in Fiji's capital Suva and in the town of Sigatoka do not support the idea that Fiji is a typical plural society where the different population groups live next to rather than with each other, and only interact occasionally in the public sphere. Fijians and Indo-Fijians only contextually experience themselves as homogeneous or unified ethnic groups. An imagined or real common decent and cultural similarities stand at the core of such an ethnic identity. From this perspective I argue that inter-ethnic conflicts and ethno-nationalism form major elements of Fiji's coup culture only in certain political contexts in which existing ethnic stereotypes and prejudices are deployed by Fijian (or Indo-Fijian) politicians in the particular interest of the respective ethnic group they represent. This group in turn needs to contextually experience and display a shared ethnic identity.

The perspective outlined here allows us to critically engage with Fijian ethno-nationalism because it helps us to draw a more nuanced picture of Fijian politics at a national level. Without doubt ethnic divisions feature prominently in Fiji, but under certain circumstances these divisions are less shaped by ethnic differences because ethnicity can also be manipulated by Fiji's coup protagonists to blur or hide other causes of the coup culture. In other words, ethnic identities are employed by Fijians only in certain contexts. This means that we cannot understand the local setting by focusing on ethnic identities as primordial and unchanging, or by claiming that ethnic Fijian identity is a recent invention. Ethnic identity in Fiji is in this particular context a political project 'articulated in the interest of specific political agendas and contextually configured for political reasons' (Schieder 2012b: 54). On the one hand my argument is based on ethnographic observations, and on the other it relies on the idea that cultural divisions or differences and the mere existence of multiple ethnic groups within a state or state-like territory do not necessarily lead to conflicts between these groups.[15] Ethnic identities in Fiji, articulated in specific contexts and expressed in terms of Fijian ethno-nationalism, are at once essentialist claims and more or less deliberate attempts at social (re)construction. Therefore, as Newbury and Newbury have similarly pointed out for Rwanda, 'it is politics that makes ethnicity significant (or, indeed, insignificant), not ethnicity which invariably defines politics' (Newbury and Newbury 1999: 313). In order to understand this complex interplay of essentialist and socially-constructivist notions of ethnicity, and how it is used by Fiji's coup protagonists for their political agendas, we need to explore Fiji's coup culture further by looking at its other constituting factors and forces.

Intra-ethnic Divisions and Power Struggles as Aspects of the Coup Culture

A closer look at Fiji's recent history reveals that intra-ethnic political divisions and power struggles within the Fijian community (and also Indo-Fijian community) are a second major cause of the coup culture. According to Rechtman (1992), archaeological evidence shows that a number of internal and external factors led to the formation of powerful Fijian chiefdoms in the late eighteenth century. However, while pre-colonial divisions and conflicts were suppressed during Fiji's colonial period with the help of some prominent chiefs who hailed mainly from eastern and north-eastern Fiji, formerly loosely structured regional hierarchies and shifting power relations within and between Fiji's pre-colonial chiefdoms were cemented and perpetuated from the end of the nineteenth century onwards (Schieder 2012a: 245–61). According to Alumita Durutalo (2005), political parties and democratic elections can be understood as modern instruments for settling old scores. These new types of political activity have been gradually incorporated into contemporary cases of Fijian dynastic rivalries that are still based on regionalisms, descent and marriage alliances.

I will give an example of intra-Fijian power struggles and Fijian chiefly title rivalries from the island of Bau, but such centrifugal forces are at work between and within other Fijian chiefdoms and *matanitu* (confederacies incorporating several chiefdoms) as well.[16] The descendents of Ratu Sir George Cakobau, the last installed paramount chief of Bau (*Vunivalu mai Bau*), and arguably Fiji's most prominent chief of the nineteenth century, can be divided into two sets of siblings who are distinguished according to their respective mothers. Together they form a set or 'household' (*i tokatoka*) of potential title heirs from the quarrelling Tui Kaba line. Some of the main frictions within the chiefly Tui Kaba line are caused by the rivalries of Adi Samanunu and Adi Litia Cakobau on one side, and Ratu Apenisa Cakobau on the other. These rivalries were present in state politics during the 1990s, with Adi Litia and Adi Samanunu supporting Rabuka's Fijian Political Party and Ratu Apenisa supporting Rabuka's main political rival, Josevata Kamikamica. In the elections of 1999, however, Adi Litia and Ratu Apenisa both stood for the Fijian Political Party, a move which can be explained from an intra-ethnic perspective as these two sets of paternal half siblings are members of the *mataiwelagi* household, which represents a powerful Bauan descent line in opposition to the *naisogolaca* descent line. Both trace their direct descent to Ratu Seru Cakobau. The *naisogolaca* household, however, is a younger branch of the Tui Kaba line, and is closely related to the Mara dynasty which featured prominently in the government around 2010 (Tuimaleali'ifano 2000; Weber 2008; Firth and Fraenkel 2009). This opposes the households on segmentary lines. In conclusion, it becomes obvious that for a deeper understanding of Fiji's coup culture much can be gained by examining the inter-relationship of Fijian chiefly title rivalries and modern party politics from a historical perspective. This approach reveals the complex interplay of title disputes and state politics which underscore the rivalries within the Tui Kaba line.

In addition, a historical perspective on Fiji's coup culture reveals that political coups are no recent phenomenon in Fijian politics. A look at pre-colonial modes of warfare and the usurpation of political power shows that stealth, treachery, conspiracy and plotting were fundamental strategies used to pursue rivalries outside and especially within the close range of potential candidates for Fijian chiefly titles (Clunie 2003). For example, the inter-connections of status rivalry and title disputes within and between the chiefdoms of Bau and Rewa in the nineteenth century are explored by Marshall Sahlins (2004). Shelley Ann Sayes (1982) analysed similar mechanisms for usurping political power and leadership in the chiefdom of Cakaudrove. These accounts show that the idea of an 'overthrow', expressed through the Fijian word *vuawiri*,[17] was an essential feature of Fijian dynastic politics in pre-colonial times. Moreover, the Fijian expression *vere vaka Bau*, 'plotting and conspiring in the Bauan way' (Fraenkel 2000: 302), to which people referred during the Speight coup in 2000, also has its roots in pre-colonial Fiji.

Hence, George Speight's putsch in May 2000 was, among other things, a struggle on the part of the political confederacy Kubuna to regain the pre-colonial political status it had gradually lost after the British annexed the Fiji Islands.[18] Similarly, the 1987 coups were triggered by intra-ethnic Fijian rivalries because one aim of Rabuka and the coup perpetrators was to restore the previously hegemonic political status of the Tovata confederacy, which was established and institutionalised in twentieth-century Fiji (Howard 1991). Finally, the 2006 coup was supported by members of the Mara dynasty which gradually lost its political influence with the rise of Sitiveni Rabuka in the 1990s and the ousting of Ratu Sir Kamisese Mara, Fiji's long-serving prime minister and president during the 2000 putsch attempt (Weber 2008: 43).[19]

Again, it is important to understand that the rhetoric of ethnicity and ethnic politics is used by Fiji's coup protagonists for their political projects and power struggles, which at times revolve around intra-ethnic and not inter-ethnic divisions. However, Fiji's coup protagonists conceal these significant intra-ethnic divisions because they are able to mobilise Fijians as an ethnic group against a rival Indo-Fijian ethnic group. Here it is important to emphasise that the past (local rivalries, intra-ethnic power struggles, marriage and war-related alliances) is not the essence of Fiji's coup culture but a substrate on which political actors draw. While intra-ethnic Fijian divisions based on a primordial understanding of Fijian culture and tradition play a major role in coup dynamics and future prospects, these regional divisions themselves do not determine Fiji's coup culture. Rather, it is the way in which culture and tradition are deployed and articulated for political projects that makes them important.

Class Divisions and Conflicts as Aspects of the Coup Culture

An analysis of the manifold social divisions which underlie the political thought and action that fuels Fiji's coup culture is incomplete without taking into consideration the class dimension as well. As in neighbouring Pacific island societies (cf. Besnier 2009, 2011), Fiji's urban communities, which today comprise just over half the country's total population, are influenced by cosmopolitan middle-class ideas and practices. An ethno-historical approach indicates that class divisions are not a recent development in Fijian society. They have existed since the arrival of the first European settlers and colonial administrators, and gradually evolved in urban Fiji against the background of the development of a capitalist economy.

Under the system of indirect rule, a new chiefly class developed, which had privileged access to financial and material resources and the means of production. This in turn led to the growth of a new type of chiefly leader whose socio-political status was still based on birth rights and mechanisms of descent, but was at the same time built on education and financial capital. The emergence of a new type of Fijian chief led over time to a shift in chiefly priorities, from the interests of their respective social groups to their own. Additionally, carefully selected Fijian commoners were chosen to work in the Native Fijian Administration, thus limiting access to upward social mobility to those commoners (and chiefs) who were willing to support and cooperate with the colonial regime, and openly embrace new economic and political values and ideas. Together, these Fijian commoners and colonial chiefs served as agents of an evolving colonial capitalist economy. These beneficiaries of Fiji's colonial rule established an indigenous petit bourgeoisie whose interests are remarkably different from the values and needs of Fijians in more rural settings. However, until Fiji's independence in 1970, the social status of Fijian colonial agents remained mainly legitimised by their political rather than their economic position, and especially their dependence on the system of indirect rule (Naidu 1987; Halapua 2003; White 2006).

In post-independence Fiji, class divisions became accentuated, and they also developed a multi-ethnic dimension. For example, the eastern Fijian chiefly oligarchy (Howard 1991), together with Fijian commoners, local Europeans and the Indo-Fijian upper class (mainly Gujaratis, but also some Sikhs and Muslims), formed the engine of Ratu Sir Kamisese Mara's Alliance Party. This party dominated Fiji's political landscape until Mara and his companions lost narrowly in the 1987 elections to the Fijian Labour Party, whose political agenda focused predominantly on class issues. In the wake of the 1987 events, an urban Fijian middle class constituted of both chiefs and commoners profited from the affirmative action programmes of the Rabuka governments, and it is no surprise that the leading protagonists of the 2000 putsch attempt as well as prominent political figures of the national landscape of twenty-first-century Fiji belong in one way or another to an urban, at times multi-ethnic, Fijian community that only partially identifies with the *vaka i taukei*, the communal Fijian way of life.

In summary, European influences, the establishment of a market economy, the introduction of the system of indirect rule and, later, democratisation and the development of a political elite led to the emergence of class divisions and a steadily growing class consciousness among Fiji's multi-ethnic community. While these class issues are still perceived predominantly in racial or ethnic terms, it cannot be denied that specific groups of Indo-Fijian and ethnic Fijians share interests based on their socio-economic status. However, Fiji's coup protagonists strengthen their own political and economic position by strategically deploying a racial political rhetoric which makes most economically underprivileged Fijians or Indo-Fijians perceive themselves – at least in certain political-economic contexts – as members of a respective ethnic category rather than as an exploited economic class with similar interests and problems (Schieder 2012b: 58).[20]

From this perspective, the coups of 1987 appear as reactions against the agenda and envisioned future of the Fiji Labour Party, based on class and not ethnic identity. The coups with their ethnic rhetoric were instrumental in reinstalling the political supremacy of Fiji's chiefly class and its allies vis-à-vis other ethnic groups who had stood together at the apex of Fijian state politics until the mid 1980s. George Speight's putsch in 2000 was mainly initiated and supported by a generation of upwardly mobile Fijians who had benefited from the Rabuka years and faced economic problems and legal charges after Mahendra Chaudhry's election victory in 1999. Similarly, the

2006 military takeover was planned and staged by members of the Fijian and Indo-Fijian middle class in the capital Suva. While the coup was allegedly accomplished for the benefit of all Fijians, its agenda was mainly directed towards the capital's residents, more precisely, Fijian politicians, church and community leaders who claim to represent diverse ethnic and rural communities but ultimately reside in Suva and its surroundings and only visit their home villages infrequently.

An Integrative Perspective on Political Strategies and Actions in Fiji

I identified and discussed above three of the main social factors and divisions that fuel Fiji's political instability, and showed that Fiji's coup culture is a complex, historical and multi-layered socio-cultural phenomenon. However, by discussing Fiji's past I do not intend to argue that a there is a direct and linear connection between its history of social and cultural divisions – especially in the political sphere – and its present and future. On the contrary, the social factors outlined in the last sections serve Fiji's coup protagonists as a substrate for their political rhetoric and action. In other words, we cannot explain Fiji's coup culture by focusing on a single prime mover such as ethnic conflicts or traditional Fijian rivalries. Nor can we analyse Fiji's coup syndrome by simply acknowledging the socio-cultural complexity in Fijian politics. It is agency that makes ethnic stereotypes, class divisions or pre-colonial power struggles in their modern guise a political issue.

Furthermore, the coherence of Fiji's politics of 'tradition' and 'democracy' needs to be rethought. It is commonly argued that traditional Fijian politics has a logic of its own, and because of this one central aspect of Fiji's coup culture lies in the duality of political values, political laws and notions of political leadership. Traditional values, modes of authority and customary laws exist alongside democratic values, modern legal law and the constitution. From this perspective, traditional and democratic politics form opposing forces and lead to numerous inconsistencies.[21] However, I argue that it is necessary to question explanations which describe, for example, traditional politics and democratic politics as diametrically opposed projects. In short, the analysis of Fiji's political instability should emphasise the political reality that ties a variety of models of governance and political legitimacy together. For example, Fijian chiefs and commoners alike use politics at state level as mediating tools for traditional power struggles. They thus contest the fundamental principles of the modern state and the ideology of civic nationalism from within its own boundaries and, more importantly, they are aware of this.[22] It is thus vital to recognise the local circumstances which shape Fiji's political system and to focus on Fijians' own perceptions of what foreign observers often depict as an absolute distinction between 'tradition' and 'modernity'. This gap is, in fact, of a symbiotic nature, and it allows Fiji's coup protagonists to contextually deploy 'traditional' or 'modern' agendas in order to realise their political projects.

The case of Sitiveni Rabuka who, throughout his political career (1987 to 1999), simultaneously appeared as a flamboyant Fijian ethno-nationalist, a democrat and advocate of civic values, a member of the urban Fijian middle class, an individual political agent and loyal Fijian commoner to his paramount chief (Ratu Sir Penaia Ganilau), shows clearly that Fiji's coup protagonists are not passive figures but active agents who contextually negotiate their political and economic circumstances, and, by extension existing socio-political frameworks, to pursue their own future-oriented agendas (cf. Hermann and Kempf 2005: 309–11).

While it is obvious that all the factors and forces discussed here are amalgamated into what is commonly referred to as the coup culture, I propose to focus on the coup protagonists themselves because they, in their quality as social actors, link the many elements of this coup culture through their political actions which aim to gain, regain or maintain political power and leadership. Fiji's coup protagonists have the ability to shift between multiple identities, and develop a plurality of social roles to serve their political projects. Their identities and roles derive from different socio-cultural and political systems with specific underlying ideologies, especially the Fijian chiefly system(s), the parliamentary democracy and the political aspects of a class-based urban lifestyle, to name only the ones discussed here. The identities and roles of Fiji's coup protagonists are not fixed but changeable and hybrid, and they are shaped by local discourses of power and social relations. This plurality of social lifestyles is not exclusively limited to Fiji's political elites but is visible in broader Fijian society, as Brison has recently shown for a local community in north-eastern Viti Levu (Brison 2007). In this chapter, however, I focus on how Fiji's urban society and urban elites navigate self and belonging in this plurality of social divisions.

Given their positions of power and influence, their capacity to recruit an entourage and the ability to choose and follow a specific political strategy in specific political settings, Fiji's political elites are the focal point of the coup culture. Through their agency they possess the capacity to incorporate inter-ethnic, intra-ethnic and class divisions into manifold political discourses that simultaneously shape Fiji's socio-political instability. Without denying that in a particular context or social setting one social factor (such as inter-ethnic divisions) can gain greater political importance than others, the perspective I outline here offers an integrative explanation of the many complexities and contradictions which are an integral part of Fiji's socio-political landscape. On the one hand, these complexities and contradictions can lead to what could be best described as identity crises or role conflicts of Fiji's coup protagonists.[23] On the other hand, it is exactly this complexity of existing socio-cultural and political systems that offer Fiji's coup protagonists numerous and innovative strategies by which to pursue their political projects (Schieder 2012b: 60–61).

One of these projects is the coup culture, a powerful rhetorical device through which this integration is effected. Although the notion of coup culture was only introduced in the wake of the 2006 political crisis, it nevertheless incorporates the coups of 1987 and the putsch of 2000 because Fiji's political actors (and foreign observers alike) do not perceive Fiji's coups as single, unrelated past political events which were limited to political moves to oust a government, but as correlated benchmarks in a political continuum that is created and maintained by Fiji's political actors.

The Future of Fiji's Coup Culture

At the 2009 Fiji (Parliamentary) Update in Canberra, Katerina Teaiwa argued that analysts must become more creative in approaching Fiji's ongoing socio-political instability: 'We need more options than just "for or against" … We cannot just roll out a series of economic or political facts which paint the bleak picture we expect to see' (Teaiwa 2009). In her statement Teaiwa rightly calls for more diversity among, and collaboration between scholars and disciplines, so that the 'situation on the ground is illuminated from multiple spheres and through multiple lenses' (ibid.).

Similar claims were repeatedly voiced by those willing to discuss Fiji's coups, elections and political problems with me during my stay in Fiji. In this chapter I have responded to their claims by focusing on the socio-cultural framework of Fiji's political instability and emphasising the agency and rhetoric of those political actors who were responsible for Fiji's political takeovers in 1987, 2000 and 2006. Previous approaches to Fiji's complicated political landscape offered by political scientists, sociologists and even anthropologists (e.g. Rutz 1995; Kelly and Kaplan 2001; Norton 2009) tend to reduce Fiji's political problems to a number of dichotomous patterns, such as democracy versus tradition or ethno-nationalism versus civic nationalism, and describe Fiji's political actors as caught between different socio-political and ideological frameworks. Thus, they deny Fiji's coup protagonists the necessary vision and ability to make sense of a political situation which is more complex than discussion of an ethnic (or racial) prime-mover theory or an analysis of the limits of diametrically opposed policies can reveal.

One possible way to acknowledge agency in contemporary and future Fijian politics and incorporate a nuanced discussion of the past, culture and tradition as political resources is to re-read Fiji's political history through the political rhetoric of a coup culture. This concept stands at the very heart of Fiji's ongoing socio-political instability and affects the country and its future in various negative ways. I have attempted to argue that the coup culture is a central topic of the present but also future political strategies of Fiji's political actors. With regard to the many complexities and contradictions within Fijian society, and the various ways in which Fiji's coup protagonists make sense of them, it becomes obvious that, while the political rhetoric of the current political leaders emphasises a coup-less future for Fiji, a future-focused approach to Fiji's coup culture allows us to question the original agenda of the interim government and draw a rather pessimistic picture, a picture that may in fact not produce the coup-free political landscape as imagined by the current government. This is because Fiji's coup protagonists still frame their political agenda around ethnic sentiments, as well as regional and class discourses. To put it differently, Fiji's coup protagonists, including those who were never arrested and continue to exercise their influence quasi-anonymously, hiding behind the visible faces of 1987, 2000 and 2006, are still operating within the framework of a discourse which focuses on colour, class and custom. A coup-less future for Fiji would need to begin by questioning and dismantling past-oriented, ethno-nationalist and race-focused discourses, and by consolidating the political agendas of the many political actors in Fiji who regard the coup culture as their very own political project, and use it to shape their political futures in definite ways.

Acknowledgements

This chapter has benefited from discussions of Fiji's coup culture held in Japan throughout 2012. I thank Lynda Newland and Jon Fraenkel for their comments on an earlier draft, as well as Teresia Teaiwa, Amelia Bonea, Will Rollason and an anonymous reviewer for their useful comments and criticisms. I am also indebted to Yoshiko Ashiwa, Norio Niwa, Akira Okazaki and Steven Ratuva.

Notes

1. The following account of the events that led up to Fiji's 2006 coup and its aims and aftermath is intended only as a short summary. A detailed discussion can be found in several annual political updates on Fiji (e.g. Durutalo 2007; Fraenkel 2008, 2009, 2010; and especially in Fraenkel, Firth and Lal 2009).
2. Ethnic identities are mainly perceived in racial terms in Fiji. Yet, I argue like Emde (2005) that discourses of race in Fiji are conflated with an anthropological understanding of ethnicity because the expression of belonging and of differentiating 'us' and 'them' depends mainly on customs, traditions and languages and not on physical appearance.

3. Frank Bainimarama, 'Speech at the 62nd Session of the UN General Assembly', 29 September 2007. Retrieved from: http://www.scoop.co.nz/stories/WO0709/S00767.htm, last accessed 28 November 2013.
4. For the full text of the People's Charter for Change, Peace and Progress, see: http://www.fijipeoplescharter.com.fj/finalcharter.pdf, last accessed 14 January 2011.
5. For the full text of the decree, see: http://www.fiji.gov.fj, last accessed 26 January 2011.
6. While I acknowledge other usages of the concept 'coup culture' – for example, as a means of political mobilization by more passive political actors – I would like to emphasise that the present chapter focuses on coup culture as articulated by selected Fijian political elites. Space limitations do not allow a detailed discussion of my approach to political elites, which follows Laura Nader's call for 'studying-up' (and sideways) in addition to studying-down (Nader 1972). However, I would like to mention that by elites I mean agents or cultural brokers who, on account of their charisma, education and social status, and their political vision, all of which grants them an entourage of followers and supporters, are able to mobilize capital, be it material, ideological or human, to follow a certain strategy or goal. By doing this they develop and maintain their 'own particularistic set of interests, norms and practices to differentiate [themselves] from the masses' (Shore 2002: 2–3). For anthropologists, who often have a rather ambivalent relationship to the study of (modern) political elites due to what Nader describes as ethical problems (Nader 1972: 294, 303) and Shore as a methodological dilemma (Shore 2002: 10), the perspective I outline here can be of great value to illuminate contemporary political conflicts in Oceania. We need to engage with modern political elitism and elite agencies because only through in-depth studies of how elites mobilise the past as well as cultural resources for their political projects can complex political divisions and conflicts such as those in Fiji be fully understood. Moreover, focusing on the agency of political elites serves as an excellent starting point for rethinking mechanisms of the creation and maintenance of social identities in a country where the political elite is constituted of networks that cross ethnic, regional, kinship and class divisions.
7. I use Rapport and Overing's definition of agency as 'individual consciousness, its ability to constitute and reconstitute itself, and … the capability, the power, to be a source and originator of acts' (Rapport and Overing 2000: 1; cf. Barnard and Spencer 1996: 595). Agency allows individuals (social agents) to act within the framework of a number of choices. I consider agency and structure, and by extension culture, as complementing elements of social existence. Agency allows social agents to navigate and negotiate structure and to contextually create new socio-cultural boundaries and meanings without changing the structural framework fundamentally. As Ratner points out, 'agency depends

upon cultural [social] processes for its realization, forms culture [and social groups], and has a cultural [social] form' (Ratner 2000: 413). Thus, an anthropological engagement with social actors urges us to understand the social norms and social divisions which underpin their agency and how these norms and divisions are negotiated, reproduced or transformed by social agents (cf. Ortner 2006: 129–54).

8. In this chapter I focus particularly on the indigenous Fijian perspective. I have discussed the political implications of the heterogeneity and social divisions of Fiji's society from an Indo-Fijian perspective elsewhere (Schieder 2011).
9. In addition, the term coup culture was recently used by Siollun (2009) to refer to Nigeria's political instability.
10. Interview with Sitiveni Rabuka, Suva, 4 January 2009.
11. Interview with Ratu Joni Madraiwiwi, Suva, 27 November 2008.
12. According to the 2007 census, Fiji's total population of 837,271 comprises 475,739 Fijians (56.8 per cent) and 313,798 Indo-Fijians (37.5 per cent), with the remaining 47,734 (5.7 per cent) coming from other ethnic groups. Urban residents comprise 50.7 per cent of the total population.
13. The Fijian word *taukei* describes a free-born native person and/or the owner of a thing (material or non-material) in the traditional context. As a class, the *i taukei* represent the landowners who share common descent and are considered to be the first to have arrived in a certain locality. Any other individual who arrives later is called a *vulagi*, a 'visitor' or 'foreigner'. *Vulagi* are only allowed to use land but do not have rights of ownership. The relationship between *vulagi* and *taukei* is best understood in terms of guest and host. Within the context of the Taukei Movement, the relationship between *taukei* and *vulagi* acquired a new meaning, with Indo-Fijians regarded as 'guests' who had exceeded the rights ascribed to them by their Fijian hosts (Ravuvu 1991).
14. The term Indo-Fijian refers to the descendants of different groups of migrants who came to Fiji from South Asia. The first to arrive were indentured labourers (*girmitiyas*). They were recruited from various parts of North and South India (present-day Bihar, Uttar Pradesh, Bengal, Tamil Nadu, Andhra Pradesh and Kerala). The term Indo-Fijian also incorporates migrants from Gujarat and Punjab (Chauhan 1988).
15. For a detailed discussion on this issue, see Eller (2002).
16. For a broader picture, the disputes and divisions between east and west Fiji (Bose and Fraenkel 2007) or coastal Fiji and the hinterland (Nicole 2006) have to be taken into account.
17. Steven Ratuva (personal communication).
18. The *matanitu* Kubuna and its political centre of Bau is one of the three traditional Fijian confederacies. The other two are the Tovata ko Lau and Burebasaga.
19. While the Mara dynasty was prominently involved in the 2006 coup and succeeding interim governments, since 2010 this influential group has lost

its grip on Fijian state politics. For example, Ratu Sir Epeli Ganilau, Ratu Sir Kamisese Mara's son-in-law, resigned from his ministerial post in 2010. Mara's son Ratu Tevita fled to Tonga in May 2011 after he was charged with mutiny and accused of aligning himself with a group of fellow officers and politicians who aimed to overthrow Bainimarama.

20. The majority of Indo-Fijians are still farmers, some of whom belong to the poorest strata of Fiji's population despite the stereotypical political rhetoric of the economically successful Indo-Fijian. On the other hand, a significant number of Indo-Fijians can also be found among the working and urban middle class, sharing with their Fijian counterparts common economic and political interests. In short, this distinction undermines the idea of monolithic ethnic identities in Fiji. It is my observation that, especially in urban areas, class issues overcome ethnic sentiments in many day-to-day situations.
21. See e.g. Lawson (1991). The tradition versus democracy debate reflected in analyses which regard ethnic conflicts as the prime mover of Fijian politics is no more than a scholarly echo of crude popular descriptions of island economic and socio-political systems which fail to allow local actors alternative political futures for their country, and especially for themselves.
22. I have offered a critical perspective on older anthropological studies on agency in Fijian politics elsewhere (cf. Schieder 2012b: 59–60).
23. Miyazaki (2000, 2004) refers to an 'abeyance of agency' in a different Fijian context.

References

Barnard, A. and J. Spencer (eds). 1996. *Encyclopaedia of Social and Cultural Anthropology*. London: Routledge.

Besnier, N. 2009. 'Modernity, Cosmopolitanism and the Emergence of Middle Classes in Tonga', *Contemporary Pacific* 21(2): 215–62.

_______ 2011. *On the Edge of the Global: Modern Anxieties in a Pacific Island Nation*. Stanford: Stanford University Press.

Bhim, M. 2011. Stifling Opposition: An Analysis of the Approach of the Fiji Government after the 2006 Coup. State, Society and Governance in Melanesia Discussion Paper 6. Canberra: Australian National University.

Bose, A., and J. Fraenkel. 2007. Whatever Happened to Western Separatism? In J. Fraenkel and S. Firth (eds), *From Election to Coup in Fiji: The 2006 Campaign and its Aftermath*, pp.225–42. Canberra: Australian National University Press.

Brison, K. 2007. *Our Wealth Is Loving Each Other: Self and Society in Fiji*. Lanham, MD: Lexington Books.

Chauhan, I.S. 1988. *Leadership and Social Cleavages*. Jaipur: Rawat Publishers.

Clunie, F. 2003. *Fijian Weapons and Warfare*. Suva: Fiji Museum.

Dean, E., and S. Ritova. 1988. *Rabuka: No Other Way*. Sydney: Doubleday.

Durutalo, A. 2005. Of Roots and Offshoots: Fijian Political Thinking, Dissent and the Formation of Political Parties 1960–1999. Ph.D. diss. Canberra: Australian National University.

——— 2007. Fiji. *Contemporary Pacific* 19(2): 578–82.

Eller, J. 2002. *From Culture to Ethnicity to Conflict: An Anthropological Perspective on International Ethnic Conflict.* Ann Arbor: University of Michigan Press.

Emde, S. 2005. Feared Rumours and Rumours of Fear. *Oceania* 75(4): 387–402.

Firth, S., and J. Fraenkel. 2009. The Fiji Military and Ethno-nationalism: Analyzing the Paradox. In J. Fraenkel and S. Firth (eds), *From Election to Coup in Fiji: The 2006 Campaign and its Aftermath*, pp.117–38. Canberra: Australian National University Press.

Fraenkel, J. 2000. The Clash of Dynasties and the Rise of Demagogues: Fiji's Tauri Vakaukauwa of May 2000. *Journal of Pacific History* 35(3): 295–308.

——— 2006. Regulating Bipolar Divisions: Ethnic Structure, Public Sector Inequality and Electoral Engineering in Fiji. In Y. Bangura (ed.), *Ethnic Inequalities and Public Sector Governance*, pp.73–97. London: Macmillan.

——— 2008. Fiji. *Contemporary Pacific* 20(2): 450–60.

——— 2009. Fiji. *Contemporary Pacific* 21(2): 337–52.

——— 2010. Fiji. *Contemporary Pacific* 22(2): 415–33.

Fraenkel, J., S. Firth and B. Lal (eds). 2009. *The 2006 Military Takeover in Fiji: A Coup to End all Coups?* Canberra: Australian National University Press.

Furnivall, J. 1948. *Colonial Policy and Practice: A Comparative Study of Burma and Netherlands India.* New York: New York University Press.

Garrett, J. 1997. *Where Nets Were Cast: Christianity in Oceania Since World War II.* Suva: Institute of Pacific Studies.

Geraghty, P. 1983. *The History of the Fijian Languages.* Honolulu: University of Hawaii Press.

Halapua, W. 2003. Militarism and Moral Decay in Fiji. *Fijian Studies* 1: 105–26.

Hermann, E. and W. Kempf. 2005. Introduction to Relations in Multicultural Fiji: The Dynamics of Articulations, Transformations and Positionings. *Oceania* 75(4): 309–24.

Howard, M. 1991. *Fiji: Race and Politics in an Island State.* Vancouver: University of British Columbia Press.

Kaplan, M. 2004. Neither Traditional nor Foreign: Dialogics of Power and Agency in Fijian History. In H. Jebens (ed.), *Cargo, Cult, and Cultural Critique*, pp.59–78. Honolulu: University of Hawaii Press.

Kelly, J., and M. Kaplan. 2001. *Represented Communities: Fiji and World Decolonization.* Chicago: University of Chicago Press.

Lal, B. 1992. *Broken Waves: A History of the Fiji Islands in the Twentieth Century.* Honolulu: University of Hawai'i Press.

Lawson, S. 1991. *The Failure of Democratic Politics in Fiji.* Oxford: Clarendon Press.

_______ 2004. The Military versus Democracy in Fiji: Problems of Contemporary Political Development. In R.J. May and V. Selochan (eds), *The Military and Democracy in Asia and the Pacific*, pp.131–47. Canberra: Australian National University Press.

Legge, J.D. 1958. *Britain in Fiji 1858–1880*. London: MacMillan.

Miyazaki, H. 2000. Faith and Its Fulfillment: Agency, Exchange, and the Fijian Asthetics of Completion. *American Ethnologist* 27(1): 31–51.

_______ 2004. *The Method of Hope: Anthropology, Philosophy, and Fijian Knowledge*. Stanford: Stanford University Press.

Nader, L. 1972. Up the Anthropologist: Perspectives Gained from Studying-up. In D. Hymes (ed.), *Reinventing Anthropology*, pp.284–311. New York: Random House.

Naidu, V. 1987. Fiji: The State, Labour and Aristocracy and the Fiji Labour Party. In R. Crocombe (ed.), *Class and Culture in the South Pacific*, pp.210–29. Suva: Institute of Pacific Studies.

Newbury C., and D. Newbury. 1999. A Catholic Mass in Kigali: Contested Views of the Genocide and Ethnicity in Rwanda. *Canadian Journal of African Studies* 33(2/3): 292–328.

Nicole, R. 2006. Disturbing History: Aspects of Resistance in Early Colonial Fiji 1874–1914. Ph.D. diss. Christchurch: University of Canterbury.

Norton, R. 2009. The Historical Trajectory of Fijian Power: State, Society and Governance in Fiji. Melanesia Discussion Paper 6. Canberra: Australian National University.

Ortner, S. 2006. *Anthropology and Social Theory: Culture, Power, and the Acting Subject*. Durham, NC: Duke University Press.

Rapport, N., and J. Overing. 2000. *Social and Cultural Anthropology: The Key Concepts*. London: Routledge.

Ratner, C. 2000. Agency and Culture. *Journal of the Theory of Social Behaviour* 30(4): 413–34.

Ratuva, S. 2008. Issues and Discussion Paper: Ending the Coup Culture. National Task Team 1 on Good Governance. Working Group 3: The Role of Fiji's Security Forces in National Development. Unpublished paper, by courtesy of author.

Ravuvu, A. 1991. *The Facade of Democracy: Fijian Struggle for Political Control 1830–1987*. Suva: Institute of Pacific Studies.

Rechtman, R. 1992. The Evolution of Sociopolitical Complexity in the Fiji Islands. Ph.D. diss. Los Angeles: University of California.

Robertson, R., and A. Tamanisau. 1988. *Fiji: Shattered Coups*. Leichhardt: Pluto Press.

Rutz, H. 1995. Occupying the Headwaters of Tradition: Rhetorical Strategies of Nation Making in the Pacific. In R. Foster (ed.), *Nation Making: Emergent Identities in Postcolonial Melanesia*, pp.71–93. Ann Arbor: University of Michigan Press.

Sahlins, M. 2004. *Apologies to Thucydides: Understanding History as Culture and Vice Versa*. Chicago: University of Chicago Press.

Sayes, S. 1982. Cakaudrove: Ideology and Reality in a Fijian Confederation. Ph.D. diss. Canberra: Australian National University.

Scarr, D. 1988. *Fiji: The Politics of Illusion. The Military Coups in Fiji*. Kensington: New South Wales Press.

Schieder, D. 2011. Jenseits der pluralen Gesellschaft. Zur politischen Relevanz der Heterogenität in Fidschis 'indischer' Bevölkerung. *Mitteillungen der anthropologischen Gesellschaft in Wien* 141: 277–90.

——— 2012a. *Das Phänomen der* coup culture*: Politische Konflikte auf den Fidschi-Inseln*. Wiesbaden: Harrassowitz.

——— 2012b. 'Fiji Has a Coup Culture': Discussing Fiji's Ongoing Political Instabilty. *Paideuma* 58: 45–67.

Shore, C. 2002. Introduction: Towards an Anthropology of Elites. In C. Shore and S. Nugent (eds), *Elite Cultures: Anthropological Perspectives*, pp.1–21. London: Routledge.

Siollun, M. 2009. *Oil, Politics and Violence: Nigeria's Military Coup Culture (1966–1976)*. New York: Algora.

Sutherland, W. 1992. *Beyond the Politics of Race: An Alternative History of Fiji to 1992*. Canberra: Australian National University Press.

Tarte, S. 2009. Reflections on Fiji's 'Coup Culture'. In J. Fraenkel, S. Firth and B. Lal (eds), *The 2006 Military Takeover in Fiji: A Coup to End all Coups?* pp.409–14. Canberra: Australian National University Press.

Teaiwa, K. 2009. 'Fiji Future Requires Diversity of Views: Expert'. Paper delivered at the Fiji (Parliamentary) Update meeting, Australian National University, Canberra. Retrieved from: http://news.anu.edu.au/?p=1525, last accessed 28 November 2013.

Tuimaleali'ifano, M. 2000. Veiqati Vaka Viti and the Fiji Islands Elections in 1999. *Journal of Pacific History* 35(3): 253–67.

——— 2007. Indigenous Title Disputes: What They Meant for the 2006 Election. In J. Fraenkel and S. Firth (eds), *From Election to Coup in Fiji: The 2006 Campaign and its Aftermath*, pp.262–71. Canberra: Australian National University Press.

Weber, E. 2008. *Fidschi: Diskurse und Akteure der Gewalt*. Neuendettelsau: Pazifik Informationsstelle.

White, C. 2006. Moving up the Ranks: Chiefly Status, Prestige, and Schooling in Colonial Fiji. *History of Education Quarterly* 46(4): 532–70.

9

The Devouring of the Placenta

The Criss-crossing and Confluence of Cosmological, Geomorphological, Ecological and Economic Cycles of Destruction and Repair in Ruatoria, Aotearoa/New Zealand

Dave Robinson

The People, the Parent and the Placenta

In February 2009, shortly before completing my ethnographic field research, I met with Papa Anaru at his home on the outskirts of Ruatoria, a small rural township on the East Coast of Aotearoa/New Zealand's North Island, where the Māori *iwi* (kin group), Ngāti Porou, are *tangata whenua*, 'people of the land'. My meeting with Papa Anaru, a Ngāti Porou *kaumātua* ('elder'), had been arranged to discuss, amongst many other topics, his perspectives on Ruatoria's resident group of Ngāti Porou Rastafari, upon whom my ethnographic research centred.

Having at that time completed nearly twenty-five months of field research among the Ngāti Porou Rastafari who self-identify as the Dread, I was already well acquainted with many aspects of Māori culture. Nevertheless, as we were midway through these long and wide-ranging discussions, Papa Anaru reminded me – as Māori are often inclined – that as *tangata whenua*, Ngāti Porou are also the *kaitiaki* (custodians) of the East Coast. From a Māori perspective, he explained, it is therefore Ngāti Porou's cultural obligation to manage the interdependent well-being of people and the natural-cum-spiritual environment they inhabit. Papa Anaru then followed his reminder with the announcement that in June of that year he would be leading a group of Ngāti Porou on what he described as a 'journey to do the cleansing. The total cleansing of the mountain, the river, the areas we have to go to bring back harmony'.

Papa Anaru's intriguing announcement was not, however, the first mention I had heard of his planned cleansing ceremony. The previous day, one of his close associates had pre-empted my introduction to this topic of discussion when revealing her intention to participate in a ceremony being organised by Papa Anaru for the specific purpose of lifting the sickness afflicting *te tangata me te whenua* ('the people and the land'). I was informed that the need for the ceremony had arisen as a direct consequence of Ngāti Porou's continuing failures as *tangata whenua*. More specifically, Ngāti Porou's failure to respect the spiritual interdependence of this term's composite elements – *tangata*, meaning 'people' and *whenua*, a term that not only represents the Māori variant of the widespread Austronesian term for 'land', but also possesses the parallel meaning of 'placenta'.

In the context of Papa Anaru's planned cleansing of the mountain and river, the parallel meaning of placenta is particularly instructive for two important reasons. Firstly, the conceptualisation of land as placenta – the organ that in mammals develops from both maternal and embryonic tissues during pregnancy – situates land as something analogous to the interface that enables the unborn child to metabolise sustenance from its mother. As such, it is arguable that land, from the Māori cosmological perspective, corresponds to placenta, because, like placenta, land makes possible the interconnectedness between the recipient of nurture – namely, each Māori kin group and the primordial female parent, Papatūānuku, the Earth Mother.

The second reason is in direct relation to the first. For recognition that the existence of *tangata whenua* is contingent upon the exchange of metabolic substance between the body of Papatūānuku and the bodies of the kin group leaves one better placed to appreciate the concerns that gave rise to Papa Anaru's organisation of a cleansing ceremony. I contend that it was the cosmological requirement to preserve the interconnectedness between the kin group and Papatūānuku that underlies Papa Anaru's and his fellow participants' obligation to restore the harmony that had previously existed between Ngāti Porou and their *whenua papatipu* (ancestral land).

Furthermore, as *kaitiaki* (custodians) of ancestral land, Ngāti Porou's obligations can neither be taken lightly nor overlooked without incurring the wrath of *atua* (supernatural beings, often glossed 'gods') who preside over the dominions of the natural-cum-spiritual environment. Indeed, one of several ways Ngāti Porou articulate this obligation to manage the interdependence between the people of the land and their ancestral land is through the proverb: *Toitū te marae a Tāne, Toitū te marae a Tangaroa, Toitū te iwi* (meaning, 'Be undisturbed the house of Tāne, be undisturbed the house of Tangaroa, be undisturbed the kin group').[1] Here, the two houses that Ngāti Porou are urged not to disturb for fear of disturbing their kin group are the dominions of the *atua* Tāne and Tangaroa, the divine guardians of (native) forests and ocean respectively.

From the perspective of those intending to participate in Papa Anaru's cleansing ceremony, the East Coast's native forests have been subjected to unremitting disturbance since the widespread deforestation that accompanied the adoption of European farming practices. What is more, the disturbance of Ruatoria's surrounding forests also necessitated the disturbance of the nearby Waiapu River, from whose riverbed increasingly large quantities of ore is continually being extracted to repair the region's roads. The cumulative impact of these environmental disturbances has led many among the cleansing ceremony's intended participants to demonstrate that which Alfred Gell dubbed the Māori predisposition towards 'divine victimage' (Gell 1993: 242).[2] In this instance, Ngāti Porou anxieties associated with the retribution of the gods had given rise to a belief that the rivers are devouring the land.

It is also significant that, with the exception of the numerous farms that populate the East Coast, Ruatoria and its neighbouring settlements are all either located along the shoreline adjacent to the mouths of rivers and streams, or in close proximity to floodplains situated within fifteen miles of the ocean. Ruatoria itself is located approximately four miles from the coast, on the southern plain of the Waiapu River Valley. Given these settlement characteristics and the regular occurrence of landslides in the region, it is not surprising that grave concerns surrounding the river's facilitation of land into the ocean are rendered paramount in local discourse.

Papa Anaru had explained that the cleansing ceremony would entail the recital of *karakia* (ritual chants) and the application of water to purify the land. As previously stated, the aim would be to demonstrate to the gods and ancestors Ngāti Porou's acknowledgement of the sacred life-giving properties of the land, its waterways and native forests, while simultaneously placating Papatūānuku for the wrongs being inflicted upon her. Together, these measures were deemed an important first step in recommencing Ngāti Porou's responsibility of *kaitiakitanga* (guardianship) over their ancestral land. The men, I was informed, would initiate proceedings at the summit of the Ngāti Porou's sacred mountain, Hikurangi Maunga, and along the watercourses of the Tapuaeroa and Waiapu rivers to the tiny coastal settlement of Rangitukia. From there the proceedings would then be handed over to the women, whose role it would be to conclude the ceremony at the point where the mouth of the Waiapu River issues into the southern Pacific Ocean.

On the day that followed my meeting with Papa Anaru, I shared my newfound awareness of the cleansing ceremony with two members of the Dread. The first to respond was Te Hokowhitu, who immediately dismissed any chance of the ceremony's success, owing to its failure to offer adequate placation to the gods and ancestors. Then it was the turn of Te Ahi, who is regarded by most as the principal figure among the Dread. He deliberated carefully before opining: 'Our *kaumātua* (elders), they know *tikanga* (literally, 'correct ways', glossed as custom), and they're good for a *mōteatea* (traditional chant). They can calm the sea when it's a rough day and people are going like this'. Te Ahi accompanied the conclusion of this sentence by gesticulating the uncertainty of the people by quivering the down-turned palm of his outstretched right hand, before briefly pausing to continue. 'You know, they're good for that, but at the same time…' Te Ahi then winced as he suspended the sentence with his thoughts poised in the same mode of careful deliberation from which his response had first emerged.

The purpose of this introduction has been to detail the ongoing anxieties that have arisen in response to a perceived deterioration in the spiritual interdependence between Ngāti Porou and their ancestral land. Moreover, having adopted the idiom of the 'devouring of the placenta' as a heuristic starting point, I now situate the Dread's long-standing, yet evolving strategies to combat the devouring of the placenta within the context of Papa Anaru's cleansing ceremony and approximately a century and a half of European settlement on the East Coast of Aotearoa/New Zealand. I will show that where once the Dread's approach motivated destructive forms of direct action against farms owned by Pākehā (New Zealanders of European descent), the group is now formulating what they refer to as their 'plan' or 'blueprint', which allows for potential confluence to emerge between streams of Māori and Pākehā thought previously assumed incompatible. In this regard, the Dread's formulation of an alternative 'blueprint' to that with which they first set out reflects that which the famed Ngāti Porou scholar, Āpirana Ngata, characterised as the long held Māori recognition that their communities must continually adapt in order to survive and thrive in the face of change.[3]

Somewhat reflective of Ngata's position, the underlying argument being advanced in this chapter is that it is neither inevitable nor inconceivable that the seemingly opposed cosmological understandings and/or economic agendas of the Dread (and by extension Māori) need continue to exist in a tensive relationship with the New Zealand settler state. Rather, the intention here is to extricate the historic criss-crossing of a long assumed antithesis between Māori cosmological understandings and Western scientific conceptions of geomorphology, ecology and economic practices. I will show that there now exists the potential for future ecological and economic confluence to emerge between the Dread, their Ngāti Porou neighbours in Ruatoria and key aspects of New Zealand government policy concerning land use, with which the group were previously opposed.

It is equally important to note that underpinning the approach to my argument is Jørgen Prytz Johansen's classic observation that 'there is a fundamental difference between our [the European] experience of time and that of the Māori' (Johansen 1954: 152–53). Subsequent authors have since enlivened Johansen's observation by contrasting the Euro-American model of linear historical time with the intrinsic double aspect of its Māori counterpart. From the Māori perspective, the dimensions of 'the past' (the ancestral world) and the central concern of this collection, 'the future' (the world of the living), are collapsed into a single field of unified knowledge, which encompasses individuals within a framework that is both historic and ahistoric.

Individually, the Māori past and the Māori future are each identified by Māori as bearing a paradoxical force of their own. The past, designated *nga rā o mua* (the days in front), is conceived as being to the fore of human consciousness, because only the past is perceptible, while the complimentary term *kei muri* denotes both the future and that which lies behind, as the future cannot be seen (Metge 1976: 70; Walker 1993: 6; Binney 1995: 507). As a corollary, the Māori, says Johansen, 'relives history' (1954: 161; see also Sahlins 1987: 58). Therefore, Māori individuals, writes Ranginui Walker, are conceptualised as 'traveling backwards in time to the future, with the present unfolding in front as a continuum into the past' (Walker 1993: 6). Similarly, this essay confronts the issue of the Ngāti Porou future by, at various points, engaging with the Ngāti Porou past.

In constructing the argument, I shall begin with a brief outline of the Dread before continuing my exploration of prevailing Māori cosmological understandings pertaining to the significance, relatedness and origin of land. These Māori conceptions will then be juxtaposed with various counter representations of Aotearoa/New Zealand's geomorphology and the origins of human settlement offered by the scientific approaches of late-nineteenth-century Western anthropologists and geologists, and twentieth-century farming and commercial forestry practices. Finally, I will illuminate why and how, from the Dread's perspective, the imperative to restore native forests is considered key to reasserting the interconnectedness of people and land in both a literal and a cosmological sense.

Both, the Dread and the supporters of Papa Anaru's cleansing ceremony seemingly agree that what is at stake for Ngāti Porou is a return to the harmonious state of nurture that previously existed between *tangata* (people) and *whenua* (placenta/land). Nevertheless, as the responses of Te Ahi and Te Hokowhitu of the Dread imply, the two approaches differ quite considerably. For, as I will now discuss, in contrast to the ceremonial prowess that would be on display in Papa Anaru's cleansing of the mountain and river, the Dread's pursuit of cosmological objectives begins by targeting the practical and material requirements of Ngāti Porou on the East Coast.

Alienating the Placenta

Between the mid 1980s and early 1990s, the Dread targeted numerous pastoral and agricultural farms owned by Pākehā with a spate of direct action that was designed to render these enterprises commercially unviable. The Dread's opposition to local Pākehā pastoralists and agriculturalists was fuelled by decades of simmering Māori discord over the alienation of Ngāti Porou *whenua papatipu* (ancestral land), appropriated by Pākehā settlers during the late nineteenth and early twentieth centuries. It was those tracts of *whenua papatipu* allegedly appropriated using the disputed practice of leasing in perpetuity which were the specific focus of the Dread's direct action.

During the mid nineteenth century, already simmering disputes surrounding the legitimacy of many land transactions between Māori and Pākehā erupted following the British settler state's introduction of the Native Land Acts of 1862 and 1865. In essence, both acts were explicitly designed to dismantle 'the communism of tribal right' (Webster 1990: 206; see also Ward 1974: 148; Williams 1999: 70–71) exercised by customary Māori land titles, and supplanting it with a system based 'as nearly as possible [on] the ownership of land according to British law'.[4] These acts empowered *rangatira* (chiefs) to sell communal land, held in trust on behalf of their respective *hapū* (sub-tribe) and/or *iwi* (tribe) (Sinclair 1957; Goldman 1970; Ballara 1982; Mahuika 1992; Rosenfeld 1999).

Drawing on nineteenth-century Māori and settler accounts, academics have argued that in many cases the *rangatira* designated as agents in these early land transactions had not intended the absolute alienation of their land, but had only allocated *tuku whenua* (land use rights), which were not transferable. Rather, land rights afforded by the principle of *tuku whenua* were contingent upon its continued occupation or use by those receiving it, and were premised on the Māori cultural understanding that the land would eventually be returned. As the commander of a US expedition, Charles Wilkes, recorded in 1840:

> So far as the chiefs understand the agreement, they think they have not alienated any of their rights to the soil, but consider it only a personal grant, not transferable. In the interview I had with [a Ngā Puhi leader named] Pomare … I found he was not under the impression that he had given up his authority, or any portion of his

land permanently; the latter he said he could not do, as it belonged to all his tribe. (Wilkes 1850: 376)

Accounts such as the example given above support the notion that lands, which non-Māori had mistakenly (Metge 1998) or duplicitously (Mutu 1992) considered to be *hoko* (rendered as to 'buy', 'trade', 'exchange') under the conditions of freehold title, were merely intended as *tuku* (meaning to 'allow', 'lease' or 'let go').

On the East Coast, long-standing Ngāti Porou grievances concerning the alienation of Māori lands by European settlers had been communicated to the Dread by some of the group's *kaumātua* (elders). For the Dread, such grievances possess a dual emphasis. Firstly, the Dread claim modern farming practices introduced by Pākehā appropriators of Ngāti Porou ancestral land are destroying the material and spiritual environment. Secondly, the Dread hold the Pākehā privatisation of ancestral land responsible for undermining Ngāti Porou's autochthonous relationship to what had traditionally been communal land, by alienating Ngāti Porou from access to numerous spiritually and cosmologically significant sites, such as the kin group's ancestral mountain, Hikurangi Maunga.

In battling to regain access to Hikurangi Maunga and other spiritually significant sites appropriated for farmland, a key strategy employed in the Dread's campaign of direct action entailed land repossessions[5] and the cutting of boundary fences that demarcated disputed lands. In so doing, the Dread repudiated Pākehā land acquisitions by making unimpaired incursions onto 'privately owned' farmland, while defending themselves against accusations of trespassing and vandalism with the assertion of having an ancestral birthright to roam freely about their kin group's lands. However, in spite of the Dread's actions being initially directed towards Pākehā landowners, events in and around Ruatoria soon escalated to the point where they subsumed and divided the entire town in which the vast majority of residents, Ngāti Porou and Pākehā alike, are closely related kin.

Throughout the numerous confrontations that followed, many members of the Dread were repeatedly jailed for their actual or alleged involvement in a litany of offences. Alongside convictions for trespassing and criminal damage, members of the Dread were also imprisoned for acts of livestock theft, assault, possession of cannabis, an incident that involved the kidnapping of a local police officer and a series of arson attacks that involved the burning of more than thirty buildings. The cumulative effect of these events, in conjunction with the Dread's unorthodox Ngāti Porou-Rastafari identity, resulted in the group's virtual ostracism by the overwhelming number of residents among Ruatoria's majority Ngāti Porou and minority Pākehā community. Nevertheless, a tiny, albeit significant minority of the

Dread's exploits were appreciated by some small sections of Ruatoria's Ngāti Porou community. For example, the Dread's late 1980s campaign to repossess Hikurangi Maunga on behalf of Ngāti Porou is credited in some local quarters as having kick-started the process that, in November 1990, saw the return of the mountain from a New Zealand state-owned forest park to Ngāti Porou ownership. In the words of a prominent Ruatoria resident with whom I spoke: 'One of the good things about the Rastas was that, because of them, loads of Pākehā sold up their land and left. This enabled us [Ngāti Porou] to buy our land back. Buying land is not the right way to get the land, but at least we got our land back'.

Far less appreciated, however, were the Dread's overtures to rename Hikurangi Maunga, which, from the Dread's Rastafari[6] perspective, corresponds to the Mount Zion of the Old Testament. On many separate occasions, members of the Dread independently conveyed this understanding to me in the following, almost identical terms: 'The Bible says Zion is a mountain in the east. Not the Near East or the Middle East, but the Far East, and where's further east than Aotearoa?' Cumulatively, therefore, Hikurangi Maunga possesses a dual Rastafari and Ngāti Porou significance for the Dread. On the one hand, as a biblical symbol of God's covenant, communicated in the verse: 'They that trust in the Lord shall be as mount Zion which cannot be removed, but abideth for ever' (Psalms 125: 1), and on the other hand, as I will now discuss, as a pronouncement of Ngāti Porou's autochthonous origins from the depths of the ocean.

Dismissing the Placenta

The reasons underlying why the retention of Māori land was – and by many including the Dread – is still considered to be of paramount importance, and therefore deemed inalienable, are buttressed by *whakapapa* (genealogy). This *whakapapa* connects *tangata* (people) to *whenua* (land) through a long sequence of *tīpuna* (ancestors) and *atua* (supernatural beings) to the progenitors of all things, Ranginui, the Sky Father, and Papatūānuku, the Earth Mother. Understood as such, Māori sensitivities surrounding land tenure reveal themselves as far more than mere property claims, but are in fact cosmological statements detailing the autochthonous history of people, the tangible world they inhabit and the all-pervasive spiritual environment with which they coexist.

Having said that, many early European chroniclers dismissed Māori cosmological explanations of the relationship between people and land, either on the grounds that they were mere analogies or with an air of disdain. Consider, for example, the opinion expressed by the Reverend William Yate of the Church Missionary Society, who in the early nineteenth century stated:

'Their ideas of Mawe (Māui), the being who, they tell us, fished-up the island from the bottom of the sea, are truly ridiculous' (Yate 1835: 142). A similar perspective was forwarded by the colonial governor of New Zealand, George Grey, in his dismissal of ancient Māori narratives as 'puerile' and 'absurd'.[7] The alternative dismissal of origin narratives as inherently symbolic was encapsulated by the scholar Peter Buck's appraisal that Māori cosmology constituted 'a Polynesian figure of speech', which later generations came to adopt as literal explanations (Buck 1939: 47; 1974: 5). In the words of Pomare and Cowan, this assumed language of metaphor was illustrative of the Polynesian fondness 'for clothing facts with a garb of poetic fiction and allegory' (Pomare and Cowan 1987: 14).

Between these periods of mid-nineteenth-century dismissal by disdain and mid twentieth-century dismissal by analogy, the Austrian geologist Eduard Suess had offered a substitute scientific explanation for the geological origin of Aotearoa/New Zealand. Suess proposed that Aotearoa/New Zealand's two principle islands emerged between 130 and 85 million years ago during the break up of an ancient southern hemisphere super-continent called Gondwanaland (Suess 1904). Shortly after the publication of Suess's work, a perhaps lesser known, although equally intriguing formulation was forwarded by William Morris Davis, who developed a theory concerning the evolution of landforms, called the 'geomorphic cycle' or 'erosion cycle'. Davis proposed that the geological history of all terrestrial landscapes progressed through a predetermined sequence of modifications, which he termed 'construction', 'destruction' and 'baselevel' (Davis 1894: 72). The cycle was described as beginning with the stage of 'youth', which marked the development of uplift to produce mountains, hills and valleys. Next proceeded the stage of 'maturity', characterised by a roughening of land that induced 'the channeling of streams' that widened valleys until they eventually consumed the intervening hills. In the final, 'old-age' stage of the cycle, landscapes were reduced to an eroded sea level plain called a 'peneplain'. The geomorphic cycle was then assumed to recommence with the uplift of youth (Davis 1888: 15).

Alongside European dismissals of Māori cosmological explanations surrounding the origin of Aotearoa/New Zealand, the late nineteenth century also witnessed notable theories to explain the peopling of Aotearoa/New Zealand. Among them, that of Edward Tregear (1885) provoked heated debate among academics in both Europe and New Zealand with his hypothesis that the island's Māori inhabitants were in fact migratory offshoots of the Aryan race descended through peoples of India. However, the dominant late-nineteenth-century explanation of Māori racial origin and migration was that which the ethnologist Stephenson Percy Smith first advanced in a three-part series of articles (Smith 1898a, 1898b, 1899).[8] From collecting and analysing tribal *whakapapa* (genealogies), Smith calculated estimates of 'average' Māori life spans for each generation. From the resulting dates and figures, Smith composed the 'Great Fleet' narrative, which chronicled the Māori colonisation of Aotearoa/New Zealand by successive waves of Polynesian immigrants.

Smith's chronology began with the Polynesian discovery of Aotearoa/New Zealand in AD 925 by Kupe, a navigator from Ra'iatea in the Society Islands, who was followed by the first settlers, Toi and his grandson Whatonga, in the mid twelfth century. The sequence is then said to have culminated in 1350, when a fleet of seven canoes, which Smith labelled the 'Great Fleet', set out on a colonising expedition from their ancient Polynesian homeland of Hawaiki. Smith's chronicle remained the authoritative account of Māori migration and the human settlement of Aotearoa/New Zealand until the final quarter of the twentieth century. Following this, however, numerous authors (e.g. Simmons 1976; Sorrensen 1979) challenged Smith's textual reconstruction as a misreading of various tribal traditions, and accused him of amalgamating them into one tidy but completely fabricated account. In recent decades, further discoveries in geology, archaeology, linguistics and ecology have fuelled new research, and informed the development of theories surrounding the migration of Polynesian peoples from South America. Nevertheless, few Māori appear prepared to unequivocally relinquish their Hawaiki canoe narratives for alternative scientific explanations. A case in point is Ngāti Porou's explanations of their *tangata whenua* origins, which remain inextricably linked to Aotearoa/New Zealand's geomorphology, and as I will now discuss, are often articulated in far simpler terms than any proposed by Western science.

Hanging from the Fishhook of Māui

My initial encounter with Ngāti Porou's origin narrative occurred during the early period of my research, when my rearticulation of the orthodox Hawaiki migration narrative to a member of the Dread was summarily met with a swift rebuttal, delivered in a gentle and earnest tone: 'That may be so, but we of Ngāti Porou have always been here. We have been here since Māui fished up Te Ika a Māui (literally, The Fish of Māui)'. Over the course of my fieldwork I came to appreciate the Dread's affinity with Māui as penetrating far deeper than the cultural pride or enjoyment garnered from the mythic hero of metaphorical or fanciful stories to which Buck (1939, 1974) and Pomare and Cowan (1987) referred. Neither do the Dread identify Māui narratives as 'ridiculous', 'puerile' or 'absurd'. On the contrary, when I first quizzed the Dread's Te Ahi on the influence of Māui upon the group, he simply responded by saying, 'Māui has been an inspiration ever since we [Ngāti Porou] were hanging from his hook'. To fully appreciate this seemingly unique Ngāti Porou perspective it is first necessary to briefly outline the original cosmogonic process of cleavage and separation that brought the Māori cosmos into being.

In the opening chapter of George Grey's classic account of Polynesian mythology (Grey 1956), the author recounts the decision taken among the six all-male offspring of Ranginui and Papatūānuku to force apart their ceaselessly embracing parents. This decision was pre-empted, writes Grey, by the siblings' desire to escape their cramped and uncomfortable conditions within the creases and crevices of their parents clasped bodies, which stifled their movement, growth and potential to reproduce. The eventual act of cosmogonic cleavage and separation entailed severing Ranginui's limbs so that his body could be pushed upwards and away from that of Papatūānuku. Next, to assuage their parents' grief, the siblings overturned the body of Papatūānuku, inadvertently shattering her limbs – thereby creating the fragmented earthly appearance of continents and islands. Finally, to attain divine placation for their act of violent rupture, the siblings clothed and beautified the nakedness of their parents – Ranginui with the light and warmth of sun (*te rā*), moon (*te marama*) and stars (*te whitū*), and Papatūānuku in a garment of forests, sometimes referred to as, 'the cloak of Papatūānuku'.[9]

According to Ngāti Porou tradition, it was a fragment of Papatūānuku's body that the irrepressible demigod and heroic Ngāti Porou ancestor, Māui, recovered from the ocean's depths, while on a fishing expedition with his five elder brothers.[10] This fragment, in the form of a gigantic fish, was named Te Ika a Māui (The Fish of Māui). The narrative, as related to the Ngāti Porou *kaumātua* (elder), Anaru Reedy, by the *tohunga* (ritual expert) Mohi Ruatapu (Reedy 1993: 123; see also Best 1924: 144), describes how Māui utilised the enchanted jawbone of his ancestor, Muri-ranga-whenua, as a fishhook baited with blood from a self-inflicted punch to his nose. Māui then cast his line overboard and, detecting a fish had seized his baited hook, recited a magical *karakia* (ritual incantation) while gradually hauling the hooked fish towards the surface. After a protracted struggle, the ocean's surface was broken by part of the fish, which Ngāti Porou identify as the summit of the sacred mountain, Hikurangi Maunga. The rising of Hikurangi Maunga stranded Māui's *waka* (canoe), named Nukutaimemeha, on its peak, where to this day Ngāti Porou assert its petrified remains lay inverted in a small lake named Te Roto o Hine Takawhiti (Lake of Hine Takawhiti), which is located at the summit of the mountain (Ngata 1989: 2).

What is more, upon surfacing, Te Ika a Māui exposed a population of *iwi atua* (supernatural beings), who are described as busily going about their daily tasks, which included tending the domestic fires that burned on open hearths outside the many houses (Tylor 1920: 344; Alpers 1964: 55–56). It was on the *maihi* (bargeboards) of one of these abodes that Māui's hook had attached itself. Consequently, some members of Ngāti Porou claim that their autochthonous descent stems from the cohabitation of Māui and his brothers with these inhabitants, the *iwi atua*, sometimes referred to as 'fairy people' or *tūrehu*, *patupaiarehe* or *pakepakehā* (Cowan 1921: 96). This autochthonous lineage, distinguished by Ngāti Porou as *tangata tūturu* (permanent people), contrasts with later Māori arrivals (Smith's Hawaiki migrants if you will), termed *tangata hīkoi*, which refers to people who arrived from elsewhere (Harmsworth et al. 2002: 73).

Crucially, before any portion of the fish could be consumed, Māui had first to conduct obligatory rites in order to placate the gods. As he departed to perform this task, Māui instructed his brothers to refrain from consuming any part of the fish until its *tapu* (sanctity) had been lifted. However, on Māui's exit, his brothers immediately began cutting away at the fish. Had they not ignored Māui's instruction it is said that the surface of the fish would have remained flat and smooth. As it was, the butchered fish solidified into land, creating Aotearoa/New Zealand's rugged and mountainous terrain.

It is ironic that in the fishing of the land from the ocean and its butchering by Māui's brothers, the Māori narrative of Te Ika a Māui displays extraordinary parallels to the stages of 'youth' (the upward emergence of land) and 'maturity' (the roughening of the land) featured in Davis's theory of the geomorphic cycle outlined above. Recall, Davis's hypothesis was an example of the very theories that were advanced during the late nineteenth and early twentieth centuries to supplant the so-called 'garb of poetic fiction' (Pomare and Cowan 1987: 14) with Western scientific knowledge.

Following Te Ika a Māui's inauspicious origin at the transgressive hands of Māui's brothers, Māori recognise that much of Aotearoa/New Zealand is now considered challenging for the needs of people. Furthermore, as descendants of the autochthonous inhabitants who were raised up with the fish, Ngāti Porou now once again consider themselves to be bearing witness to the defilement of the land by the relatively recent wave of Pākehā migrants. It is in further contemplation of tensions emerging from the Pākehā introduction of modern farming, forestry and mineral extraction and further similitudes with Davis's latter stage of maturity – the consumption of hills and mountains by rivers executing the return of the land to the ocean – that I now turn my attention.

Removing the Cloak of Papatūānuku

The late-nineteenth-century introduction of pastoral and agricultural farming by the growing number of European settlers necessitated a rapid increase in the quantity of Māori land being leased to Europeans, and subsequently deforested for farming purposes. Until the 1840s, an estimated 80 per cent of the hills and river valley areas of the East Coast were covered in native forests and dense areas of scrubland. Today that figure stands at approximately 33 per cent (Harmsworth et al. 2002: 11, 111).[11] Denuded of much of its native vegetation, the East Coast's composition of unstable rock types and fragile soils has become increasingly exposed to the regular occurrence of high rainfall, erosion-generating storms and severe flooding (Coulter and Hessell 1980; Tomlinson 1980; Glade 1998). These events have been instrumental in the decline of biodiversity and acceleration of environmental degradation. The latter, brought on by the cumulative impact of landslides, gully erosion and the silting of rivers and streams, in turn degrades natural watercourses and causes downstream flooding.

These patterns of increased sediment transport are highly visible on many of the hills around Ruatoria, where unvegetated patches of hillside caused by the regular occurrence of landslides are indicative of the movement of sluiced farmland being washed into the ocean. Moreover, in view of this disappearance of land into the ocean, it is no surprise that many Ngāti Porou residents living in and Ruatoria articulate concerns that the rivers are devouring the land. From a Māori cosmological perspective, such anxieties also raise the parallel spectre that Aotearoa/New Zealand's North Island, conceptualised as Te Ika a Māui (the fish of Māui), is slowly returning to the ocean depths from which it originally emerged.

In the 1960s, the New Zealand government responded to the issue of environmental degradation by commissioning an investigation into the devastating impact of erosion occurring in the Poverty Bay–East Cape district. The committee's findings were published in 1967 as the Taylor Report, which delineated a 'blue line' identifying an area beyond which farming was impractical and where forestry (for production or protection) was strongly recommended to stabilise land. Following the publication of the Taylor Report, the East Coast's regional authority, the Poverty Bay Catchment Board, together with the New Zealand Forest Service, initiated a policy of lease-purchasing and planting all the designated 'worst land' with non-native Monterey pine (*Pinus radiata*). It was proposed that the planting of Monterey pine would not only alleviate erosion, but would also contribute to Aotearoa/New Zealand's burgeoning need for timber, while providing much needed jobs and income for communities on the East Coast. To further encourage the widespread planting of commercial forests, schemes such as the East Coast Forestry Programme offered landowners grants to plant erosion-prone land with pine (Harmsworth et al. 2002: 135).

By the end of the last decade, approximately 26 per cent of the Waiapu River catchment area, in which Ruatoria is situated, had been planted in exotic pine forest (Jessen et al. 1999). However, the success of commercial forestry as an erosion-control measure has so far offered inconsistent results, a principle reason being that the fast-maturing growth of Monterey pine enables commercial forestry companies to harvest afforested areas supposedly reserved for 'permanent erosion control' within thirty years of the trees having been planted. The eventual replanting of pine forests in harvested areas does little to allay Ngāti Porou, many of whom remain concerned by the detrimental impact that harvesting one, two or three crop rotations in quick succession has upon the future health of the land. Indeed, periods between crop rotations have regularly served as reminders of the susceptibility of harvested land, as soil awaiting replanting is washed away by heavy annual rains.

Alongside the advent of commercial forestry came the transformation of the East Coast's road network to facilitate the removal of harvested timber. This involved upgrading the loose-shale road that weaves its way around the region to the current tar-sealed State Highway 35. However, far from satisfied with their upgraded road network, many *tangata whenua* have grown increasingly concerned by the increase in speeding heavy goods vehicles on the narrow, undulating highway. Throughout my fieldwork, several local residents articulated the seemingly widespread view that Highway 35 is Aotearoa/New Zealand's most expensive stretch of highway. This assertion certainly appears to be borne out by the constant state of repair in which the highway habitually finds itself. Crews of predominantly Māori employees of the New Zealand Transport Agency (NZTA) appear permanently engaged in the simultaneous repair of different sections of the East Coast's logistical artery. The range of work being carried out regularly entails the removal of debris from roadsides, stabilising hillsides, repairing damaged road surfaces and stabilising riverbanks to reduce the likelihood of the rivers bursting and flooding the highway.

In the most recent bid to counteract the regular occurrence of landslides and subsidence instigated by heavy seasonal rainfall and exacerbated by articulated logging and livestock trucks, the NZTA has turned to the technique of Deep Soil Mixing (DSM) to stabilise slopes along the most severely affected sections of the road network.[12] Meanwhile, earlier proposals to invest in a local timber processing plant in order to provide jobs and add value to the East Coast's fabled 'wall of wood' have consistently failed to materialise.[13] Consequently, it is unsurprising that *tangata whenua*, such as the Dread, view the net effect of afforestation policies as providing little more than an alternative form of exploitative agriculture, the proceeds of which flow like a tributary into Aotearoa/New Zealand's agricultural export economy. In short, the East Coast's ecology is rendered vulnerable by an economy that is currently overly reliant upon timber harvested from

Ruatoria and surrounding areas and then transported to overseas destinations as untreated logs along a local state highway, perpetually cobbled together with gravel extracted from the bed of the Waiapu River. The latter intervention not only contributes to the environmental degradation of the banks of the Waiapu and the transmogrification of its watercourse, but it also commutes the aforementioned 'wall of wood' into a procession of timber flowing outwards along Highway 35.

Te Ika a Māui's Geomorphological Return to the Ocean

Following the criss-crossing of nineteenth-century Western scientific theories and Māori origin narratives (outlined above), the past two decades have witnessed the confluence of scientific research and a cosmological concern that the rivers are devouring the land. As has also been discussed, the afforestation policies of successive New Zealand governments offer clear acknowledgement that landslides occurring on the East Coast's already fragile slopes are being aggravated by the destabilising effects of deforestation and agriculture. Of considerable geomorphological significance has been recognition that Aotearoa/New Zealand lays at the southern end of the so-called Pacific 'ring of fire' – the line that marks the frequent quakes and volcanic eruptions that occur virtually along the entire Pacific Rim. Significant also is the location of Aotearoa/New Zealand, which straddles the boundary between two tectonic plates, the Pacific and Australian. It is also significant that in the offshore area around the East Coast, the more dense Pacific Plate is pulled down beneath the lighter Australian Plate in a process known as subduction. For these reasons, Aotearoa/New Zealand, and the East Coast in particular, are subject to significantly higher than average levels of seismic activity. Consequently, in real terms, the extent of land instability onshore is but a microcosm of the submarine instability occurring offshore.

One such outcome of the Pacific region's long-standing seismic activity is the undersea landslide located off Aotearoa/New Zealand's East Coast, called the Ruatoria Avalanche, which is some 40 kilometres wide by 80 kilometres long (Lewis and Pettinga 1993). Moreover, the recently arrived at scientific consensus identifies the enormous quantity of land-derived sediments from the Waiapu River as contributing to this steep underwater slope on the ocean floor. It is this underwater movement of debris that renders the ocean floor susceptible to crumbling and slipping, and when it does so it creates the phenomena of undersea avalanches. The latent danger here is that when a section of ocean floor collapses on an undersea landslide such as the Ruatoria Avalanche, it constitutes the effect of pulling down the ocean above. The force exerted from the sudden motion of plunging water is then liable to rebound, potentially triggering the displacement of a large volume of water in the form of a tsunami.

For these reasons, the Dread attribute Ruatoria's inability to absorb climatic phenomena as a consequence of the exploitative capitalist practices operated by local commercial farming, forestry and mineral extraction. Reflecting on the economic motivations underpinning the ongoing cycle of resource exploitation and the ominous threat of ecological devastation, the Dread's Te Ahi, had this to say: 'I call it environmental sabotage, but who's gonna pay for it and how they gonna fix it after all these years of clear cutting [deforestation] and agriculture. They [the government and private industry] won't fix it because there's no money in it. They're just here to make their dollar'.

The activities described by Te Ahi are further compounded by the aforementioned industries' apathetic attitude towards *te tangata me te whenua* (the people and the land). Such a view elicited the following summary of land alienation and socio-economic exclusion by the Dread's Te Hokowhitu: 'They [Pākehā] had a blueprint for our land that didn't include us [*tangata whenua*]. Just a dole office, a pub, a police station and a courthouse'. Moreover, consonant with Ngāti Porou's identification as *tangata whenua*, the Dread also identify these problems of alienation, exploitation and devastation as not merely confined to the use of land and the value of its mineral resources.

Since the 1950s, ever-increasing numbers of Ngāti Porou have been migrating from their *whenua papatipu* (ancestral land) to Australia or New Zealand's major cities. Ruatoria's current recorded population of 756 people represents a decrease of 81, or 9.7 per cent, since the 2001 census. During my field research, neighbouring Australia was experiencing an economic boom that created a wealth of employment prospects for New Zealanders, both Māori and Pākehā. In Ruatoria, opportunities in Australia's buoyant mining sector, which required skilled manual labourers, machinery operators and HGV drivers, appeared particularly attractive to a sector of the Ruatoria labour market that constitutes approximately one-third of the township's employed men and women. Others from Ngāti Porou ventured across the Tasman Sea simply to try their hand at securing a higher salary for performing similar employment.

I encountered one such example of the latter incentive at a Ruatoria petrol station, during an interchange initiated by a curious pump attendant eager to determine my reason for residing on the East Coast. On revealing my purpose, the attendant announced her bemusement that I could find anything of interest to research in Ruatoria, before confessing her expressed desire to leave the township and move to 'Aussie', based on her uncle's report that she could earn AUS$25 an hour in the same job. Without needing to enquire how much she was currently earning, I quietly accepted her declaration as indicative of the pessimism associated with life in Ruatoria that I had often heard expressed by many of the township's young residents. Reflecting on the excellent academic record of Ruatoria's Ngata College in facilitating the migration of many young Ngāti Porou, Te Ahi decried: 'We train them [young people] up, not for here, but to go to the cities'. Nonetheless, the young were not alone in seizing opportunities 'across the ditch', as the Tasman Sea is often referred to. I also witnessed an auction of livestock, farm equipment and machinery belonging to an elderly Ngāti Porou farmer who had elected to sell up and try his luck in Perth, where many of his *whanaunga* (blood relatives) had already settled.

Ruatoria's outward migratory trend is reflective of the broader situation for Ngāti Porou as a whole, where according to figures from the 2006 Australian Census, approximately one-sixth, that is to say 12,500 members of Ngāti Porou's registered population of 71,895, currently live in Australia.[14] Of Aotearoa/New Zealand's cities outside Ngāti Porou's traditional territory, the country's most populous city, Auckland, is registered as having the largest population of Ngāti Porou anywhere (13,215), followed by the nation's capital, Wellington (11,268). The East Coast's largest city, Gisborne, has a registered population of 12,402,[15] while a further 4,212 live in rural areas on the East Coast.[16] Ruatoria's modest population therefore belies the fact that the township constitutes one of the most significant centres of population in the sparsely inhabited heartland of Ngāti Porou, whose territory incorporates an estimated 102,000 hectares of Māori multiple-owned land.

With the subsequent decline in the Ngāti Porou population has come opportunities for Pākehā to obtain large freehold land blocks, ranging in size from anywhere between 2,000 and 30,000 acres. A constant source of anxiety for the slowly dwindling number of *tangata whenua*, such as the Dread, is therefore the quantity of land being neglected, leased or sold to non-Ngāti Porou, who, not being *tangata whenua* by definition, are considered to lack the requisite spiritual connection to the *whenua*. Of course, for every member of Ngāti Porou that sought to take advantage of the perceived bounty on offer in Australia or elsewhere, there are others who maintain they will never leave Aotearoa/New Zealand's East Coast. For example, several local people expressed to me, with a mixture of dismay, disdain and/or humour, their concerns over the prospect of Māori children growing up in Australia as 'Mozzies' (Māori Australians) with little or no sense of Māori culture.

For the Dread, the consequences of leaving the East Coast are not only undesirable, but also potentially catastrophic for the well-being of the land. It is with arresting this trend of increasing migration by Ngāti Porou in mind that the Dread first engaged in projects based around the building of adobe houses that would eventually culminate in the construction of a *papa kāinga* (traditional community homestead), consisting of housing and areas of permaculture.[17] It was in the 1970s that the Dread first encountered the idea of building adobe houses from a local college teacher, Joe Tawhai. However, it was not until 1996 that a small contingent of the Dread that included Te Ahi, Te Hokowhitu, Ihu Kaya and Shiloh travelled to the town of Nelson, on Aotearoa/New Zealand's South Island, to learn adobe-building techniques from an engineer named Richard Walker. According to Te Ahi, 'Walker saw the mud-brick as a Third World idea and wanted the technology to benefit poor people'. During the 1980s and 1990s, the Dread professed to having retained the idea of adobe housing while simultaneously pursuing direct action against Pākehā farmers. Te Ahi keenly points out that throughout this period the Dread's now deceased prophet and leader, Jah Rastafari, kept the adobe *kōrero* (discussion) alive. However, it was not until the Dread began emerging from periods spent in and out of jail that the adobe idea came to life. In the words of Te Ahi:

> When we got out of jail, the bros[18] were sleeping under the stars and the women and children were in the cars. The bros refused to work for the forestry and we didn't want to move to the city either [...] We were always thinking, 'who's gonna save us?' To me it's like the *kotahitanga* (unity movement) was left behind with the *rawakore*, 'the poor and the needy'. All those that didn't make the cut to go out there to get an education and stayed at home were the *kotahitanga*. And those ones that stayed at home, they had to put together the *whakaaro* (plan). They had the vision. How do we save ourselves, keep the land together.

The cornerstone of the Dread's plan is, in the first instance, to foster self-reliance by building and teaching the specialised skills required in the construction of sustainable adobe homes. In this regard, the Dread's plan is premised upon the anticipated return of Ngāti Porou newly released from prison and those soon-to-be disillusioned with life in the cities of Aotearoa/New Zealand and Australia, who now wish to return to the East Coast. As Te Ahi further explained: 'The whole plan was to set it up [the adobe housing project] so that when the *whānau* (extended family) come back, there's a house [for them] to come back to. It's like when my sister died, I had to bring my nephew back form Auckland, being he's the oldest boy and none of her [other] kids are back here'.

Unfamiliar with such an occurrence and curious as to its motivation, I enquired whether Te Ahi's request for his nephew's return to Ruatoria was prompted by customary practice – perhaps, I considered, as a means for facilitating the retention of a family's occupation rights following the death of the last residing member of the family line. To this, Te Ahi responded:

> Nah, that was my idea 'cos I knew that if none of the sister's kids came back at that time, they'll never come back. Then their relationship to the land will be lost. So I put it to his father that I feel we should bring the nephew back to carry on, keep the sister's family side on the ground. Otherwise they'll grow up in the city, their kids will grow up in the city. They won't know their roots. That was the whole idea about the mud brick [adobe housing]. So that won't happen to us. Because it could happen to any of us, we could get moved out.

In reconciling people with the land from which they have been alienated, the Dread's adobe house-building scheme not only redeems the obligatory association between people (*tangata*) and land (*whenua*) – invoked by the designation *tangata whenua* – but it also exhibits the potential to perform two further conciliatory functions. Firstly, utilising the land as a building resource, the Dread's strategy aims to reconcile the connection between the bodies of people and the body of Papatūānuku, the Earth Mother. In so doing, there lays the hope that the threat of geomorphological and ecological destruction can be averted by resituating the salvation of the people in the placenta/land – the cosmological interface that enables the resident kin group to metabolise sustenance from the body of Papatūānuku.

The second function constitutes a means of reconciling the Dread with their non-Rastafari Ngāti Porou kin in Ruatoria, from whom they have virtually been ostracised since the turbulent events associated with their activism of the 1980s and 1990s. Indeed, the Dread now consider themselves well placed to contribute to the cycle of repair on the East Coast. By no means lost on the group's members, this potential turnaround in fortunes was evidenced in Te Ahi's bold declaration, 'at one time the bros were seen as a problem in Ruatoria and told we were scaring people away, but the tables are turned. We are a solution'.

The adobe scheme, although the cornerstone of the group's strategy, is but a part of the Dread's self-conscious recognition that they are 'a solution'. Indeed, the construction of sustainable adobe housing also contributes to a far more ambitious plan for the future of *tangata whenua* on the East Coast. It is these plans for the future that presents the potential for economic and ecological confluence to emerge between the Dread's imperative to restore 'the cloak of Papatūānuku' (native forest) under the *kaitiakitanga* (guardianship) of Ngāti Porou on the one hand, and the environmentally green aspirations of recent New Zealand governments on the other. What unites both sets of aspirations, I argue, is the shared commitment to a 'sustainability revolution' (Clark 2006: 5), which, prompted by international agreement, aims to contribute to the combating of climate change through the restoration of permanent forests. It is to the Dread's engagement with these national and international developments that I now turn.

Restoring the Cloak of Papatūānuku

To date, the Kyoto Protocol remains the most significant international agreement on combating climate change through the reduction of greenhouse gas (GHG) emissions. Aotearoa/New Zealand's engagement with the Kyoto Protocol is, from the heuristic of confluence adopted in this chapter, one that illuminates a coming together of the ecological concerns articulated by Ngāti Porou living along the rivers and coastline around Ruatoria and those of the New Zealand government. For example, I have so far posited that the regular occurrence of landslides happening in close proximity to Ngāti Porou settlements has heightened concerns that the rivers are devouring the land. In situating a wider recognition of the concerns associated with Aotearoa/New Zealand's settlement characteristics within recent national political discourse on climate change, I suggest we need look no further than a public address given by the country's former prime minister, Helen Clark.

In the midst of her address, Clark announced: 'We believe in being part of the solution to global problems, and, as a major primary producer, we have much to lose from unstable and extreme climatic conditions. We are also a nation with a very long coastline where communities dwell' (Clark 2006: 5). In her address, Clark also bookended her reflections on the problems of meeting binding emissions reduction targets placed on industrialised countries by explaining: 'New Zealand has ratified the Kyoto Protocol, even though it poses major challenges to us … But future generations won't forgive us if our legacy to them is an irretrievably damaged planet' (ibid.: 5). Interestingly, Clark also announced that Aotearoa/New Zealand was 'engrossed in a comprehensive revamp of [its] climate change policies – ranging across policies for forestry and agriculture and the energy and transport sectors' (ibid.: 5). Certainly, most industrialised countries who ratified the Kyoto Protocol have focused their efforts on combating global warming by implementing policies designed to tackle GHG emissions generated as by-products of energy consumption, industry and transport sectors. However, Aotearoa/New Zealand's rurally biased economy has subsequently pursued an alternative approach.

Successive New Zealand governments have so far maintained Helen Clark's commitment to a comprehensive strategy that has been necessitated by the nation's highly unusual emissions profile, in which approximately one half of the country's GHG emissions are constituted from methane (CH_4) and nitrous oxide (N_2O). Both these GHGs are by-products of the commercial farming practices so disliked by the Dread, with methane generated through entric fermentation and manure management on the one hand, and nitrous oxide from animal effluent and fertiliser on the other. In adopting this approach to reducing the nation's GHG emissions, New Zealand governments have been eager to stress local environmental benefits such as reductions in erosion-induced outcomes of deforestation discussed earlier, while pursuing the goal – originally laid out by Helen Clark – of becoming carbon neutral, that is, producing a net output of zero GHG emissions (ibid.: 5).

It was against this background that in November 2008, New Zealand pioneered what it hopes will become a gold standard in carbon-offset projects for the international community to follow. By including GHG emissions generated by forestry and farming alongside those from the previously mentioned sectors of energy, industry and transport, the ambitious introduction of the nation's emission trading scheme (ETS) aims to address the issue of all GHG emissions from all sectors of the Aotearoa/New Zealand economy. Of specific interest to the Dread's imperative to restore 'the cloak of Papatūānuku' has been the incorporation of the Permanent Forest Sink Initiative (PFSI) into a wider package of measures introduced under New Zealand's ETS legislation. PFSI has specifically been devised to address concerns about deforestation by once again encouraging the growing of new, permanent forests, only this time with the express purpose of carbon sequestration and long-term carbon storage. With these objectives in mind, PFSI actively encourages the reforestation of marginal, erosion-prone land, which with the benefit of hindsight should never have been denuded of its native vegetation.

Under ETS legislation, the New Zealand government has committed to pay internationally tradable carbon credits, called New Zealand Units (NZU), to landowners who establish permanent forests that comply with the requirements of the Kyoto Protocol's forestry rules.[19] These NZUs can either be traded domestically or converted into internationally tradable Kyoto-compliant emissions units such as Emission Reduction Units, Certified Emission Reductions, Removal Units or Assigned Amount Units.[20] This built-in flexibility will, the New Zealand government anticipates, enable ETS to maximise the significant economic opportunities offered by emissions-intensive companies and/or countries, who face increasing legislative pressure to buy emissions units to offset their own GHG excesses, with obligations under international frameworks such as the Kyoto Protocol. PFSI therefore represents a new economic opportunity for landowners to participate in carbon-farming by creating permanent forest sinks that remove GHG's from the atmosphere.

In part, the Dread's pursuit of the economic and ecological opportunities potentially on offer with PFSI were inspired by the Kīngitanga (the Māori king movement), whose unsuccessful appeals for Māori self-governance throughout the 1870s and 1880s enlisted legislative support from Section

71 of the New Zealand Constitution Act of 1852 (Buddle 1860; Meijl 1993; Ballara 1996; Rosenfeld 1999). The 1852 act, although never implemented by the Crown, remained on New Zealand's statute until it was repealed by the Constitution Act of 1986. From the Kīngitanga standpoint, however, the ignored 1852 act had appeared, in principle at least, sympathetic to the movement's appeals for the preservation of Māori laws and customs, stating:

> And Whereas it may be expedient that the Laws, Customs, and Usages of the Aboriginal or Native Inhabitants of New Zealand, so far as they are not repugnant to the general principles of Humanity, should for the present be maintained for the Government of themselves, in all their relations to and dealings with each other, and that particular districts should be set apart within which Laws, Customs, or Usages should be so observed. (Taiwhanga 1888: 9)

In recourse to the members of the Kīngitanga, whom he refers to as both *tīpuna* (ancestors) and 'our old people', Te Ahi explained:

> I'm always looking for the plan, because our *tīpuna* had the plan there, which was self government, and they were using Article [i.e. Section] 71 of the constitution, but then they said if that don't work we got to go back to the blueprint, back to the drawing board. That's what our old people – that died before I ever met them – taught me. They taught me that they've got all their plans there, but if that don't work son, you're back onto the drawing board. You got to redraw the blueprint. The blueprint from what though, eh? Well easy, from the Resource Management Act. 'Cos the Resource Management [Act] says you gotta go back to the Treaty of Waitangi, you know, to consider these things, today. Ten years ago that was never heard of, but it's now in law, but no one [in Ruatoria] knows the law because no one reads those books. Even when it comes to many of our *kaumātua* (elders), I don't know how far they're up against the Resource Management Act.

As Te Ahi's account suggests, the Dread now aim to capitalise on Part 2, § 5, 6, 7 and 8 of the Resource Management Act (RMA). First passed in 1991, Part 2 of the RMA, subtitled, 'Purpose and Principles', was drafted with particular regard to Māori cultural values, and leads by stating: 'The purpose of this Act is to promote the sustainable management of natural and physical resources … in a way, or at a rate, which enables people and communities to provide for their social, economic, and cultural wellbeing and for their health and safety'.[21]

Nearly a century and a half after the Kīngitanga movement's ultimately unsuccessful appeals for Māori self-governance, the Dread's redrawn 'blueprint' identifies the RMA and the New Zealand government's PFSI legislation as a means of accomplishing the reunion of *tangata* (people) and *whenua* (land) by restoring 'the cloak of Papatūānuku' – that is, native forests. At the expense of non-native pine forests, which they refer to dismissively as 'penis radiata', the Dread now aim to attract investment in large-scale greenhouses to propagate native trees alongside native plants and flowers, which together will be able to encourage the return of native species of birds, fish and animals. At its economic heart, the Dread's proposed blueprint entails the creation of local training and employment opportunities in planting and environmental management, alongside fencing and pest control. Each of these areas would enable the Dread's project to harness existing local expertise in hunting and agricultural labour.

In a situation where the overwhelming majority of individuals that constitute the Dread are shareholders in Ngāti Porou land, members of the group consider themselves to be in an increasingly enviable position with regards to negotiating investment with interested third-party financiers. In the last few years, for example, Credit Suisse and London-based ethical investor Sustainable Forest Management (SFM) have announced a US$200 million investment in funding their target of 100,000 hectares of permanent forests in Aotearoa/New Zealand for the purpose of amassing carbon credits.[22] That said, it is unlikely that private equity companies, even those professing ethical considerations such as SFM, will be willing to extend their 'long-term target' to match the expectations of the Dread. Their support of the New Zealand government's proposal to transform large expanses of the East Coast into a 'green canopy' that duly functions as 'the lungs of Aotearoa', is wholly contingent upon the trees planted being native species. As Te Ahi puts it: 'To do this [replant native forests] would require investment and training of local people and require a 200-, 300- or 500-year plan, not a fifty-year plan.

In spite of achieving considerable success in securing grants for the initial phase of their adobe house-building project, the Dread have subsequently encountered further difficulties. Their bid to sustain the development of their adobe scheme has so far failed to achieve its full potential, having encountered local difficulties. The second phase of the project, which entailed the building of an adobe brick-making factory at a location named the Crossroads, was eventually stifled by lingering resentment from sections of the local community staunchly opposed to the Dread. This stalling of the project has led one Ngāti Porou resident to dismiss the Dread as having had their opportunity. Proclaiming, 'their venture failed because they were unable to match the expectations of local people who are not ready to embrace concepts like mud-brick houses'. Nonetheless, the Dread respond to such comments rather philosophically. Reflecting upon the episode in which the Dread were evicted from the Crossroads, an area of unused land to which a family member had previously granted them land-use rights (*tuku whenua*), Te Ahi reasoned:

> It's a sad story when our own *whānau* (extended family) said, 'kick them [the Dread] out of there'. 'Cos we had everything; the roof was already paid for, [we had] all our windows and doors made out of native timber we scored [salvaged]. We were that close, if the *whānau* never said 'don't dig anymore holes at the Crossroads', the adobe brick factory would have been finished. I don't like it, but what can I say, he's the owner of the place.

Te Ahi then paused for an additional moment before concluding in his characteristically deliberate manner: 'Sometimes I think, was it 'cos people were jealous of what we were doing? But, then, I put it down to the adobe brick is from the earth, and the earth goes through its stages and its seasons. That's why when it's ready it'll come back'.

Concluding Cycle

In elucidating the linkages and ruptures in the cycles of environmentally destructive activity perpetuated by Pākehā and the Dread's pursuit of ecologically sustainable repair, this chapter has criss-crossed between Māori cosmology and Western geomorphology; national and international politics and local protest; and global and local notions of environmental sustainability and economics. The attention paid to these foci reveals the Dread's 'blueprint' for repairing the relationships between the composite elements of *tangata* (people) and *whenua* (placenta, land) on the one hand, and *tangata whenua* (the people of the land) and their primordial female parent, Papatūānuku – the Earth Mother – on the other. Furthermore, in addition to their long-standing opposition to state intervention and the activities of commercial farming, forestry and mineral extraction from the bed of the Waiapu River, the Dread's blueprint also reveals a submerged critique of their elders' response to the devouring of the placenta.

In addressing present-day cosmological concerns, it is the Dread's attention to past, present and future economic, scientific and political factors that sets their blueprint apart from the purely cosmologically focused cleansing ceremony organised by Papa Anaru. Therefore, rather than participating in traditional cleansing ceremonies, the Dread's alternative response champions the return to a condition of cosmological well-being through the reinstitution of native forests, 'the cloak of Papatūānuku'. In this way, the Dread aim to fulfil their stated key intention of holding the land together in a literal sense, while simultaneously generating sustainable employment, income and housing for *tangata whenua*. Moreover, endowing Ngāti Porou with a means to remain or return to their ancestral land, as *kaitiaki* (guardians), will enable the kin group to once again manage its affairs in accordance with the practices, values and obligations of *tangata whenua*.

As previously stated, this chapter has also been concerned with the repair of relationships. On the one hand, attention has been paid to relationships occurring at the micro level, for example, the Dread's relationship to non-Rastafari Ngāti Porou in Ruatoria and the relationship between *tangata whenua* and Pākehā on the East Coast of Aotearoa/New Zealand. Then, on the other hand, attention has also been paid to relationships occurring at the macro level, that is to say, the Dread's future economic relationship with the New Zealand state and its participation in the global 'sustainability revolution', and Ngāti Porou's cosmological relationship to Te Ika a Māui (North Island).

However, as the commentaries with which I ended illustrate, many Ngāti Porou in Ruatoria remain unconvinced or unwilling to support the Dread's transition from a self-professed problem that scared people away to being a potential solution to the alienation and destruction of ancestral land and the ongoing predicament of Ngāti Porou outward migration, unemployment and poor housing or homelessness. Consequently, the Dread have so far found it difficult to sustain the support of their Ngāti Porou neighbours, whose participation is without doubt integral to the group's response to ecological, geomorphological and cosmological crises, unwanted political interventions, and demographic and economic uncertainties that blight the future of *tangata whenua* in and around Ruatoria.

If successful, the Dread's aim to restore 'the cloak of Papatūānuku' would go a long way in satisfying the objectives of Papa Anaru's cleansing ceremony – namely, facilitating a return to the harmonious state of nurture that previously existed between people (*tangata*) and placenta (*whenua*, land). If, on the other hand, the current situation persists, whereby little or no practical or intellectual support is offered to the cosmological concerns of *tangata whenua* battling to bring to a halt the devouring of the placenta, then from the perspective of Ngāti Porou the consequences threaten the wholesale destruction of ancestral land.

Irrespective of whether the cause of this destructive scenario is articulated in scientific or cosmological terms – that is to say, through the discourse of soil erosion and tsunami or explanations rooted in the enactment of divine retribution – the danger is that the placenta, or if you prefer, land, will continue to be eroded/devoured by the ocean. In a purely cosmological respect, the devouring of the land by the ocean would then complete Aotearoa/New Zealand's cycle from the ocean floor, wherein Te Ika a Māui (The Fish of Māui) would find itself reclaimed by the ocean from whence Māori, and indeed the American geomorphologist William Morris Davis, claim the land first emerged.

Notes

1. The proverb (*pepeha*) is given in Harmsworth, Warmenhoven, Pia Pohatu and M. Page (2002: 31).
2. See also Earle (1832), Shortland (1856), Thomson (1859), Goldie (1904), Hanson (1982), Sahlins (1981, 1985, 1987), and Gell (1995).
3. Āpirana Turupa Ngata. The Genealogical Method as Applied to the Early History of New Zealand. Unpublished paper presented at a meeting of the Wellington Branch of the Historical Association, Wellington, 1929. Wellington: Alexander Turnbull Library, qMS NGA, pp.7–8.
4. The quoted phrase is taken from the preamble to the Native Land Act (1862).
5. Here, I apply use of the term 'repossession' rather than 'occupation' to communicate the Dread's perspective that disputed lands were illegally transferred into Pākehā private ownership.
6. The term 'Rastafari', pronounced 'Rasta-FAR-I' with 'I' enunciated as in the English letter 'I', is used throughout this chapter to refer to the movement itself, as well as to groups or individuals. Many adherents of Rastafari reject derivative terms such as 'Rastafarian' and 'Rastafarianism'. The latter is regarded as particularly objectionable, as the suffix '-ism' is considered to be constitutive of false or destructive ideologies and religions, such as 'capitalism', 'racism', 'Catholicism' or 'communism'.
7. Grey's remarks come from the unpaginated preface to Grey (1956).
8. Smith republished the aggregate of his findings in a single volume (Smith 1910).
9. For having introduced me to this expression, I owe a sincere debt of gratitude to my Ngāti Porou mentor, Joe McClutchie.
10. In some accounts, Te Ika a Māui is described as a stingray, which, although a class of fish generally distinguished in Māori by the term *whai*, is highly significant. Unlike most fish that lay eggs, stingrays belong to a class of fish termed 'viviparous'. Among viviparous species, pregnant females not only give birth to live young, but to do so they develop an organ analogous to, though not identical with, the placenta found in mammals. Like the placenta in mammals, this organ connects the mother's blood supply to that of the embryo.
11. It is important to note that, while Māori undoubtedly participated in forest clearance during the pre-Pākehā era, the felling of native forests increased dramatically with the introduction of Western technologies and systems of land use.
12. DSM is a technique first introduced to Aotearoa/New Zealand in 2002, whereby deep shafts are dug into the affected land and filled with a mixture of soil blended with cement and/or other materials. The technique is applied to sites where previous attempts have failed to stabilise slopes using methods

such as conventional retaining walls, mass excavation and re-compaction, buttress toe supports and deep cut-off drainage.

13. East Coast's Wall of Wood. *New Zealand Herald*, 20 February 2008.
14. Figures retrieved from: http://www.ngatiporou.com/Whanaungatanga/Whanui/default.asp, last accessed 18 December 2013.
15. Figures retrieved from: http://www.ngatiporou.com/Whanaungatanga/Whenua/default.asp, last accessed 18 December 2013.
16. Figures retrieved from: http://www.ngatiporou.com/Whanaungatanga/Kainga/default.asp, last accessed 18 December 2013.
17. Permaculture is a system of cultivation intended to maintain permanent agriculture or horticulture by relying on renewable resources and a self-sustaining ecosystem.
18. Generally reserved for fellow members, the designation 'bro', derived from 'brother', represents one of the Dread's favoured fictive kinship terms.
19. $275m to Help Landowners Branch Out. *New Zealand Herald*, 23 May 2007.
20. In December 2012, New Zealand's climate minister, Tim Groser, announced the country's decision to opt out of the second phase of the Kyoto Protocol, saying that the New Zealand government has now shifted its attention from the 1997 Kyoto deal to a new global climate pact that would also include developing nations. At present, however, it remains unclear if or how this decision will effect New Zealand's future participation in the Kyoto trading mechanism for emissions credits (Groser: NZ 'Ahead of the Curve' in Quitting Kyoto Protocol. *Channel 3 News*. Retrieved from: http://www.3news.co.nz/Groser-NZ-ahead-of-the-curve-in-quitting-Kyoto-Protocol/tabid/1160/articleID/278937/Default.aspx, last accessed 18 December 2013.
21. Quoted from the Resource Management Act (1991). Retrieved from: http://www.legislation.govt.nz/act/public/1991/0069/latest/whole.html#DLM231904, last accessed 18 December 2013.
22. $275m to Help Landowners Branch Out. *New Zealand Herald*, 23 May 2007.

References

Alpers, A. 1964. *Māori Myths and Tribal Legends*. Auckland: Blackwood and Janet Paul.

Ballara, A. 1982. The Pursuit of Mana: A Re-evaluation of the Process of Land Alienation by Maoris, 1840–1890. *Journal of the Polynesian Society* 91(4): 519–42.

_______ 1996. *Te Kīngitanga: The People of the Māori King Movement*. Auckland: Auckland University Press.

Best, E. 1924. *The Māori*, Vol. 1. Wellington: Board of Māori Ethnological Research.

Binney, J. 1995. *Redemption Songs: A Life of Te Kooti Arikirangi Te Turuki*. Auckland: Auckland University Press, Bridget Williams Books.

Buck, P. (Te Rangi Hīroa). 1939. *Anthropology and Religion*. New Haven: Yale University Press.

——— 1974 [1949] *The Coming of the Māori*. Wellington: Whitcomb and Tombs.

Buddle, T. 1860. *The Māori King Movement in New Zealand, with a Full Report of the Native Meetings Held at Waikato, April and May 1860*. Auckland: New Zealander Office.

Clark, H. 2006. Modern New Zealand in a Changing World. Unpublished address given at the London School of Economics, 10 November.

Coulter, J.D., and J.W.D. Hessell. 1980. *The Frequency of High Intensity Rainfalls in New Zealand*, Part II: *Point Estimates*. Wellington: New Zealand Meterological Service, Ministry of Transport.

Cowan, J. 1921. The Patu-paiarehe: Notes on Māori Folk-tales of the Fairy People. *Journal of the Polynesian Society* 30(118): 96–102.

Davis, W.M. 1888. Geographic Methods in Geologic Investigation. *National Geographic Magazine* 1: 11–26.

——— 1894. Physical Geography in the University. *Journal of Geology* 2: 66–100.

Earle, A. 1832. *A Narrative of a Nine Months' Residence in New Zealand, in 1827; Together with a Journal of a Residence in Tristan D'Acunha, an Island Situated Between South America and the Cape of Good Hope*. London: Longman, Rees, Orme, Brown, Green, and Longman.

Gell, A. 1993. *Wrapping in Images: Tattooing Polynesia*. Oxford: Clarendon Press.

——— 1995. Closure and Multiplication: An Essay on Polynesian Cosmology and Ritual. In, D. de Coppet and A. Iteanu (eds), *Cosmos and Society in Oceania*, pp.21–56. Oxford: Berg.

Glade, T. 1998. Establishing the Frequency and Magnitude of Landslide Triggering Rainstorm Events in New Zealand. *Environmental Geology* 35(2/3): 160–74.

Goldie, W.H. 1904. Maori Medical Lore: Notes on the Causes of Disease and Treatment of the Sick among the Maori People of New Zealand, as Believed and Practised in Former Times, together with Some Account of Various Ancient Rites Connected with the Same. *Transactions and Proceedings of the Royal Society of New Zealand* 37: 1–120.

Goldman, I. 1970. *Ancient Polynesian Society*. Chicago: University of Chicago Press.

Grey, G. 1956 [1855]. *Polynesian Mythology and Ancient Traditional History of the Māori as told by their Priests and Chiefs*. Auckland: Whitcombe and Tombs Limited.

Hanson, F.A. 1982. Female Pollution in Polynesia. *Journal of the Polynesian Society* 91(3): 335–82.

Harmsworth, G., Tui Warmenhoven, Pia Pohatu and M. Page. 2002. Waiapu Catchment Report: Māori Community Goals for Enhancing Ecosystem Health FRST Contract. Unpublished report.

Jessen, M.R., T. Crippen, M.J. Page, W.C. Rijkse, G.R. Harmsworth and M. McLeod. 1999. *Land Use Capability Classification of the Gisborne-east coast Region: A Report to Accompany the Second-Edition New Zealand Land Resource Inventory.* Lincoln: Manaaki Whenua Press.

Johansen, J. 1954. *The Māori and his Religion in its Non-ritualistic Aspects.* Copenhagen: Ejnar Munksgaard.

Lewis, K.B., and J.R. Pettinga. 1993. The Emerging, Imbricate Frontal Wedge of the Hikurangi Margin. In P.F. Ballance (ed.), *Sedimentary Basins of the World*, Vol.2: *South Pacific Sedimentary Basins*, pp.225–50. New York: Elsevier.

Mahuika, A. 1992. Leadership: Inherited and Achieved. In M. King (ed.), *Te Ao Hurihuri: Aspects of Māoritanga*, pp.86–114. Auckland: Reed.

Meijl, T. 1993. The Māori King Movement: Unity and Diversity in Past and Present. *Bijdragen tot de Taal-, Land- en Volkenkunde* 149(4): 673–89.

Metge, J. 1976. *The Māoris of New Zealand: Rautahi.* London: Routledge and Kegan Paul.

_______ 1998. Kia Tupato! Anthropologists at Work. *Oceania* 69(1): 47–60.

Mutu, M. 1992. Cultural Misunderstanding or Deliberate Mistranslation? Deeds in Māori of Pre-treaty Land Transactions in Muriwhenua and their English Translations. *Te Reo: Journal of the Linguistic Society of New Zealand* 35: 57–107.

Ngata, A.T. 1989 [1944]. Lecture 4, Rauru Nui a Toi Lectures. Unpublished manuscript.

Pomare, M., and J. Cowan. 1987 [1930–1934]. *Legends of the Māori*, Vol. 1: *Mythology, Folk-lore, Tradition and Poetry.* Auckland: Southern Reprints.

Reedy, A. (ed.). 1993. *Ngā Kōrero a Mohi Ruatapu, Tohunga Rongonui o Ngāti Porou: The Writings of Mohi Ruatapu.* Christchurch: Canterbury University Press.

Rosenfeld, J.F. 1999. *The Island Broken in Two Halves: Land Renewal Movements Among the Māori of New Zealand.* Pennslyvania: Pennsslyvania State University Press.

Sahlins, M. 1981. *Historical Metaphors and Mythical Realities.* Ann Arbor: University of Michigan Press.

_______ 1985. Hierarchy and Humanity in Polynesia. In A. Hooper and J. Huntsman (eds), *Transformations of Polynesian Culture*, pp.195–217. Auckland: Polynesian Society.

_______ 1987. *Islands of History.* Chicago: University of Chicago Press.

Shortland, E. 1856. *Traditions and Superstitions of the New Zealanders.* London: Longman, Brown, Green, Longmans and Roberts.

Simmons, D.R. 1976. *The Great New Zealand Myth: A Study of the Discovery and Origin Traditions of the Māori.* Wellington: Reed.

Sinclair, K. 1957. *The Origins of the Māori Wars.* Wellington: New Zealand University Press.

Smith, S. 1898a. Hawaiki: The Whence of the Māori, Being an Introduction to Rarotonga History. *Journal of the Polynesian Society* 7(3): 137–77.

——— 1898b. Hawaiki: The Whence of the Māori, Being an Introduction to Rarotonga History, Part II. *Journal of the Polynesian Society* 7(4): 185–223.

——— 1899. Hawaiki: The Whence of the Māori, Being an Introduction to Rarotonga History, Part III. *Journal of the Polynesian Society* 8(1): 1–48.

——— 1910. *Hawaiki: The Original Home of the Māori; with a Sketch of Polynesian History*. Christchurch: Whitcomb and Tombs Ltd.

Sorrensen, M.K. 1979. *Māori Origins and Migrations: The Genesis of Some Pākehā Myths*. Auckland: Auckland University Press.

Suess, E. 1904. *The Face of the Earth (Das Antlitz Der Erde), Volume 1*, trans. H. Sollas. Oxford: Clarendon Press.

Taiwhanga, S.D. 1888. *Proposals of Mr Sydney David Taiwhanga, M.H.R., for the Colonization and Settlement of Māori Lands*. Wellington: Edwards and Co.

Thomson, A.S. 1859. *The Story of New Zealand: Past and Present – Savage and Civilized*, Vol. 1. London: John Murray.

Tomlinson, A.I. 1980. *The Frequency of High Intensity Rainfalls in New Zealand*. Wellington: National Water and Soil Conservation Organisation.

Tregear, E. 1885. *The Aryan Māori*. Wellington: George Didsbury, Government Printer.

Tylor, E.B. 1920. *Primitive Culture: Researches into the Development of Mythology, Philosophy, Religion, Language, Art and Custom*, Vol 1. London: John Murray.

Walker, R.J. 1993. A Paradigm of the Māori World View of Reality. Unpublished paper delivered at the David Nichol Seminar IX, 'Voyages and Beaches: Discovery and the Pacific 1700–1840', Auckland, 24 August 1993.

Ward, A. 1974. *A Show of Justice: Racial 'Amalgamation' in Nineteenth Century New Zealand*. Auckland: Auckland University Press.

Webster, S. 1990. Correspondence: Response to Metge. *Journal of the Polynesian Society* 99(2): 205–8.

Wilkes, C. 1850. *Narratives of the United States Exploring Expeditions During the Years 1838, 1839, 1840, 1841, 1842*, Vol. 2. Philadelphia: Lea and Blanchard.

Williams, D.V. 1999. *Te Kooti Tango Whenua: The Native Land Court 1864–1909*. Wellington: Huia.

Yate, W. 1835. *An Account of New Zealand, and of the Formation and Progress of the Church Missionary Society's Mission in the Northern Island*. London: Seeley and Burnside.

10

The Human Face of Climate Change

Notes from Rotuma and Tuvalu

Vilsoni Hereniko

When I was growing up on Rotuma during the 1950s and 1960s, there was so much food in the ocean that I was practically stepping on it whenever it was low tide and I wandered around on the coral of the lagoon, which was now above water. For me then, the ocean was the equivalent of a well-stocked supermarket, except that everything in it was free. There were beautiful shells of all kinds everywhere I looked, and there were colourful fish stranded in the pockets of water among the coral. With spear in hand, I filled my basket with the gifts of the ocean before I returned home. It did not matter that I was walking on fragile coral that shattered as I strode to shore, wearing rubber boots sent from Fiji (and often borrowed from neighbours) that protected my bare feet.

Over the years, each time I returned to Rotuma I noticed that the ocean's resources had become depleted due to over-fishing, I noticed the effects of El Niño on the coral, and I noticed ignorance. Every time anyone went fishing, they returned with as much fish as they could catch, and with no thought of tomorrow. Since there was no refrigeration then, excess fish was distributed to households nearby, and families feasted without any thought about the ocean's resources possibly running out. As the ocean became warmer and the coral started to die and solidify, the fish started to move further away in search of more friendly habitats. Human predators continued to hunt and gather, ignorant of the changes in the climate that were causing the sea to rise. Aware of the depleted resources but lacking the will to change bad habits that work against conserving the coral and the ocean's finite resources, most Rotumans continue to plunder their birthright.[1]

Will the ocean ever forgive us for what we have done to it? How can we have been so deaf to its cries for respect over the years? How can we not realise that if we do not conserve the ocean's marine resources for our children, there won't be any left for our children's children? We have been bad stewards of our birthright, so why then should we be surprised if one day the ocean should rise up against us? Although scientists tell us that industrialised nations are primarily to blame for climate change, most Pacific Islanders would probably have behaved in the same way in the same circumstances. It is a function of human nature to care more about our own self-interests than those who are yet to be born, unless we are given incentives to do otherwise or punished for our wrongdoings.

The kind of experience and knowledge of the ocean that I have mentioned above inform my response to sea-level rise and climate change on Rotuma, and to a lesser extent, Tuvalu. I have visited Tuvalu only once; this visit made me realise that Tuvaluans and Rotumans have much in common, particularly in our cultural values and religious beliefs. There are historical and political differences of course, but these do not have any bearing on the issues that are important in this chapter.

Tuvalu is an independent country of four reef islands and five atolls. It covers 26 square kilometres with a population four times greater that of Rotuma (home to about 2,500). Rotuma, on the other hand, is approximately 465 square kilometres. The island is volcanic, and the hills in the interior of Rotuma are far enough from the ocean and high enough to protect everyone from a tsunami. About two thirds of Rotuma's population are Methodists, with the other third Catholics. The vast majority of Tuvaluans, meanwhile, belong to the Church of Tuvalu, which has links to the Congregational Church. Other denominations include Seventh-Day Adventists, Bahai and Jehovah's Witnesses, but their numbers are small.

In this chapter my focus is on affective or emotional truth. As human beings, our reactions to danger or disaster are not always informed by rational or factual truth, but quite often by cultural and religious beliefs. Quite often our actions are informed more by our emotional make-up than by our rational minds. Based on my experience, this *modus operandi* is more pronounced among Pacific Islanders than say, for example, their European or American counterparts. This comment is not intended to privilege the rational mind above our emotional feeling, but merely to make an observation that is relevant to understanding the tenor and focus of this chapter.[2]

I write from the perspective of a freethinking Pacific Islander (not an anthropologist or social scientist boxed in by a discipline) who has a direct stake in the issue of climate change. I have a home on Rotuma that is only metres away from the Pacific Ocean, which has the potential to destroy it and all my relatives living in it. I have strong feelings about the sea level rising and how it might impact on my home, my compatriots and my precious island. Writing from within this context, I make no claims to being 'objective'; besides, complete objectivity is a myth.

The selection and ordering processes that go into the writing of any chapter, academic or otherwise, make any claims to objectivity more of a goal than a reality. I would grant, however, that there are certain degrees of objectivity, and that there is value in being scientific because of the facts that this perspective can reveal. The vast majority of chapters in this volume fall into this category; their contributions to our understanding of the Pacific may be different but are just as important as this one, which places people and culture at its centre and makes no claims to being objective.[3]

The Human Face of Climate Change

It seems that everyone today is concerned about climate change, particularly in relation to Oceania and its thousands of low-lying islands. If you are like me, then you will have gone to a number of seminars and read some of the recent literature on climate change to educate yourself on what is probably the most important concern for those of us who live in what the late Epeli Hau'ofa has appropriately called 'our sea of islands' (Hau'ofa 1999). In my experience, I have noticed that the tendency in seminars and in the published literature is to focus on facts, figures and statistics gleaned from academic research to prove that our climate is indeed changing. The sea level has indeed risen, the weather patterns have indeed changed, the ice is indeed melting, and we are indeed headed for a calamity by the end of this century. I find the pie charts with percentages that demonstrate which industrial countries are most responsible for the plight our world is in today illuminating. More than once I have noticed my heart beating faster at the thought that, once again, it is the poorest and smallest nations in the developing world that will suffer the worst consequences of the greed, selfishness and arrogance of the bigger and more powerful nations. I cannot help but compare this feeling of helplessness to former colonies in Oceania being colonised a second time.

In the last ten years, a number of documentary films, several of which are set in Tuvalu, have brought home to us the imminent danger Pacific Islanders face as a result of sea-level rise. Images of waves flooding coastal homes, precious land disappearing under water and Tuvaluans migrating en masse to New Zealand are reminders that things will get worse and worse. Will they ever get better? The jury is still out on this question, but in the meantime the future looks bleak indeed. I am an optimist by nature, but on the issue of climate change I see very little hope for our children's children. They will inherit from us a world that is worse off than when we found it, and they will be forced to take on the challenges of saving it because those of us who are responsible for its sorry state will have gone by then. Admittedly, most of us who live in Oceania regard our contribution to carbon dioxide emissions as negligible, and see no reason at all why we should shoulder any of the blame for sea-level rise or other evidence of climate change. After all, Oceania does not even appear in most of those pie charts I have seen.

In the contemporary Pacific, on Rotuma and in Tuvalu, ordinary folks are responding to climate change as best they can, oblivious to the scientific research that is shared at academic conferences or at global events such as the 2009 Copenhagen climate summit. Theirs is motivated by self-preservation in the face of impending disaster, informed by the dictates of their culture or their religious beliefs. Theirs is the focus of this chapter, which asks the following questions: How do ordinary folks on Rotuma and Tuvalu respond or adapt to climate change? How do they think about its causes and effects? Like two sides of the same coin, climate change consists of scientific evidence on one side and, on the other, real humans trying their best to survive or prepare for the future. We have heard a lot about the statistics and the hard scientific evidence that proves that our global climate is changing. It is now time to give climate change a human face.

Rotuma

Many people on Rotuma believe that the weather has become unpredictable. Rotuma is hotter and wetter than before; there are reports of plants withering in the heat of the sun, and of fish dying during low tide. In addition, Rotumans are aware of natural disasters in neighbouring Pacific islands like Samoa, the Solomon Islands and Vanuatu, and they are thankful that so far Rotuma has been spared, even though Rotumans have had to flee the coastline several times in recent years as a result of possible tsunami inundation.

In 2010, a tsunami warning for the people of Rotuma created panic among the general population, who learn about a possible tsunami in several ways. Hawaii, where I have lived for the past twenty years, is where the monitoring of tsunami activity occurs. Once determined, information concerning a possible tsunami approaching Rotuma is relayed to the Fijian government, which has ultimate authority over the island. The announcement is made over the radio, and carried on television and in the daily newspapers in Fiji.

Better still, Rotumans in Fiji call their relatives on the island by phone and advise them on what to do. Through the so-called 'coconut wireless', the news spreads like wildfire on Rotuma, at times corroborated or contradicted by the 'official' account that sooner or later policemen provide as they travel from one village to another proclaiming impending disaster. The advice given is minimal; basically, it is to flee from the coastline. Residents are usually left to figure out where to flee to, and what to take.

After the most recent tsunami threat, I called my sister in Rotuma to find out how our family had responded to the tsunami warning. She said they were woken up early in the morning by a policeman and ordered to run inland as soon as possible. Almost all Rotuman homes, incidentally, are situated along the coastline of the island. My sister, who was living with a nephew, his wife and their three very young children, revealed that they grabbed some torches, threw some clothes and the remains of the previous night's meal in a basket, and fled into the bush. Fleeing immediately is the normal reaction to a tsunami warning on Rotuma if one is wise because the information cannot be trusted as totally accurate. After all, it is better to be safe than sorry.

Hours later, as the first rays of the sun cast its light through the trees in the forest where they huddled, my relatives learned that the tsunami warning was a false alarm, and that they, and the island's other inhabitants, should head back toward their homes on the coast, and to the ocean that hours earlier had been a source of terror. When I asked my sister why they couldn't just run to the hill a twenty-minute walk away and where the government station is situated, she replied that we had no relatives living on the hill that they could impose themselves upon or inconvenience. Besides, she added, what would happen if they arrived only to find that the home they had fled to for shelter was already full of people? Where then could they find a roof above their heads, she asked me.

A month later, I called my sister again to inquire about how they were coping. She told me then that my nephew was helping the neighbours build thatched houses in the bush. I wanted to know what the houses were for, and she told me that they were preparing for the next tsunami. According to her, they have endured three false tsunami warnings in the last two years. Now they have decided to prepare for the next one. When it comes, she added, they would know exactly where to run for shelter. They would not be *kelea'ehanis*, a Rotuman term that loosely translates as 'pitiful people'. In other words, having a house to run to for shelter would demonstrate preparedness on their part, and would spare them feelings of *masraga* (embarrassment); it might even enhance their reputation in the eyes of other Rotumans. They would be seen as smart and wise, not stupid and lazy. She then surprised me by saying that there are now many families around the island who have done the same and, like them, they are now spending considerable time in the bush enjoying their 'second homes' and cooler temperatures.

Meanwhile in Suva, Fiji's capital, Rotumans compose songs about climate change, particularly the threat of tsunamis, and dance away as they sing lyrics such as the following:[4]

Sa'au la mata'ua
Raksa'a fupum e 'on laloga
Kainag mamaf 'os mauri sasi ta 'utum
Mataua 'ae la se rou
Fuag ri ne 'os temamfua
Haifaegaga te ran te sokoan

Haumea se isa climate changing
Sasi jarava kalua Rotuma
Ta'e fatu otou Rotuma
Ka la mao tapen Rotuma
Hoi te mamfua fuak vahia

An English translation of the above lyrics runs as follows:

Danger has arisen from beneath the ocean
Arise from your slumber because a tsunami's approaching
Beware so you can save yourself and your inheritance
A global summit will now discuss climate change.

Our climate is now changing
A deep blue ocean surrounds Rotuma
I will always remember Rotuma
How could I ever forget Rotuma
This foundation our ancestors have bequeathed us.

An important observation about the lyrics above is that the focus is on preparing for impending disaster and the possible loss of the inheritance bequeathed to present-day Rotumans by their ancestors. The song draws attention to a major concern without giving specific instructions of how to prepare for such a calamity. More emotional than practical, the lyrics also draw attention to a concern of Rotumans, and Oceanians too, that is often left out in our efforts to find solutions for rising sea levels: although the living may be able to relocate to other lands such as Australia or New Zealand, what do we do with the bones of our ancestors?

Tuvalu

Some Tuvaluan Christians believe that God would never allow another flood to occur.[5] And because God does not lie, He will continue to maintain Tuvalu. In spite of the evidence before their eyes of waves flooding certain homes, or precious land disappearing under water, these people would rather cling to their religious beliefs than to believe the statistics that show that the sea level surrounding their islands, which are only 4 metres above sea level, will rise by 1.5 meters in the next fifty years.

At a recent screening in Honolulu of a new documentary entitled *Beautiful Islands* (Kana 2009), which examines the effects of sea-level rise on three islands (Tuvalu, Venice and Shismaref in Alaska), a member of the audience asked during the post-screening discussion how some Tuvaluans could possibly put their faith in God to save their country from disappearing. I replied that, for many Pacific Islanders, Tuvaluans included, the bible is more dependable than any of the big industrial countries such as the USA, China or Russia, countries that have contributed the most to carbon dioxide emissions. How could they believe that the USA, for example, will reduce its carbon dioxide emissions when the affluent lifestyles of its citizens and its leaders have been largely responsible for the sea-level rise in the waters surrounding their tiny islands? Surely it would be more prudent to put one's faith in God than in human beings?

In Tuvalu, as in Rotuma, people pray regularly that their islands will be protected, spared from the terrible effects of climate change, whether it is sea-level rise, hurricanes, earthquakes or tsunamis. And when disasters strike, they more often than not interpret these to mean that they have sinned, or had committed wrongs that have offended God, and that God is reminding them of His power and dominion over nature and all human life. In Fiji, for example, a church minister once claimed that the devastation caused by a certain hurricane was due to the practice of homosexuality among some of its citizens.[6] Blaming 'sinful' behaviour when natural disasters occur, incidentally, is one that some Christian ministers in Oceania continue to propagate in an effort to justify our collective need for religion.

Conclusion

Most people on Rotuma and Tuvalu know little about the causes of climate change, including sea-level rise, as well as how to prepare for possible disasters. There is a need, therefore, to ensure that information that filters down to them from their leaders is understood and followed at the grassroots level. In the case of Rotuma, its leaders need to devise a coordinated action plan for its residents, particularly in the case of a possible tsunami.

People need to be better informed and trained about what to do, where to go and how they might survive for several days after a disaster.

As for Tuvalu, one dares not contemplate the consequences of a tsunami, given that Tuvalu consists of atolls that are barely above sea level. Many Tuvaluans have already chosen to migrate overseas, but this option is not available to everyone, particularly to those who do not have the financial resources. Until such a time that the Tuvaluan government can afford the cost of relocating a whole population to another Pacific island or country, a belief in God for those who remain in Tuvalu makes the most sense to me.

Unlike Rotuma, where there are hills in the interior that can provide a safe haven, Tuvaluans have no physical safe haven to run to in the event of a tsunami. This of course is not their fault – the type of land they live on is what their ancestors have passed on to them. A belief in an omniscient, omnipotent and omnipresent and benevolent God is therefore the only option for Tuvaluans who have chosen to remain. It is not that most Rotumans do not believe in an Almighty God. Of course they do, but they also believe that, while they are praying, they should also be running to the hills to maximise their chances of survival. If the shoe were on the other foot, Rotumans would react to the threat of sea-level rise in much the same way as many Tuvaluans. They would put their faith totally in God.

Epilogue

When I first wrote this chapter, I discussed what Pacific Islanders, myself included, could do to reduce our carbon footprint. In that discussion I suggested that we might consider reducing the amount of smoke produced every time we make our traditional earthen ovens or cook using firewood, and also suggested that efforts be made to provide women in rural areas with smokeless stoves. The response I got from colleagues was that the contributions of Pacific Islanders to climate change are minimal, and that it is the larger industrial nations that needed to change their behaviour. Though I have reiterated this point above, if we consider that Pacific Islanders have been making their earthen ovens since leaving Asia to settle the Pacific about 50,000 years ago, is it really unreasonable to think that the amount of smoke emitted comprises a sizeable carbon footprint? In addition, since women and children are the ones who suffer the most from cooking with wood in open fires, surely a shift to using smokeless stoves would represent a health benefit to our women and children.

A refusal to acknowledge that we in the Pacific have contributed (even if in a relatively small way) to climate change is tantamount to a refusal to acknowledge that we have also contributed to the destruction of our coral reefs by walking on them, for example, and by over-harvesting our oceanic resources. Until Pacific Islanders are willing to make certain changes in their lifestyles that will better conserve marine resources or lessen the carbon dioxide in the atmosphere, we will continue to act as helpless victims, dependent on the kindness and largesse of more powerful nations. The sooner we realise that we are also contributors to our own demise, the sooner we will empower ourselves to be part of the solution and not part of the problem.

Notes

1. There is a group of concerned young people from Fiji called Laje Rotuma who have visited the island on various occasions to carry out conservation work on coral reefs as well as educate Rotumans about how to protect the environment. Their message appears to me to have more impact among school children. The main offenders (throwing debris such as plastic and batteries into the ocean) are the adults.
2. Why this is the case is unclear to me, but it may be a function of living on small islands surrounded by a large expanse of sea, as well as the influence of oral traditions combined with beliefs in the power of the natural and supernatural world to affect life on a daily basis.
3. Recognising that there is value in a subjective perspective rooted in experience and lived reality, for the original presentation of the arguments made in this chapter I showed video footage of land resources and people's homes being inundated by sea-level rise at the beginning of my presentation as well as at the end. The opening video examined sea-level rise in Tuvalu in the context of global concerns and scientific data on climate change issues. My talk concluded with a clip taken from the documentary *Beautiful Islands* (Kana 2009) that contained interviews with Tuvaluans expressing their religious belief that God will never allow Tuvalu to sink beneath the ocean because God promised Noah that a second flood would never take place. Unfortunately, it is not possible to include the video footage in a written essay. However, I have tried to make up for this by bookending my essay with an introduction and an epilogue, which are frankly subjective in character.
4. I am grateful to Harieta Bennet for providing me with the lyrics of this song.
5. For two films that make reference to this religious perspective, see Kana (2009) and Bayer and Salzman (2005).
6. This issue can be seen in Goldson (2008).

References

Bayer, J and J. Salzman (dir.). 2005. *Time and Tide*, 59 mins. Wavecrest Films.

Goldson, A. (dir.). 2008. *An Island Calling*, 76 mins. Occasional Productions.

Hau'ofa, E. 1999. Our Sea of Islands. In V. Hereniko and R. Wilson (eds), *Inside Out: Literature, Cultural Politics, and Identity in the New Pacific*, pp.27–38. Lanham, MD: Rowman and Littlefield.

Horner, C. (dir.). 2004. *The Disappearance of Tuvalu: Trouble in Paradise*, 75 mins. European Television Center, in association with Planete and Planete Future.

Kana, T. (dir.). 2009. *Beautiful Islands*, 75 mins. Horizon Features.

O'Connor, M and Jones-Middleton, S (dir.). 2001. *Paradise Drowned: Tuvalu, The Disappearing Nation*, 47 mins. New Zealand Natural History.

Yifan Li, Yu Yan (dir.). 2005. *Before the Flood*, 59 mins. Fan & Yu Documentary Studio.

Notes on Contributors

Annelin Eriksen is Professor of Social Anthropology and head of the research project 'Gender and Pentecostal Christianity', funded by the Norwegian Research Council, at the Department of Social Anthropology, University of Bergen. Her research centres on Melanesian ethnography, Christianity, politics, the state and gender. She is the author of *Gender, Christianity and Change in Vanuatu: An Analysis of Social Movements in North Ambrym* (Ashgate, 2008). In addition, she is co-editor of the journals *Norsk Antropologisk Tidsskrift* and *Social Analysis*.

Courtney Handman is Assistant Professor of Anthropology at Reed College, Portland, OR. She received her PhD in anthropology from the University of Chicago in 2010 following doctoral research in Papua New Guinea from 2005 to 2007. Her research and writing focuses on the anthropology of Christianity and linguistic anthropology.

Vilsoni Hereniko is a playwright and film-maker and holds a professorship at the Academy for Creative Media at the University of Hawaii. He is a former director of the Oceania Center for Arts, Culture and Pacific Studies at the University of the South Pacific in Fiji, as well as the Center for Pacific Islands Studies at the University of Hawaii. Originally from the island of Rotuma, he is also a former editor of the journal *Contemporary Pacific*.

Lisette Josephides is Professor of Anthropology at Queens University, Belfast. She has conducted lengthy fieldwork in Papua New Guinea, where she lived for seven years while also teaching at the university in Port Moresby. Her first book, *The Production of Inequality* (Tavistock, 1985) investigated political and economic processes in egalitarian Melanesian societies, arguing that gender relations modelled and disguised relations of inequality. Her research interests have now extended to philosophical approaches in anthropology (especially phenomenology, theories of the self, morality, ethics and emotions). Her latest book *Melanesian Odysseys* (Berghahn, 2008) combines interests in narrative genres and theories of the self, communicative practices within a contested and changing moral and political universe, and local and anthropological knowledge.

Craig Lind is a post-doctoral research fellow at the Centre for Pacific Studies, Department of Social Anthropology, University of St Andrews, where he contributes to the work of the European Consortium for Pacific Studies (ECOPAS). He carried out fieldwork in Vanuatu between 2002 and 2004, where he worked with Paama islanders on Paama Island and in urban settlements around Vanuatu's capital, Port Vila. His research and teaching interests include kinship, movement, sand-drawing, personhood, Christianity and 'place-making'. Lind is currently drafting a monograph concerning the place of Paama in Vanuatu and social anthropology.

Arno Pascht is based at the Institut für Ethnologie, University of Cologne. He conducted extensive field research in the Cook Islands between 1998 and 2001. His particular interests lie in legal and political anthropology, and the anthropology of ethnicity. He is the author of *Die Erben Tangiias und Karikas. Landrechte auf Rarotonga* (Bayreuth, Univ., Diss, 2009) on land rights and legal anthropology, and *Ethnizität: Zur Verwendung des Begriffs im wissenschaftlichen und gesellschaftlichen Diskurs; eine Einführung* (München: Akademischer Verlag, 1999) which considers the meaning and use of ethnicity in scholarly and popular discourse.

Anthony Pickles is Junior Research Fellow at Trinity College, Cambridge. His PhD research concerned gambling in Goroka Town, Papua New Guinea. His interests are in enumeration, money and currency, consumption, exchange, value, cosmology, social change, pattern and indigenous models of efficacy and contingency. He has published a number of chapters and journal articles, most recently in the *Journal of the Royal Anthropological Institute*.

Dave Robinson is a PhD student at the London School of Economics and Political Science and has conducted field research in Aotearoa/New Zealand. His doctoral research focuses on Maori Rastafari with special reference to myth, land, genealogy and biblical narratives.

Will Rollason is Lecturer in Anthropology at Brunel University, UK, having received his PhD in anthropology from the University of Manchester in 2008. He has published on mimesis, race and the postcolony in Papua New Guinea in the context of sports, marine resource harvesting and clothing. His is the author of *We are Playing Football* (Cambridge Scholars Press, 2011).

Dominik Schieder is Fritz Thyssen Foundation Postdoctoral Fellow at the Frobenius Institut, Goethe University, Frankfurt, and Visiting Fellow at the London School of Economics. He holds an MA and PhD from Bayreuth University. Schieder has conducted research in Fiji, Japan and India. Schieder's current research focuses on transnational Fijian migration as well as Fijian rugby and its global presence. He recently completed a project with Fijians in Japan as Japan Society for the Promotion of Science Postdoctoral Fellow at Hitotsubashi University, Tokyo.

Index